Cognitive Technologies

For further volumes:
http://www.springer.com/series/5216

Souhila Kaci

Working with Preferences: Less Is More

 Springer

Prof. Souhila Kaci
LIRMM (Laboratoire d'Informatique, de
Robotique et de Microélectronique de Montpellier)
161 rue ADA
F34392 Montpellier
Cedex 5
France
kaci@lirmm.fr

Managing Editors
Prof. Dov M. Gabbay
Augustus De Morgan Professor of Logic
Department of Computer Science
King's College London
Strand, London WC2R 2LS, UK

Prof. Dr. Jörg Siekmann
Forschungsbereich Deduktions- und
Multiagentensysteme, DFKI
Stuhlsatzenweg 3, Geb. 43
66123 Saarbrücken, Germany

Cognitive Technologies ISSN 1611-2482
ISBN 978-3-642-26883-0   ISBN 978-3-642-17280-9 (eBook)
DOI 10.1007/978-3-642-17280-9
Springer Heidelberg Dordrecht London New York

ACM Computing Classification: I.2, J.4, F.4

Cover design: KünkelLopka GmbH, Heidelberg

Printed on acid-free paper

Springer is part of Springer Science+Business Media (www.springer.com)

To my parents

Preface

Because preferences naturally arise and play an important role in many real-life decisions, they are the backbone of various fields. Preferences are fundamental in scientific research frameworks such as artificial intelligence, economics, and social choice theory, as well as applications, e.g., recommender systems, and e-commerce. Although preferences have been developed in diverse disciplines, their different usages share a common purpose, namely, to identify appealing choices from among those available.

In particular, preferences are a core and hot topic in artificial intelligence, for which we are witnessing plenty of work and dedicated international events. I have been involved with preferences for many years. My contributions to this topic were guided by two important questions I attempted to answer: *"How does one deal with users' preferences?"* and *"How can work on preferences in artificial intelligence be successfully exported to fields dealing with preferences?"* Each of these questions has motivated significant work. In particular, artificial intelligence researchers have extensively addressed the first question from representation issues when the number of choices is large. This led to a large number of different frameworks for preference representation. I contributed to this topic with new insights into preference representation. Nevertheless, I refrained from committing to any specific proposal (including mine). Instead, I studied, analyzed and compared the different frameworks and concluded that they are not competing but complementary. In fact, each has its merits but cannot adequately and/or naturally cope with all problems related to preference representation. Having studied different frameworks for preference representation allowed me to broaden my research contributions and address the second question. The purpose of this question is twofold. First, I aimed at understanding the usage of preferences in both artificial intelligence and other disciplines. Then, I aimed at highlighting the benefits of various successful preference representations developed in artificial intelligence and exporting them to other fields, allowing efficient handling of preferences. We promote the use of simple but satisfactory compact preference representation languages (less is more). This topic is of growing importance in the artificial intelligence community.

As I had always been keen on problems related to preferences, I moved for one year to a psychology lab (Cognition, Langues, Langage, Ergonomie, CLLE, Toulouse) as a researcher visitor. Preferences are not new topic in psychology. Different problems related to preferences have been identified and studied in this field. However, the relevance of the works in this field for artificial intelligence is largely unexplored. My collaboration with psychologists aims at exploring the connection between theoretical sciences and experimental sciences for preference handling in order to highlight the beneficial synergies among these fields.

Given that preferences have been extensively investigated from different perspectives, clearly a complete synthesis of this work does not fit in one book. On the other hand, one may wish to have an overview of these works. This book grew from an attempt to offer a coherent exposition of some problems related to preferences. The core part of this book is dedicated to preference representation and related problems. The second part is dedicated to the use of preference representation in various preference-based frameworks.

The book is reader-friendly. All concepts, definitions and results are explained in a simple way and illustrated with examples. The intended audience is students, novice researchers, and senior researchers in various fields, such as artificial intelligence, database management, operations research and psychology.

Lens,   *Souhila Kaci*
October 2010

Acknowledgements

My work has benefited from discussions with many people from different research communities. I am not able to remember the names of all the people I should acknowledge (the list is too long). I would like to thank my collaborators and friends whose comments helped me improve this book. Many thanks go to Richard Booth, Rui da Silva Neves and Leon van der Torre.

I am enormously grateful to Youssef Hamadi for his support and encouragement to get this book through.

Special thanks go to my family for their unconditional support, encouragement and love.

Contents

Acronyms

List of abbreviations.

QCL	Qualitative Choice Logic
GAI	Generalized Additive Independence
GAI-net	Generalized Additive Independence Network
CPT	Conditional Preference Table
CP-net	Conditional Preference Network
CI-net	Conditional Importance Network
TCP-net	Conditional Preference Network with Tradeoffs
UCP-net	Conditional Preference Network with Utilities
CSP	Constraint Satisfaction Problem
SCSP	Soft Constraint Satisfaction Problem

List of symbols.

$\in$	membership
$\subseteq$	subset
$\subset$	proper subset
$\cap$	intersection
$\cup$	union
$\setminus$	difference
$\emptyset$	emptyset
$2^{\mathscr{A}}$	power set
$\times$	cartesian product
$\models$	satisfaction
$\neg$	negation
$\vee$	disjunction
$\hat{\times}$	ordered disjunction
$\wedge$	conjunction
$\forall$	universal quantifier
$\exists$	existential quantifier
$\top$	tautology

$\succeq$	at least as preferred as
$\succ$	strictly preferred to
$\sim$	incomparable with
$\approx$	as preferred as
min	minimal value
max	maximal value
$\geq$	greater than or equal
$>$	strictly greater
$\leq$	smaller than or equal
$<$	strictly smaller

Chapter 1
Introduction

What is a preference?

According to the dictionary, a preference is "(i) the act of preferring, (ii) the desire to have, do or choose one thing rather another, because you like it better, or because it is more convenient for you, (iii) a preferred choice: His preference is vanilla, not chocolate, (iv) a practical advantage given to one over others" (Collins Cobuild English Language dictionary, Dictionary.com).

Preferences are everywhere in our daily lives. They occur as soon as we are faced with a choice problem, e.g., "which ice cream flavor would you prefer?", "which investment funds would you choose?", etc. Among multiple choices, it is often necessary to identify one or more choices that are more appealing than others. Preference is inherently a multidisciplinary topic which brings together artificial intelligence researchers, philosophers, psychologists, economists, operations researchers, etc. In particular, preferences are becoming of greater interest in many areas in artificial intelligence, such as non-monotonic reasoning, multi-agent systems, constraint satisfaction, decision making, social choice theory and decision-theoretic planning.

The last few years were witness to different international events dedicated to preferences in artificial intelligence, which showed a growing interest in problems related to preferences in this framework:

- Workshop on Preferences in AI and CP: Symbolic Approaches, 2002 (with AAAI in Edmonton)

- Special issue on "Preferences in AI and CP", Computational Intelligence, Blackwell, 2004 (U. Junker, J. Delgrande, J. Doyle, F. Rossi, T. Schaub)

- Preferences: Specification, Inference, Applications, Dagstuhl seminars (2004)

- Multidisciplinary Workshop on Advances in Preference Handling (2005 with IJ-CAI in Edinburgh, 2006 with ECAI in Riva del Garda, 2007 with VLDB in Vienna, 2008 with AAAI in Chicago, 2010 with ECAI in Lisbon)

- Special issue on "Preferences and Soft Constraints", Journal of Heuristics, Springer, 2006 (S. Bistarelli, F. Rossi)

- Special issue on "Preference Handling for Artificial Intelligence", AI magazine, 2008 (J. Goldsmith, U. Junker)

- Special issue on "Representing, Learning, and Processing Preferences: Theoretical and Practical Challenges", Artificial Intelligence, Elsevier (C. Domshlak, E. Hüllermeier, S. Kaci, H. Prade)

Related problems

Research problems related to the study of preferences arise in their life cycle. We use in this book the generic term "user" to refer to an agent, an expert, etc.

When speaking about preferences, an obvious and natural question which arises is "what are users' preferences?", i.e. "where do preferences come from?". Preferences may be acquired through an interactive process with the user. This is called preference elicitation. They may also be acquired from data describing the user's behavior or her past preferences. This is called preference learning. Both frameworks are gathered under a generic terminology, namely, *preferences acquisition*. Once this is accomplished, the next step is the mathematical expression of preferences in terms of a preference relation over choices. In other words, this relation describes preferences between pairwise choices. The properties of such a relation are important. From among many questions, one may ask whether the relation is transitive, i.e., if the relation tells us that the choice c_1 is preferred to the choice c_2 and that the latter is preferred to the choice c_3, can we conclude that c_1 is preferred to c_3? Another question is about whether the relation is complete, i.e., is any choice comparable to any other choice? Constructing a preference relation and describing its properties is called *preferences modeling*. In most applications, preferences modeling calls for representation issues, which capture and manipulate the user's preferences described by a preference relation. The support of a preference relation is called a language, which we refer to as a preference representation language. This step is called *preference representation*. The last step in the preferences life cycle is *preferences reasoning*. This may involve, on the one hand, problems related to reasoning about preferences, e.g., preferences aggregation when we need to combine preferences of multiple agents, and preference revision when a new user's preferences must be added to her old preferences. On the other hand, preferences reasoning may involve problems related to reasoning with preferences, e.g., argumentation framework, decision theory, game theory, and database theory where preferences play an important role and need special attention.

To summarize, the preferences life cycle consists of four steps, namely, preferences acquisition, preferences modeling, preference representation and reasoning about and with preferences. Each step constitutes a major research topic.

Book content

Recent years have witnessed intensive work in each topic. This book aims at providing a coherent exposition of the above-cited problems, from preferences modeling and representation to reasoning with preferences.

Preference representation

Modeling users' preferences has long been tackled in decision theory. In this framework, a preference relation is represented by a numerical function which associates a utility value with each choice to express how satisfactory it is. However, it was early on recognized that the direct assessment of a preference relation is not the proper way to represent users' preferences. In fact, we generally have to deal with an exponential number of choices whose explicit enumeration and evaluation is time-consuming. Moreover, due to their cognitive limitation, it is not reasonable to expect that users are always able to compare all pairwise choices or evaluate how satisfactory each choice is.

Fortunately, choices we have to rank-order are not always holistic but are generally described by a set of attributes, e.g., cost, color, price, etc. On the other hand, in our daily lives, users more likely specify their preferences with respect to the attributes (or factors) they wish to consider. For example, a user planning a trip for her holiday may choose on the basis of destination, price and airline company. Thus she may prefer Venice to Barcelona and would prefer a cheap company. Lastly she may prefer travel with KLM to Barcelona and with Alitalia to Venice. The ultimate goal is to deal with such partial descriptions of preferences to find the most preferred trip (in terms of destination, price and airline company) or to compare two trips. This task is called preference representation. It is accomplished by compact preference representation languages which represent partial descriptions of preferences and rank-order the possible choices. Therefore, a preference relation is not explicitly exhibited but implicitly represented by a compact preference representation language. Preference representation has come to be an increasingly central framework in artificial intelligence. The challenge in developing a good compact preference representation language is in being faced with different conflicting aspects: it should (i) cope with sophisticated users' preferences, (ii) faithfully represent users' preferences in the sense that it rank-orders choices in a way as close as possible to users' specifications of preferences over choices if they were able to provide them, (iii) cope with possibly inconsistent preferences and (iv) offer attractive complexity properties, i.e., the spatial cost of representing partial descriptions of preferences and the time cost of comparing pairwise choices or computing the best choices.

The last decade has seen a widespread number of compact preference representation languages aiming as best as possible to comply with the above-cited desiderata. Fundamentally these languages differ in the form of partial descriptions of preferences they support. In fact, users' preferences show up in different formats: comparative preference statements, e.g., "I like London more than Paris"; quantitative weighted preference statements, e.g., "I like Berlin with weight .7"; or qualitative weighted preference statements, e.g., "I really like Amsterdam". This leads to a first categorization of compact languages into weighted languages (qualitative or quantitative) and unweighted languages. Moreover, an analysis of comparative preference statements leads to a finer categorization. In fact, in some situations, users exhibit independency or dependency properties when expressing comparative preference statements. For example, a user may independently specify his preferences for the color of his pants and his jacket. On the other hand, his preference for the color of his shoes may depend on the color of his pants and his jacket. Independency and dependency are nice properties as they can be graphically shown, making explicit the relations between attributes. Therefore, unweighted languages are split into conditional logics and graphical languages.

The second fundamental difference is related to the way the languages rank-order the choices. Do they compare all possible choices or do they allow incomparabilities? Before we try to understand which comparisons are allowed by compact languages, this second difference calls for an essential question: How do languages compare choices? In fact, the answer to this question depends on our interpretation of preferences. Preferences can be viewed as hard constraints, in which case the user likes the choices which satisfy all her preferences and dislikes all the other choices. However, this behavior is wishful thinking since choices which satisfy all preferences may not exist when preferences are inconsistent, i.e., they cannot be fulfilled together. Moreover, even if preferences are consistent, choices which satisfy all of them may be not feasible. In such situations, a user is generally ready to accept less satisfactory choices such as those which better fulfill her preferences. In this case, preferences are viewed as soft constraints. Therefore, we move from a simple case of preferences being satisfied or not to a more graded issue. In other words, this means that some preferences are more important than others.

Let us now go back to the second fundamental difference between compact languages. In real life, users may not wish (or be able) to compare some choices, thus allowing ties or incomparabilities. They may also reject incomparability and wish to compare all possible choices. Compact languages reflect this idea. Some of them compare all possible choices, and others not.

The first part of this book is dedicated to preference representation and related problems. In Chapter 2 we present the necessary notation and background for the mathematical encoding of preferences (preferences modeling). Chapter 3 constitutes an important part in the book. It offers a panoramic view of the well-known compact preference representation languages from each category we previously identified, namely, weighted languages, conditional logics and graphical languages.

Chapter 4 aims at explaining the behavior of some key languages in rank-ordering choices. As we previously said, given that preferences are considered as soft constraints, some preferences are more important than others. This importance is directly perceived in weighted languages, e.g., "I like Berlin with weight .7". In contrast, it is implicitly present in unweighted languages. For example, do the preference statements "prefer fish to meat", "if red wine is served, prefer meat to fish" and "if white wine is served, prefer cake to ice cream" have equal importance? It appears that "if red wine is served, prefer meat to fish" is more important than both "prefer fish to meat" and "if white wine is served, prefer cake to ice cream", which are in turn equally important. In Chapter 4 we consider some key unweighted languages and show their underpinning semantics with respect to the importance of preferences.

Chapter 5 approaches the preference representation framework from a different angle. While compact preference representation languages are mainly grounded in the interpretation of preferences in philosophy, we know relatively much less about preferences in psychology. Since preferences refer to subjective aspirations of the users, we believe that it is worth trying to understand preference representation from a cognitive psychology point of view. Preferences are not a new topic in psychology. Many works have focused on the study of preferences in human decision making and judgment. Chapter 5 concludes the first part of this book by providing some entry points to these studies. Surprisingly many well-known problems in artificial intelligence have been widely addressed in psychology, e.g., the construction of preferences and the transitivity of preferences, among many other problems.

Reasoning with preferences

Preference representation can be limited to an independent decision-aiding problem, in which case the purpose is to compute the best choices or to compare them. However the scope of preference representation is much wider than an isolated decision-aiding problem. Indeed, representing preferences and dealing with preference queries may be of interest in many fields of artificial intelligence, social choice theory, operations research and database management, to mention just a few. So far, preferences have been used in these fields in a very limited way, generally assuming that preferences over choices are explicitly available via a value function or a rank-ordering. It seems that researchers now realize the importance of revisiting the above fields and showing how they can profitably benefit from the use of compact preference representation languages. This is the focus of the second part of this book. In particular, we first shed light on argumentation theory and database frameworks and provide an overview of how preferences have been progressively integrated into these frameworks.

Argumentation theory is a reasoning process based on constructing arguments, determining conflicts between arguments and determining acceptable arguments. In some applications, an argument may be seen as a reason for or against the truth of particular statements. The following academic example describes a problem that can be represented with argumentation theory.

During a discussion between reporters (A, B, C, D, E, F) about the publication of information I concerning the person X, the following arguments are presented:

- A: I is important information; we must publish it.

- B: I concerns the person X; X is a private person and we cannot publish information about a private person without her agreement, and X does not agree with the publication.

- C: X is a minister, so X is a public person, not a private person.

- D: X has resigned, so X is no longer a minister.

- E: Her resignation has been refused by the chief of the government.

- F: I concerns a problem of public health, so I is important information.

Clearly, in order to employ consistent reasoning, one cannot use together the arguments provided by A and B. In fact, they argue for mutually exclusive statements, i.e., publishing information I and not publishing that information, respectively. We say that two arguments are conflicting when one cannot forward both arguments without contradicting oneself. Among other conflicts, we also have that C and B are conflicting since the latter states that X is a private person while C concludes that X is not.

The above example gives a particular definition of an argument in terms of a set of information in favor of or against a given statement. However, the original definition of an argument states that an argument is an abstract entity whose origin and structure are not known. The role of an argument is only described by its conflicts with other arguments. This is commonly known as Dung's framework. The abstract nature of Dung's framework accounts for a broad range of its applications. For example, this framework has been shown to be suitable for reasoning about inconsistent knowledge (see the above example), decisions, and multi-agent systems. Whatever the structure of an argument (i.e., abstract or not), the major problem is how to solve conflicts. Should we trust reporter A or reporter B? Reporter B or reporter C? In our daily lives, we generally encounter situations in which not all arguments are equal in strength. For example, an argument provided by an expert is stronger than an argument provided by a non-expert. Preferences play an important role in solving conflicts in argumentation theory. When two arguments are conflicting, an argument is accepted against the other argument if it is preferred. Different ways are possible for computing a preference relation over arguments depending on their structure and origin. More precisely, an argument is preferred when it is built from more important or prioritized information. The latter may be pervaded with implicit priorities (e.g., defeasible information) or explicit priorities (e.g., weighted formulas). The preference relation may also be induced by the values (points of view, criteria, etc.) promoted by the arguments. Chapter 6 provides an overview of the main argumentation frameworks based on preferences. Surprisingly, some compact preference representation languages are used depending on the structure of the arguments and their origin.

Chapter 7 deals with preferences in database querying. When we query a database we may be faced with an undesirable result when too many answers are returned. Suppose that a user is looking for a hotel in Paris. Due to the large number of hotels in this city, providing more knowledge about the user's preferences in the query will help to eliminate irrelevant hotels and focus only on the relevant ones. Therefore, preferences act as a filter which returns relevant answers. While mainstream database problems have long focused on the retrieval of the set of the best answers, preferences are now used to return answers rank-ordered according to their satisfaction level. The introduction of preferences in database queries has seen growing interest. There are number of works on subjects ranging from numerical representations of preferences to their qualitative representations. We mainly shed light on approaches which integrate compact preference representation languages into database queries.

Chapter 8 considers the problem of reasoning with preferences from a different perspective. In contrast to Chapters 6 and 7, it does not explore the use of preferences in a particular framework. Instead, it aims at confronting compact preference representation languages to other frameworks. In particular, it focuses on conditional logics for two different purposes. In the first part of the chapter, these logics are viewed as an approach for aggregating partial preferences over attributes. The latter are seen as criteria and evaluated on the basis of a common scale of values. The analysis of this problem calls for dedicated methods for multiple criteria aggregation. In particular, the Choquet integral shows a close relationship with conditional logics as it also deals with a set of comparative preference statements over attributes. In contrast to conditional logics, the Choquet integral is a numerical aggregation approach. The chapter offers a comparison of the two frameworks.

The second part of this chapter aims to broaden the use of preferences. It makes a nice bridge with an apparently different framework, namely, temporal reasoning. Representing and reasoning about time and space are important issues in many domains, such as natural language processing, geographic information systems, computer vision, and robot navigation. Qualitative reasoning about temporal and spatial information aims to develop qualitative formalisms to reason about such information using qualitative relations. To this end, several qualitative approaches have been proposed to represent spatial or temporal entities and their relations. For example, Allen represents temporal entities as intervals over a qualitative time scale. Their relations correspond to the different relative positions of two intervals. For example, "interval I_1 meets interval I_2", "I_1 precedes I_2", etc. This formalism is commonly known as Allen's algebra. It appears that all relations in Allen's algebra can be mapped onto comparative preference statements in conditional logics. However, an interval in Allen's algebra is an abstract and non-decomposable entity only described by its start and end points. Therefore, Allen's algebra fails to represent situations where an interval is a complex entity. In a scheduling problem, an interval is a set of objects to be rank-ordered. For example, an interval may be a set of school courses, and relations describe requirements on the schedule of the courses. The chapter takes advantage of the closeness between the two frameworks and shows that the problem raised by Allen's algebra can be overcome in conditional logics.

We conclude this book with a description of related work and some hints for future work.

Part I
Preferences Modeling and Representation

Chapter 2
Preferences Modeling

2.1 Introduction

Dealing with preferences means that one needs to make a choice from a collection of possible choices. The generic term *object* is used as a formal term for choice. An object may be a trip, a candidate, a course, a time interval, etc.

Choosing an object from a set of objects implicitly means needing to compare the objects, e.g., this candidate is better than the other one, this course is more interesting than the others, I don't have a preference between giving my talk today or tomorrow, these two candidates are incomparable, etc.

Preferences modeling is formally describing these comparisons. It is the first and basic step of all works dealing with preferences in various disciplines [1, 2, 3, 5, 7]. Formally speaking, the basic ingredient of preferences modeling is a binary relation over the set of objects called preference relation. The latter expresses that an object is at least as preferred as another object. Three specific relations can be induced by a preference relation: A strict preference relation which describes a strict preference between two objects, an indifference relation which describes a similarity between two objects and an incomparability relation which holds when two objects cannot be compared in terms of a strict preference or indifference. These three relations form a preference structure. We survey different kinds of preference structures depending on the properties of the underlying preference relation.

In the last section of this chapter, we make precise the notion of an object. In this book it is generally described by a set of attributes, each attribute taking its values in a finite domain. Exceptions are made in Chapters 6 and 8 due to the context.

2.2 Crisp Preference Relations

Preferences modeling is based on a finite set of objects, denoted by $\mathcal{O}$, to be compared or evaluated [4]. The basic ingredient in this framework is a binary relation, denoted by $\succeq$, over $\mathcal{O} \times \mathcal{O}$. The notation $o \succeq o'$ stands for "o is at least as preferred as o'". Thus $\succeq$ is referred to as *preference relation*.

Given a preference relation $\succeq$ and two objects $o, o' \in \mathcal{O}$, we distinguish between three relations over o and o':

- o is strictly preferred to o', denoted by $o \succ o'$, when $o \succeq o'$ holds but $o' \succeq o$ does not. $\succ$ is called a *strict preference relation*.

- o is indifferent to o', denoted by $o \approx o'$, when both $o \succeq o'$ and $o' \succeq o$ hold. $\approx$ is called an *indifference relation*.

- o is incomparable to o', denoted by $o \sim o'$, when neither $o \succeq o'$ nor $o' \succeq o$ holds. $\sim$ is called an *incomparability relation*.

Let us now recall some basic properties concerning binary relations.

- $\succeq$ is reflexive if and only if $\forall o \in \mathcal{O}, o \succeq o$.

- $\succeq$ is irreflexive if and only if $\forall o \in \mathcal{O}, o \succeq o$ does not hold.

- $\succeq$ is complete if and only if $\forall o, o' \in \mathcal{O}$, we have $o \succeq o'$ or $o' \succeq o$.

- $\succeq$ is transitive if and only if $\forall o, o', o'' \in \mathcal{O}$, if $o \succeq o'$ and $o' \succeq o''$ then $o \succeq o''$.

- $\succeq$ is symmetric if and only if $\forall o, o' \in \mathcal{O}$, if $o \succeq o'$ then $o' \succeq o$.

- $\succeq$ is antisymmetric if and only if $\forall o \in \mathcal{O}, \forall o' \in \mathcal{O} \backslash \{o\}$, we have $not(o \succeq o'$ and $o' \succeq o)$.

- $\succeq$ is asymmetric if and only if $\forall o, o' \in \mathcal{O}$, we have $not(o \succeq o'$ and $o' \succeq o)$.

Therefore, $\succ$ is asymmetric and $\approx, \sim$ are symmetric. While the reflexivity of $\succeq$ may be considered as a natural property, it is not a necessary condition. If $\succeq$ is reflexive then $\approx$ is reflexive and $\sim$ is irreflexive.

Given $\succeq$, the triple $(\succ, \approx, \sim)$ is called a preference structure induced by $\succeq$. We also say that each relation in the triple (i.e., $\succeq, \approx$ or $\sim$) is associated with (or induced by) $\succeq$.

Given the properties of a preference relation $\succeq$, we distinguish between different types of preference structures. As far as the next few chapters are concerned, we recall two structures:

- A *total preorder:* this corresponds to a reflexive, complete and transitive preference relation $\succeq$. The associated strict preference relation and indifference relation are transitive while the associated incomparability relation is empty.

When $\succeq$ is antisymmetric, $\approx$ is the set of pairs (o,o) and the preference structure is called a *total order*. Lastly, when $\succeq$ is asymmetric, $\approx$ is empty and the preference structure is called a *strict total order*.

- A *partial preorder:* this corresponds to a reflexive and transitive preference relation $\succeq$. The associated strict preference relation and indifference relation are transitive while the associated incomparability relation is not empty.

  When $\succeq$ is antisymmetric, $\approx$ is composed of pairs (o,o) only and the preference structure is called a *partial order*. Lastly, when $\succeq$ is asymmetric, $\approx$ is empty and the preference structure is called a *strict partial order*.

A preference relation $\succeq$ is cyclic if and only if its induced strict preference relation $\succ$ is cyclic, i.e., there exists a chain of objects $o, \cdots, o'$ such that $o \succ \cdots \succ o' \succ o$. Otherwise $\succeq$ is acyclic.

$\succ$, $\approx$ and $\sim$ will always refer to the strict preference relation, the indifference relation and the incomparability relation, respectively.

Given a transitive indifference relation $\approx$ and a transitive strict preference relation $\succ$ we have the following combinations: $\forall o, o' \in \mathcal{O}$,

$$\text{if } o \succ o' \text{ and } o' \approx o'' \text{ then } o \succ o''$$

and

$$\text{if } o \approx o' \text{ and } o' \succ o'' \text{ then } o \succ o''.$$

From now on, we suppose that $\succeq$ is transitive. By abuse of language we sometimes say that $\succeq$ is a total or partial (pre)order or (strict) total or partial (pre)order. When no confusion is possible, an order is equivalently denoted by $\succeq$ or $\succ$.

When the preference relation $\succeq$ is a total preorder, the indifference relation $\approx$ induced by $\succeq$ is an equivalence relation (reflexive, symmetric and transitive). The set of equivalence classes of $\mathcal{O}$ given $\approx$ is totally ordered w.r.t. $\succ$. Let $E_1, \cdots, E_n$ be the set of equivalence classes induced by $\approx$. Then,

(i) $\forall i = 1, \cdots, n, E_i \neq \emptyset$,
(ii) $E_1 \cup \cdots \cup E_n = \mathcal{O}$,
(iii) $\forall i, j, E_i \cap E_j = \emptyset$ for $i \neq j$,
(iv) $\forall o, o' \in E_i, o \approx o'$.

$(E_1, \cdots, E_n)$ is an ordered partition of $\mathcal{O}$ given $\succeq$ iff $(\forall o, o' \in \mathcal{O}, o \in E_i, o' \in E_j$ with $i < j$ if and only if $o \succ o')$.

Example 2.1. Let $\mathcal{O} = \{o_0, o_1, o_2, o_3\}$ be the set of objects. Let $\succeq$ be a total preorder over $\mathcal{O} \times \mathcal{O}$ defined by $o_1 \succ o_3$, $o_3 \approx o_0$ and $o_3 \succ o_2$. Then, the ordered partition of $\mathcal{O}$ is (E_1, E_2, E_3) with $E_1 = \{o_1\}$, $E_2 = \{o_0, o_3\}$ and $E_3 = \{o_2\}$.

A total order can also be written as an ordered partition of $\mathcal{O}$ where each equivalence class is composed of a single object.

Note that an ordered partition of $\mathscr{O}$ associated with $\succeq$ is acyclic. For example, the preference relation $o_1 \succ o_2$, $o_2 \succ o_3$, $o_3 \succ o_2$ and $o_3 \succ o_4$ cannot be written in terms of an ordered partition.

Let $\succeq$ and $\succeq'$ be two preference relations. We say that $\succeq$ extends $\succeq'$ if and only if $\forall o, o' \in \mathscr{O}$, if $o \succeq' o'$ then $o \succeq o'$.

We compare total preorders on the basis of specificity principles [10]. The minimal specificity principle, used in system Z [8], gravitates towards the least-specific preorder, while the maximal specificity principle gravitates towards the most-specific preorder.

Definition 2.1 (Minimal or Maximal specificity principle).
Let $\succeq$ and $\succeq'$ be two total preorders over a set of objects $\mathscr{O}$ represented by ordered partitions $(E_1, \cdots, E_n)$ and $(E'_1, \cdots, E'_{n'})$, respectively. We say that $\succeq$ is less specific than $\succeq'$, written as $\succeq \sqsubseteq \succeq'$, iff $\forall o \in \mathscr{O}$, if $o \in E_i$ and $o \in E'_j$ then $i \leq j$. $\succeq$ belongs to the set of the least- (or most-) specific preorders in a set of preorders $\mathscr{D}$ if there is no $\succeq'$ in $\mathscr{D}$ such that $\succeq' \sqsubset \succeq$ (or $\succeq \sqsubset \succeq'$), where $\succeq' \sqsubset \succeq$ iff $\succeq' \sqsubseteq \succeq$ holds but $\succeq \sqsubseteq \succeq'$ does not.

In other words, $\succeq$ is less specific than $\succeq'$ when the rank of each object in $\succeq$ is not greater than its rank in $\succeq'$. Also, $\succeq$ is more specific than $\succeq'$ when the rank of each object in $\succeq$ is not smaller than its rank in $\succeq'$. Recall that the smaller the rank i, the more preferred the objects in E_i.

The following example illustrates the minimal and maximal specificity principles.

Example 2.2. Let $\mathscr{O} = \{o_0, o_1, o_2, o_3\}$ be the set of objects. Let $\succeq$, $\succeq'$ and $\succeq''$ be three preorders such that $\succeq = (\{o_3, o_2, o_0\}, \{o_1\})$, $\succeq' = (\{o_3, o_2\}, \{o_1, o_0\})$ and $\succeq'' = (\{o_3, o_0\}, \{o_1, o_2\})$. $\succeq$ is less specific than both $\succeq'$ and $\succeq''$. $\succeq'$ and $\succeq''$ are incomparable w.r.t. the specificity principle. The least-specific preorder is $\succeq$ while the most-specific preorders are $\succeq'$ and $\succeq''$.

The aim of preferences modeling is to guide a choice from the set $\mathscr{O}$ or a subset of $\mathscr{O}$. When objects are totally rank-ordered (i.e., the preference relation $\succeq$ is a total (pre)order), rationality of choice suggests that the users make a choice from among the most preferred objects w.r.t. $\succeq$, i.e., from among objects which belong to E_1 given the ordered partition $(E_1, \cdots, E_n)$ associated with $\succeq$. However, when $\succeq$ is a partial (pre)order, speaking about "most" preferred objects does not make sense. Therefore, we use the notion of undominated objects, which is suitable for both total and partial (pre)orders. We say that o dominates o' when $o \succ o'$ holds. The set of undominated (or best) objects of $\mathscr{O}' \subseteq \mathscr{O}$ w.r.t. $\succeq$, denoted by $\max(\mathscr{O}', \succeq)$, is defined by

$$\max(\mathscr{O}', \succeq) = \{o \mid o \in \mathscr{O}', \nexists o' \in \mathscr{O}', o' \succ o\}.$$

The set of the worst objects of $\mathscr{O}' \subseteq \mathscr{O}$ w.r.t. $\succeq$, denoted by $\min(\mathscr{O}', \succeq)$, is defined by

$$\min(\mathcal{O}', \succeq) = \{o \mid o \in \mathcal{O}', \nexists o' \in \mathcal{O}', o \succ o'\}.$$

The notions of best or worst objects also allow us to deal with a cyclic preference relation. For example, although the preference relation $o_1 \succ o_2$, $o_2 \succ o_3$, $o_3 \succ o_2$ and $o_3 \succ o_4$ cannot be written in terms of an ordered partition, we can conclude that o_1 is the best object and o_4 is the worst object.

2.3 Fuzzy Preference Relations

In some situations the preference relation is provided with additional information expressing the degree of plausibility of the preferences. This is called a *fuzzy preference relation*. More specifically, a fuzzy preference relation, denoted by $\mathcal{R}$, is a function from $\mathcal{O} \times \mathcal{O}$ to the unit interval $[0,1]$ such that $\mathcal{R}(o,o')$ corresponds to the degree to which the assertion "o is at least as preferred as o'" is true. Therefore, $\succeq$ is a crisp preference relation. It is a special case of a fuzzy preference relation $\mathcal{R}$ when $o \succeq o'$ holds if and only if $\mathcal{R}(o,o') = 1$.

In this extended framework, a fuzzy preference structure is defined by including a fuzzy strict preference relation denoted by P, a fuzzy indifference relation denoted by I and a fuzzy incomparability relation denoted by J.

In order to extend the properties of a crisp preference relation to the fuzzy case, the above fuzzy relations are defined from a De Morgan triple $\langle T, S, n \rangle$, where T is a t-norm, S is a t-conorm and n is a negation [6, 9] such that $S(a,b) = nT(na, nb)$.

Usually the functions T and n are respectively defined by $T(a,b) = \min(a,b)$ and $n(a) = 1 - a$. Therefore, $S(a,b) = \max(a,b)$. The properties of a preference relation listed in the previous section can be extended to the fuzzy case as follows:

- $\mathcal{R}$ is reflexive if and only if $\forall o \in \mathcal{O}$, $\mathcal{R}(o,o) = 1$.

- $\mathcal{R}$ is complete if and only if $\forall o, o' \in \mathcal{O}$, we have $\max(\mathcal{R}(o,o'), \mathcal{R}(o',o)) = 1$.

- $\mathcal{R}$ is transitive if and only if $\forall o, o', o'' \in \mathcal{O}$, $\min(\mathcal{R}(o,o'), \mathcal{R}(o',o'')) \leq \mathcal{R}(o,o'')$.

- $\mathcal{R}$ is symmetric if and only if $\forall o, o' \in \mathcal{O}$, $\mathcal{R}(o,o') = \mathcal{R}(o',o)$.

- $\mathcal{R}$ is antisymmetric if and only if $\forall o \in \mathcal{O}$, $\forall o' \in \mathcal{O} \setminus \{o\}$, we have $\min(\mathcal{R}(o,o'), \mathcal{R}(o',o)) = 0$.

- $\succeq$ is asymmetric if and only if we have $\forall o, o' \in \mathcal{O}$, $\min(\mathcal{R}(o,o'), \mathcal{R}(o',o)) = 0$.

Different proposals have been made to compute a fuzzy preference structure (P, I, J) from a fuzzy preference relation $\mathcal{R}$. We refer the reader to [9] for a detailed exposition.

2.4 The Language

Generally, users compare objects on the basis of their characteristics. For example, a car can be characterized by its color, cost and capacity. Its color may be red, white or blue. Its price may be 15,900 euros or 18,000 euros and its capacity may be five or nine persons. Therefore, the user has to compare 12 cars. However, sometimes not all possible objects are feasible due to integrity constraints. For example, a red car with capacity of nine persons and price of 15,900 euros does not exist. So the user has to make a choice from 11 feasible cars. For simplicity and without loss of generality, we do not explicitly refer to integrity constraints and suppose that all possible objects are feasible. We refer to feasibility only when it is important.

Characteristics considered to describe an object are called attributes or variables. We suppose that they take their values from a finite set.

We denote variables by uppercase letters (possibly subscripted), e.g., A, B, X_1, X_2. The domain of a variable X is denoted by $Dom(X)$.

Given a binary variable X, its values are denoted by x and $\neg x$, i.e., $Dom(X) = \{\neg x, x\}$. Sometimes, for clarity, the values $\neg x$ and x are explicitly given, e.g., *fish* and *meat* for dish, *white* and *red* for wine, etc. V denotes the set of all variables at hand.

An outcome (or object, choice, alternative), denoted by ω, is the result of assigning a value to each variable in V. Ω is the set of all possible outcomes, i.e., the Cartesian product of the domain of variables in V. $Asst(V')$, with $V' \subseteq V$, is the set of all possible assignments to variables in V'. Therefore, $\Omega = Asst(V)$.

Let $\mathscr{L}$ be a language based on V. Formulas are built on $\mathscr{L}$ using logical connectors $\wedge$, $\vee$ and $\neg$, which respectively stand for conjunction, disjunction and negation. $Mod(\varphi)$ denotes the set of outcomes that make the formula φ true. We write $\omega \models \varphi$ when $\omega \in Mod(\varphi)$. We say that ω satisfies φ. If ω does not satisfy φ, i.e., $\omega \notin Mod(\varphi)$, we write $\omega \not\models \varphi$ and say that ω is a countermodel of φ.

Given a set of formulas $\mathscr{F}$, ω satisfies $\mathscr{F}$ if and only if ω satisfies each formula in $\mathscr{F}$. ω is called $\mathscr{F}$-outcome. ω falsifies $\mathscr{F}$ if and only if ω falsifies at least one formula in $\mathscr{F}$. We say that ω is a countermodel of $\mathscr{F}$.

References

1. Allen, J.F.: An interval-based representation of temporal knowledge. In: Hayes, P.J. (eds.), 7th International Joint Conference on Artificial Intelligence, pp. 221-226. William Kaufmann, (1981)
2. Armstrong, W.E.: The determinateness of the utility function. The Economic Journal **49**, 453–467 (1939)
3. Debreu, G.: Theory of Value: An Axiomatic Analysis of Economic Equilibrium. John Wiley and Sons Inc., New York (1959)
4. Fishburn, P.C.: Utility Theory for Decision Making. Wiley, New York (1970)

5. Fishburn, P.C.: Preference structures and their numerical presentations. Theoretical Computer Science **217**, 359–389 (1999)
6. Fodor, J., Roubens, M.: Fuzzy Preference Modelling and Multi-Criteria Decision Aid. Kluwer Academic Publisher (1994)
7. Lichtenstein, S., Slovic, P.: The Construction of Preference, Cambridge University Press (2006)
8. Pearl, J.: System Z: A natural ordering of defaults with tractable applications to default reasoning. In: Parikh, R. (eds.), 3rd Conference on Theoretical Aspects of Reasoning about Knowledge, pp. 121-135. Morgan Kaufmann, (1990)
9. Perny, P, Roubens, M.: Fuzzy relational preference modelling, In: Dubois, D., Prade, H. (eds.), Chapter 1 of Volume 5 (Operations Research and Statistics) of Handbooks of Fuzzy Sets, pp. 3-30. Kluwer Academic Publishers, Dordrecht Boston London (1998)
10. Yager, R.R.: Entropy and specificity in a mathematical theory of evidence. International Journal of General Systems **9**, 249–260 (1983)

Chapter 3
Preference Representation Languages

3.1 Introduction

Preference representation is the task of capturing and manipulating user preferences described by a preference relation. The support of a preference representation is called a *language*, which we refer to as *preference representation language*.

One of the main problems a user faces when expressing her preferences lies in the number of variables, attributes, or criteria that she takes into account to evaluate the different outcomes. Indeed, the number of outcomes increases exponentially with the number of variables. Moreover, the preference relation over outcomes may exhibit some interactions between variables. Lastly, due to their cognitive limitation, users are generally not willing to compare all possible pairs of outcomes or evaluate them individually. These facts have an unfortunate consequence that any preference representation language that is based on the direct assessment of user preferences over the complete set of outcomes is simply infeasible.

Fortunately, users can abstract their preferences. More specifically, instead of providing preferences over outcomes (by pairwise comparison or individual evaluation), they generally express preferences over partial descriptions of outcomes, e.g., "I like London more than Paris", "if no smoking flights then I prefer flights with stopovers", and "I like fish with weight .8". Compact preference representation languages aim at representing such partial descriptions of user preferences which we refer to as preference statements. They use different completion principles in order to compute a preference relation induced by a set of preference statements. The consistency of this set corresponds to the induced preference relation being acyclic.

Some compact preference representation languages are based on qualitative preference statements (e.g., "I like London over Paris", "I really like London") and induce a partial or complete (pre)order over outcomes. Other languages are based on quantitative preference statements (e.g., "I like Paris with weight .7") and induce a utility function which in turn represents a complete preorder over outcomes.

Roughly compact preference representation languages can be divided into two categories: logical languages and graphical languages. Logical languages are in turn divided into two categories: weighted logics and conditional logics.

In the first part of this chapter we offer a survey of the most well-known and used languages from each category. They correspond to different ways users may express their preferences. They also use different completion principles to induce preference relations over outcomes that correspond to different reasoning lines.

The second part of this chapter deals with a particular kind of preference called "bipolar preference". Actually, preferences over a set of outcomes are sometimes expressed in two forms. On the one hand, a user may express what she considers (more or less) tolerable or unacceptable for her, and on the other hand she may express what she considers really satisfactory. The first form of preference is called negative preference and corresponds to constraints that should be respected. The second form is called positive preference and corresponds to appealing outcomes for the user. For example, consider a three-day summer school for which each invited speaker is asked to express a preferred time slot for scheduling her talk [4]. We assume that talks can be given either on Monday, Tuesday or Wednesday, and for each day the talk can be scheduled either in the morning, or in the afternoon. The invited speaker may provide two kinds of preferences. First, she specifies negative preferences, which describe unacceptable slots with levels of tolerance. For instance, she may strongly object to working on Monday (e.g., because it is the birthday of her daughter), and weakly refuse to speak on Wednesday. These negative preferences reject options and induce a first ranking on all feasible outcomes. For instance, outcomes where the talk is scheduled on Tuesday (either morning or afternoon) are the preferred ones, while outcomes where the talk is scheduled on Monday are considered as unacceptable. Next, the invited speaker specifies positive preferences. For instance, having a talk in the morning is preferred to having it in the afternoon, and scheduling it early in the morning will be even better. These positive preferences will induce a second ranking on all feasible outcomes. These preferences do not need to develop new compact representation languages (except for the graphical languages to represent positive preferences). In fact, existing languages are suitable for the representation of one or another kind of preference (i.e., negative preference or positive preference).

3.2 Numerical Language

A utility function [66], denoted by u, has been used for long to represent users' preferences. It maps the set of outcomes to the set of real numbers. More specifically, it assigns to each outcome a real number in such a way that the higher the number, the more preferred the outcome. Thus, a utility function is a numerical representation of a complete preorder such that comparing outcomes amounts to comparing their associated numbers. Formally, we write

$$\forall \omega, \omega' \in \Omega, \omega \succeq \omega' \text{ iff } u(\omega) \leq u(\omega').$$

A utility function offers a fast and easy way to compare outcomes since the user can decide easily which outcome is preferred to others. It may however be problematic when the number of outcomes is large. Moreover, the direct assessment of a numerical value over complete outcomes may not be possible, especially when there exist complex preference relations due to the interaction between variables. In such a case, a user needs to express her preferences over partial descriptions of outcomes.

Possibility theory [71] also offers a numerical representation of a complete preorder by means of a possibility distribution. The latter is a function, denoted by π, which maps the set of outcomes to the unit interval $[0, 1]$. The possibility degree of an outcome represents how satisfactory it is. The higher is the possibility degree, the more preferred the outcome.

In some situations, the use of numbers is not sufficient for representing some preference relations, in particular, when the indifference relation is not transitive. For example, an outcome ω_1 may be indifferent to ω_2, which is in turn indifferent to ω_3. However, the gap or distance between ω_1 and ω_3 is sufficient to prefer ω_1 over ω_3. Interval representation [35, 36, 53, 57, 60, 68] is a suitable framework to represent such relations, where an outcome is represented by an interval. Then, an outcome is preferred to another outcome when its associated interval lies completely to the right of the other interval. Since the purpose of this chapter is compact preference representation languages, we do not discuss this representation.

In the following sections, we survey the most well-known *compact* preference representation languages. Some of them are a compact representation of a utility function and consequently a complete preorder over outcomes. Other languages are a compact representation of a preference relation which may be a complete or partial (pre)order.

3.3 Weighted Logics

Before we explore extended logics for preference representation, we need to understand why classical propositional logic, on which these logics are built, is not satisfactory.

A user's preferences are expressed in classical propositional logic by means of propositional logic formulas. If φ represents a user's preference, this means that the user prefers outcomes satisfying φ and rejects all outcomes falsifying φ. The preference formula φ induces a complete preorder over possible outcomes as follows:

$$\forall \omega, \omega' \in \Omega, \omega \succ \omega' \text{ iff } \omega \models \varphi \text{ and } \omega' \not\models \varphi$$

and

$$\omega \approx \omega' \text{ iff } (\omega \models \varphi \text{ and } \omega' \models \varphi) \text{ or } (\omega \not\models \varphi \text{ and } \omega' \not\models \varphi).$$

Actually, a preference formula φ partitions the set of possible outcomes into two partitions: the set of good outcomes – those satisfying φ – and the set of worse outcomes – those falsifying φ.

When a user's preferences are specified by means of a set of propositional logic formulas, good outcomes are those which satisfy all preference formulas and worse outcomes are those which falsify at least one preference formula.

Example 3.1. Consider a user composing her menu based on a *main dish "M"* (fish or meat), *wine "W"* (white wine or red wine) and *dessert "D"* (cake or ice cream). We have $V = \{M, W, D\}$ with $Dom(M) = \{fish, meat\}$, $Dom(W) = \{white, red\}$ and $Dom(D) = \{cake, ice\_cream\}$. Thus, the set of outcomes is

$$\Omega = \{\omega_0 : fish - white - cake,$$
$$\omega_1 : fish - white - ice\_cream,$$
$$\omega_2 : fish - red - cake,$$
$$\omega_3 : fish - red - ice\_cream,$$
$$\omega_4 : meat - white - cake,$$
$$\omega_5 : meat - white - ice\_cream,$$
$$\omega_6 : meat - red - cake,$$
$$\omega_7 : meat - red - ice\_cream\}.$$

Suppose now that the user would prefer *fish, white wine* and *cake*. So the set of preferences is $P = \{fish, white, cake\}$. The preference relation associated with P is $fish - white - cake \succ fish - white - ice\_cream \approx fish - red - cake \approx fish - red - ice\_cream \approx meat - white - cake \approx meat - white - ice\_cream \approx meat - red - cake \approx meat - red - ice\_cream$.

Classical propositional logic allows us to express complex preferences thanks to connectors. Thus, a user may prefer *fish* and will be happy if, in addition, *white wine* or *cake* are served. Then, the set of preference formulas is $P' = \{fish, white \vee cake\}$, leading to the following preference relation:

$fish - white - cake \approx' fish - white - ice\_cream \approx' fish - red - cake \succ' fish - red - ice\_cream \approx' meat - white - cake \approx' meat - white - ice\_cream \approx' meat - red - cake \approx' meat - red - ice\_cream$.

However, this crude distinction between "good" and "worse" outcomes proves inadequate for multiple reasons. Let us go back to Example 3.1 and suppose that the menu composed of *fish, white* and *cake* is no longer available. Therefore, the set of possible outcomes is

$$\Omega' = \{\omega_1 : fish - white - ice\_cream,$$
$$\omega_2 : fish - red - cake,$$
$$\omega_3 : fish - red - ice\_cream,$$
$$\omega_4 : meat - white - cake,$$
$$\omega_5 : meat - white - ice\_cream,$$
$$\omega_6 : meat - red - cake,$$
$$\omega_7 : meat - red - ice\_cream\}.$$

Indeed, this constraint excludes the unique best outcome $fish - white - cake$. All remaining outcomes are "worse" as they falsify at least one user's preference. However, if we deeply analyze these "worse" outcomes, we can argue that some of them are better than others. More precisely, each of $fish - white - ice\_cream$, $fish - red - cake$ and $meat - white - cake$ falsifies one preference formula and each of $fish - red - ice\_cream$, $meat - red - cake$ and $meat - white - ice\_cream$ falsifies two preference formulas while $meat - red - ice\_cream$ falsifies the three preference formulas. Therefore, the preference relation $fish - white - ice\_cream \approx$ $fish - red - cake \approx meat - white - cake \succ fish - red - ice\_cream \approx$ $meat - red - cake \approx meat - white - ice\_cream \succ meat - red - ice\_cream$ is more informative and goes beyond a partitioning of possible outcomes into "good" and "worse" outcomes.

Let us now consider the set of preference formulas $P' = \{fish, white \lor cake\}$ given Ω. The user may consider that her preference for the main dish is more important than her preference for wine and dessert. Therefore, for each partition of outcomes in $\succeq'$, having $fish$ is better than not having it. The preference relation is then refined as follows: $fish - white - cake \approx' fish - white - ice\_cream \approx' fish - red - cake \succ'$ $fish - red - ice\_cream \succ' meat - white - cake \approx' meat - white - ice\_cream \approx'$ $meat - red - cake \approx' meat - red - ice\_cream$.

One can also imagine other ways to construct the preference relation.

Lastly, as we know, classical propositional logic is not suitable for handling inconsistency while a user may express contradictory preferences without being aware of that.

The reasons mentioned above motivate the need for advanced logics for preference representation. In the following subsections, we survey the most well-known logics, ranging from quantitative to qualitative ones.

Most of preference representation languages make use of binary variables. However they can be easily extended to the case of non binary variables as it is shown in Chapter 7.

3.3.1 Penalty Logic

In this logic, a user's preferences are graded and represented by means of a finite set of weighted propositional logic formulas of the form $\mathcal{N} = \{(\phi_i, a_i) \mid i = 1, \cdots, n\}$ [40, 32, 59]. For each pair (ϕ_i, a_i) in $\mathcal{N}$, ϕ_i is a propositional formula representing a user's preference and a_i is an integer representing how is important the satisfaction of ϕ_i. More specifically, the weight a_i represents the penalty of falsifying the preference formula ϕ_i. Therefore, the greater is a_i, the less satisfactory is an outcome falsifying ϕ_i. In order to evaluate the outcomes, we look for preference formulas in $\mathcal{N}$ that they falsify. An outcome ω which falsifies ϕ_i gets a *penalty degree* (i.e., a price to pay), denoted by $p(\omega)$, at least equal to a_i. Therefore, the penalty degree associated with (ϕ_i, a_i) is computed as follows:

$$p_{(\phi_i, a_i)}(\omega) = \begin{cases} 0 & \text{if } \omega \models \phi_i \\ a_i & \text{otherwise} \end{cases}.$$

The global penalty degree of an outcome w.r.t. $\mathcal{N}$ is the sum of the weights of the preference formulas falsified by that outcome. Formally, we write

$$p_{\mathcal{N}}(\omega) = \sum \{a_i \mid (\phi_i, a_i) \in \mathcal{N}, \omega \not\models \phi_i\},$$

with $\sum\{\emptyset\} = 0$.

Given a penalty distribution (or function) $p_{\mathcal{N}}$, the preference relation over $\Omega \times \Omega$ induced by $\mathcal{N}$ is defined by

$$\forall \omega, \omega' \in \Omega, \omega \succeq_{\mathcal{N}}^{pen} \omega' \text{ iff } p_{\mathcal{N}}(\omega) \leq p_{\mathcal{N}}(\omega').$$

Outcomes with a penalty degree equal to 0 correspond to the outcomes satisfying all formulas of the propositional logic base $\mathcal{N}^* = \{\phi_i \mid (\phi_i, a_i) \in \mathcal{N}\}$. The remaining outcomes are those which falsify at least one formula in $\mathcal{N}^*$. So, when there is at least one outcome with a penalty degree 0, this means that the set of preferences is consistent.

Example 3.2. Suppose a user would prefer a menu composed of both *fish* and *white wine*. She associates the level 10 with this preference. She would also prefer a menu composed of *white wine* or *cake* or both with level 6. So we have $\mathcal{N} = \{(fish \wedge white, 10), (white \vee cake, 6)\}$. In Table 3.1 we give local penalties w.r.t. each formula and the global penalty w.r.t. $\mathcal{N}$. Therefore, we have $\omega_0 \approx_{\mathcal{N}}^{pen} \omega_1 \succ_{\mathcal{N}}^{pen} \omega_2 \approx_{\mathcal{N}}^{pen} \omega_4 \approx_{\mathcal{N}}^{pen} \omega_5 \approx_{\mathcal{N}}^{pen} \omega_6 \succ_{\mathcal{N}}^{pen} \omega_3 \approx_{\mathcal{N}}^{pen} \omega_7$.

Observe that penalty logic allows compensation in the sense that falsifying a formula may be equivalent to falsifying a set of formulas with lower importance.

Example 3.3. Let $\mathcal{N}' = \{(fish, 10), (cake, 6), (white, 4)\}$. Then, the two outcomes *meat − white − cake* and *fish − red − ice_cream* have penalty degree equal to 10. The former falsifies $(fish, 10)$ while the latter falsifies $(cake, 6)$ and $(white, 4)$.

Table 3.1 The penalty distribution associated with $\mathcal{N}$

Outcomes	$P_{(fish \wedge white,10)}(\omega)$	$p_{(white \vee cake,6)}(\omega)$	$p_{\mathcal{N}}(\omega)$
$\omega_0 = fish - white - cake$	0	0	0
$\omega_1 = fish - white - ice\_cream$	0	0	0
$\omega_2 = fish - red - cake$	10	0	10
$\omega_3 = fish - red - ice\_cream$	10	6	16
$\omega_4 = meat - white - cake$	10	0	10
$\omega_5 = meat - white - ice\_cream$	10	0	10
$\omega_6 = meat - red - cake$	10	0	10
$\omega_7 = meat - red - ice\_cream$	10	6	16

3.3.2 Distance-Based Closeness to Preferences

As we have seen in the previous subsection, penalty logic is an extension of classical logic in the sense that formulas are weighted in the former, leading to a stratification of countermodels of $\mathcal{N}^*$. Penalty logic is based on the same principle as classical logic, in which an outcome either satisfies or falsifies a formula. However, some countermodels of a formula may be considered better than others. Let us consider the base $\mathcal{N} = \{(S \wedge C, 10)\}$. Suppose that the language is built on two propositional variables S and C. Then, $\Omega = \{\neg S \neg C, \neg SC, S \neg C, SC\}$. The penalty function associated with $\mathcal{N}$ is $p_{\mathcal{N}}(\neg SC) = p_{\mathcal{N}}(S \neg C) = p_{\mathcal{N}}(\neg S \neg C) = 10$ and $p_{\mathcal{N}}(SC) = 0$, leading to the preference relation $SC \succ_{\mathcal{N}}^{pen} \neg SC \approx_{\mathcal{N}}^{pen} S \neg C \approx_{\mathcal{N}}^{pen} \neg S \neg C$. Therefore, the outcomes $\neg SC$ and $S \neg C$ and $\neg S \neg C$ are equally preferred w.r.t. $\succeq_{\mathcal{N}}$. One may however argue that $S \neg C$ and $\neg SC$ are better than $\neg S \neg C$ since they satisfy either S or C while $\neg S \neg C$ falsifies both formulas. Thus $S \neg C$ and $\neg SC$ are considered closer to $S \wedge C$ than is $\neg S \neg C$. More generally, the closeness between an outcome and a formula φ is measured by a distance based on a local distance between the outcome and the φ-outcomes. Formally, we have

$$d(\omega, \varphi) = \min_{\omega' \models \varphi} \sigma(\omega, \omega'),$$

where $\sigma(\omega, \omega')$ is the local distance between ω and ω'.

Generally, the Hamming distance [25] is used as a local distance. It is equal to the number of variables whose valuation is different in ω and ω'.

Example 3.4 (Hamming distance).
Let $\omega = S \neg C$ and $\omega' = \neg SC$. The Hamming distance between ω and ω' is $\sigma(\omega, \omega') = 2$.

Example 3.5 (Distance outcome formula).
Let $\omega = S \neg F \neg C$ and $\varphi = (S \vee F) \wedge C$. We use the Hamming distance as a local distance. We have $d(\omega, \varphi) = \min_{\omega' \models \varphi} \sigma(\omega, \omega')$
$$= \min\{\sigma(\omega, SFC), \sigma(\omega, \neg SFC), \sigma(\omega, S \neg FC)\}$$

$$= \min\{2,3,1\} = 1.$$

Penalty logic has been extended to consider the distance between an outcome and preference formulas. We have [48]

$$p_{\mathcal{N},d}(\omega) = \sum \{a_i * d(\omega, \phi_i) \mid (\phi_i, a_i) \in \mathcal{N}, \omega \not\models \phi_i\}.$$

Then,

$$\omega \succeq^{pen}_{\mathcal{N},d} \omega' \text{ iff } p_{\mathcal{N},d}(\omega) \leq p_{\mathcal{N},d}(\omega').$$

Example 3.6. (Example 3.2 continued)
We have $\mathcal{N} = \{(fish \wedge white, 10), (white \vee cake, 6)\}$. We consider the Hamming distance as a local distance. In Table 3.2 we give the local distance between outcomes and preference formulas in $\mathcal{N}$ and their global distance. Therefore, we have $\omega_0 \approx^{pen}_{\mathcal{N},d} \omega_1 \succ^{pen}_{\mathcal{N},d} \omega_2 \approx^{pen}_{\mathcal{N},d} \omega_4 \approx^{pen}_{\mathcal{N},d} \omega_5 \succ^{pen}_{\mathcal{N},d} \omega_3 \succ^{pen}_{\mathcal{N},d} \omega_6 \succ^{pen}_{\mathcal{N},d} \omega_7$. For example, the ordering between ω_3 and ω_6 is reversed here due to the fact that ω_3 is closer to $(fish \wedge white, 10)$ than is ω_6.

Table 3.2 Distance-based closeness to preferences

Outcomes	$10 * d(\omega, fish \wedge white)$	$6 * d(\omega, white \vee cake)$	$p_{\mathcal{N},d}(\omega)$
$\omega_0 = fish - white - cake$	$10 * 0$	$6 * 0$	0
$\omega_1 = fish - white - ice\_cream$	$10 * 0$	$6 * 0$	0
$\omega_2 = fish - red - cake$	$10 * 1$	$6 * 0$	10
$\omega_3 = fish - red - ice\_cream$	$10 * 1$	$6 * 1$	16
$\omega_4 = meat - white - cake$	$10 * 1$	$6 * 0$	10
$\omega_5 = meat - white - ice\_cream$	$10 * 1$	$6 * 0$	10
$\omega_6 = meat - red - cake$	$10 * 2$	$6 * 0$	20
$\omega_7 = meat - red - ice\_cream$	$10 * 2$	$6 * 1$	26

3.3.3 Possibilistic Logic

Originally developed to represent uncertain knowledge, possibilistic logic [31] proved to be also suitable for preference representation. A user's preferences are represented by a set of weighted formulas of the form $\mathbb{T} = \{(\phi_i, \alpha_i) \mid \alpha_i = 1, \cdots, n\}$, where ϕ_i is a propositional logic formula representing the user's preference and $\alpha_i \in (0, 1]$ represents the minimal importance associated with ϕ_i. When α_i is equal to 1, the corresponding preference is absolute and must be satisfied. The more important a preference is, the less satisfactory are the outcomes falsifying it. A possibilistic logic base is a compact representation of a function π, called *a tolerance distribution*[1], from Ω to $[0,1]$ such that $\pi(\omega)$ represents the tolerance degree of ω. $\pi(\omega) = 0$ means that ω is not tolerated at all since it falsifies an absolute preference; $\pi(\omega) = 1$ means that nothing prevents ω from being tolerated w.r.t. the user's preferences. The higher $\pi(\omega)$ is, the more tolerated is ω.

The tolerance distribution associated with a preference formula (ϕ_i, α_i) is computed as follows [31]:

$$\pi_{(\phi_i, \alpha_i)}(\omega) = \begin{cases} 1 & \text{if } \omega \models \phi_i \\ 1 - \alpha_i & \text{otherwise} \end{cases}.$$

Possibilistic logic is a weakening of penalty logic where the sum operator is replaced by the min operator. The tolerance distribution associated with a possibilistic logic base is computed as follows:

$$\pi_{\mathbb{T}}(\omega) = \min\{\pi_{(\phi_i, \alpha_i)}(\omega) \mid \omega \in \Omega, (\phi_i, \alpha_i) \in \mathbb{T}\}, \tag{3.1}$$

which can be equivalently written as

$$\pi_{\mathbb{T}}(\omega) = \min\{1 - \alpha_i \mid (\phi_i, \alpha_i) \in \mathbb{T}, \omega \not\models \phi_i\} = 1 - \max\{\alpha_i \mid (\phi_i, \alpha_i) \subset \mathbb{T}, \omega \not\models \phi_i\} \tag{3.2}$$

with $\min\{\emptyset\} = 1$ (or $\max\{\emptyset\} = 0$).

So, in contrast to penalty logic, which considers all formulas falsified by an outcome, possibilistic logic only focuses on falsified formulas having the greatest weight.

When the tolerance distribution $\pi_{\mathbb{T}}$ is not normalized, i.e., there is no ω_0 such that $\pi_{\mathbb{T}}(\omega_0) = 1$, this means that the user's preferences cannot be satisfied all together, i.e., they are inconsistent.

Example 3.7. Let $\mathbb{T} = \{(fish \wedge white, .9), (white \vee cake, .6)\}$. The preference formulas *fish* $\wedge$ *white* and *white* $\vee$ *cake* are those used in $\mathcal{N}$ given in Example 3.2. In Table 3.3 we give the local tolerance degrees and the global tolerance degree of each outcome.

The tolerance distribution in the above example is a simple partition of the set of outcomes into outcomes which satisfy all preference formulas in $\mathbb{T}$ and those which falsify at least one preference formula, as in propositional logic. Actually, this result is due to the fact that $(fish \wedge white, .9)$ can be decomposed and replaced in $\mathbb{T}$ with the two preference formulas $(fish, .9)$ and $(white, .9)$. This can be easily checked by observing that

$$\pi_{(\phi_1 \wedge \cdots \wedge \phi_n, \alpha)}(\omega) = \begin{cases} 1 & \text{if } \omega \models \phi_1 \wedge \cdots \wedge \phi_n \\ 1 - \alpha & \text{otherwise} \end{cases}.$$

---

[1] The function π is usually called a "possibility" distribution (cf. Chapter 2). We use the term "tolerance" in the context of preference representation.

Table 3.3 The tolerance distribution associated with $\mathbb{T}$

Outcomes	$\pi_{(fish \wedge white,.9)}(\omega)$	$\pi_{(white \vee cake,.6)}(\omega)$	$\pi_{\mathbb{T}}(\omega)$
$\omega_0 = fish - white - cake$	1	1	1
$\omega_1 = fish - white - ice\_cream$	1	1	1
$\omega_2 = fish - red - cake$	.1	1	.1
$\omega_3 = fish - red - ice\_cream$	.1	.4	.1
$\omega_4 = meat - white - cake$	.1	1	.1
$\omega_5 = meat - white - ice\_cream$	.1	1	.1
$\omega_6 = meat - red - cake$	.1	1	.1
$\omega_7 = meat - red - ice\_cream$	.1	.4	.1

which is equivalent to $\pi_{(\phi_1 \wedge \cdots \wedge \phi_n, \alpha)}(\omega) = \min\{\pi_{(\phi_i, \alpha)}(\omega) \mid i = 1, \cdots, n\}$. Therefore, $\mathbb{T}$ is equivalent to $\mathbb{T}' = \{(fish,.9), (white,.9), (white \vee cake,.6)\}$ in the sense that the two bases induce the same tolerance distribution. The tolerance distribution associated with $\mathbb{T}'$ is given in Table 3.4. Now recall that the tolerance degree

Table 3.4 The tolerance distribution associated with $\mathbb{T}'$

Outcomes	$\pi_{(fish,.9)}$	$\pi_{(white,.9)}(\omega)$	$\pi_{(white \vee cake,.6)}(\omega)$	$\pi_{\mathbb{T}'}(\omega)$
$\omega_0 = fish - white - cake$	1	1	1	1
$\omega_1 = fish - white - ice\_cream$	1	1	1	1
$\omega_2 = fish - red - cake$	1	.1	1	.1
$\omega_3 = fish - red - ice\_cream$	1	.1	.4	.1
$\omega_4 = meat - white - cake$	.1	1	1	.1
$\omega_5 = meat - white - ice\_cream$	.1	1	1	.1
$\omega_6 = meat - red - cake$	.1	.1	1	.1
$\omega_7 = meat - red - ice\_cream$	.1	.1	.4	.1

of an outcome is computed w.r.t. the greatest weight associated with formulas in $\mathbb{T}$ falsified by the outcome (cf. Equation (3.2)). Indeed, $(white,.9)$ in $\mathbb{T}'$ subsumes $(white \vee cake,.6)$ in the sense that the formula $(white \vee cake,.6)$ is irrelevant in $\mathbb{T}'$. In fact, if an outcome falsifies $white$, then $white \vee cake$ is not considered. Now, if an outcome satisfies $white$, then it also satisfies $white \vee cake$. Therefore, $\mathbb{T}'$ is equivalent to $\mathbb{T}'' = \{(fish,.9), (white,.9)\}$.

Example 3.8. Let us now consider the possibilistic base $\mathbb{T}_1 = \{(fish \vee white, 1), (fish,.8), (cake,.8), (red,.5)\}$. The second column of Table 3.5 gives the tolerance distribution associated with $\mathbb{T}_1$. The two outcomes ω_6 and ω_7 are not tolerated at all as they falsify an absolute preference (i.e., an integrity constraint), namely, $fish \vee white$.

The definition of $\pi_{\mathbb{T}}$ given in Equation (3.2) faithfully models the intended meaning of the tolerance distribution associated with a possibilistic logic base. Indeed, an outcome gets a tolerance degree 0 as soon as it falsifies a formula $(\phi_i, 1)$ in $\mathbb{T}$. It gets

Table 3.5 The tolerance distributions associated with $\mathbb{T}_1$ and $\mathbb{T}_2$

Outcomes	$\pi_{\mathbb{T}_1}(\omega)$	$\pi_{\mathbb{T}_2}(\omega)$
$\omega_0 = fish - white - cake$	.5	.3
$\omega_1 = fish - white - ice\_cream$	.2	.3
$\omega_2 = fish - red - cake$	1	.4
$\omega_3 = fish - red - ice\_cream$	.2	.4
$\omega_4 = meat - white - cake$	.2	.2
$\omega_5 = meat - white - ice\_cream$	.2	.2
$\omega_6 = meat - red - cake$	0	0
$\omega_7 = meat - red - ice\_cream$	0	0

a tolerance degree 1 when it does not falsify any formula in $\mathbb{T}$. Lastly, the greater the weight associated with the formulas it falsifies (i.e., the greater the importance of the preferences it falsifies), the less tolerated it is.

Given a tolerance distribution $\pi_{\mathbb{T}}$, the preference relation associated with $\mathbb{T}$ is a complete preorder, defined by

$$\forall \omega, \omega' \in \Omega, \omega \succeq_{\mathbb{T}}^{\pi} \omega' \text{ iff } \pi_{\mathbb{T}}(\omega) \geq \pi_{\mathbb{T}}(\omega').$$

In our example we have $\omega_2 \succ_{\mathbb{T}}^{\pi} \omega_0 \succ_{\mathbb{T}}^{\pi} \omega_1 \approx_{\mathbb{T}}^{\pi} \omega_3 \approx_{\mathbb{T}}^{\pi} \omega_4 \approx_{\mathbb{T}}^{\pi} \omega_5 \succ_{\mathbb{T}}^{\pi} \omega_6 \approx_{\mathbb{T}}^{\pi} \omega_7$.

In some situations, the tolerance distribution π is not computed from a possibilistic logic base but provided by the user (although this is generally not the case due to elicitation problems). In such a case, it may be important to know some properties about sets of outcomes that are seen as preference formulas.

Definition 3.1. Let π be a tolerance distribution and ϕ be a formula.

- The tolerance measure of ϕ, denoted by $\Pi(\phi)$, is defined by

$$\Pi(\phi) = \max\{\pi(\omega) \mid \omega \in \Omega, \omega \models \phi\}. \tag{3.3}$$

- The importance degree of ϕ, denoted by $N(\phi)$, is defined by

$$N(\phi) = 1 - \Pi(\neg\phi) = \min\{1 - \pi(\omega) \mid \omega \in \Omega, \omega \models \neg\phi\}. \tag{3.4}$$

The tolerance measure $\Pi(\phi)$ evaluates the extent to which considering ϕ as a preference, given π, is tolerated. $\Pi(\phi) = 0$ means that ϕ is certainly not a preference, while $\Pi(\phi) = 1$ does not mean that ϕ is a preference but simply indicates that nothing prevents ϕ from being a preference. The importance degree $N(\phi)$ evaluates to what extent the preference ϕ is important. It behaves in a dual way, as Π. $N(\phi) = 1$ means that ϕ is highly important while $N(\phi) = 0$ means that the user did not express ϕ as a preference. This is weaker than ϕ certainly not being a preference.
Note that the importance degree $N(\phi_i)$ is not without a relationship, with the weight α_i associated with ϕ_i in $\mathbb{T}$. In fact, suppose that π is computed from $\mathbb{T}$ following Equation (3.2); we have

$$\forall (\phi_i, \alpha_i) \in \mathbb{T}, N(\phi_i) \geq \alpha_i.$$

Then a possibilistic logic base $\mathbb{T} = \{(\phi_i, \alpha_i) \mid \alpha_i = 1, \cdots, n\}$ can be equivalently written as $\mathbb{T} = \{\Pi(\neg\phi_i) \leq \alpha_i \mid i = 1, \cdots, n\}$.

From Equations (3.3) and (3.4), we have the following properties:

$$\forall \phi, \varphi, \Pi(\phi \vee \varphi) = \max(\Pi(\phi), \Pi(\varphi)), \tag{3.5}$$

$$\forall \phi, \varphi, N(\phi \wedge \varphi) = \min(N(\phi), N(\varphi)). \tag{3.6}$$

Let us now analyze how a user's preferences are handled in possibilistic logic. Suppose that π is the tolerance distribution associated with $\mathbb{T}$. First, notice that $\pi(\omega) = 0$ is more informative than $\pi(\omega) = 1$ since $\pi(\omega) = 0$ means that ω is not tolerated at all. On the other hand, $\pi(\omega) = 1$ only means that nothing prevents ω from being fully tolerated. Lastly, $\pi(\omega)$ is computed w.r.t. only formulas falsified by ω. This is supported by the inequality $\forall (\phi_i, \alpha_i) \in \mathbb{T}, N(\phi_i) \geq \alpha_i$ since we have $N(\phi_i) \geq \alpha_i$ iff $1 - \Pi(\neg\phi_i) \geq \alpha_i$ iff $\Pi(\neg\phi_i) \leq 1 - \alpha_i$ iff $\max\{\pi(\omega) \mid \omega \not\models \phi_i, (\phi_i, \alpha_i) \in \mathbb{T}\} \leq 1 - \alpha_i$. This means that the preference formula (ϕ_i, α_i) in a possibilistic logic base constrains the tolerance degree of countermodels of ϕ_i only. Indeed, possibilistic logic offers a negative reading of a user's preferences. In fact, negative preferences behave as constraints that should be satisfied. This is also asserted by noticing that the addition of preference formulas to $\mathbb{T}$ may only decrease the tolerance degree of outcomes. In the best case their degree remains unchanged. See Equation (3.1). Equation (3.6) indicates that formulas in a possibilistic logic are conjunctively combined. Once again, this is typically the behavior of constraints.

The inequality $\max\{\pi(\omega) \mid \omega \not\models \phi_i, (\phi_i, \alpha_i) \in \mathbb{T}\} \leq 1 - \alpha_i, \forall (\phi_i, \alpha_i) \in \mathbb{T}$, suggests that a family of tolerance distributions can be associated with a possibilistic logic base $\mathbb{T}$. From Equation (3.2), we can notice that $\pi_{\mathbb{T}}$ so defined is the greatest tolerance distribution satisfying the inequality $\max\{\pi(\omega) \mid \omega \not\models \phi_i, (\phi_i, \alpha_i) \in \mathbb{T}\} \leq 1 - \alpha_i$ [31]. This is the minimal specificity principle [70].

Lastly, notice that when a possibilistic logic base is inconsistent, an inconsistency degree can be computed. It is equal to the greatest weight in the base where inconsistency is met. Formally, we write

$$Inc(\mathbb{T}) = \max\{\alpha_i \mid \mathbb{T}_{\geq \alpha_i} \text{ is inconsistent}\},$$

where $\mathbb{T}_{\geq \alpha} = \{\phi_i \mid (\phi_i, \alpha_i) \in \mathbb{T}, \alpha_i \geq \alpha\}$, with $\max\{\emptyset\} = 0$.

Example 3.9. Let $\mathbb{T}_2 = \{(fish \vee white, 1), (fish, .8), (red, .7), (meat, .6), (cake, .4)\}$. The set $\{fish \vee white, fish, red\}$ is consistent but the set $\{fish \vee white, fish, red, meat\}$ is inconsistent. So, $Inc(\mathbb{T}_2) = .6$. This means that we can satisfy those preferences whose weight is greater than the inconsistency degree, namely *fish* $\vee$ *white, fish* and *red* (which is equivalent to satisfying *fish* and *red*), but these preferences cannot be fulfilled together with *meat*. Therefore, the tolerance degree of outcomes cannot exceed $1 - Inc(\mathbb{T}_2) = .4$. See the third column of Table 3.5.

Note that $\omega_2 : fish - red - cake$ and $\omega_3 : fish - red - ice\_cream$ have the same tolerance degree w.r.t. $\pi_{\mathbb{T}_2}$, namely, .4, although ω_2 satisfies $(cake, .4)$ while ω_3 does not. This is the drowning problem of possibilistic logic, where formulas at the level of the inconsistency degree and below are ignored even if they are not responsible for the inconsistency [8]. This problem does not occur in penalty logic since all formulas are considered.

In contrast to penalty logic, possibilistic logic is not weight-sensitive and preferences can be represented in a purely qualitative way. A qualitative possibilistic logic base is a set of ordered strata of the form $\mathbb{T} = (\Gamma_1, \cdots, \Gamma_n)$, where a stratum Γ_i is composed of equally important formulas, and formulas of Γ_i are more important than formulas of Γ_j for $i < j$. Here also, formulas belonging to the same stratum can be replaced by their conjunction. We say that an outcome falsifies a stratum when it falsifies at least one formula in that stratum. The tolerance distribution associated with $\mathbb{T} = (\Gamma_1, \cdots, \Gamma_n)$ is also represented in a qualitative way by means of a well-ordered partition, denoted by $\mathcal{WOP}(\pi_{\mathbb{T}}) = (S_1, \cdots, S_m)$ $(m \leq n + 1)$, such that outcomes belonging to S_i have the same tolerance degree and are more tolerated than outcomes belonging to S_j with $i < j$. $\mathcal{WOP}(\pi_{\mathbb{T}})$ is computed in the following way:

- S_1 is the set of outcomes satisfying $\Gamma_1 \cup \cdots \cup \Gamma_n$,
- S_i $(i = 2, \cdots, n)$ is the set of outcomes satisfying all formulas in $\Gamma_1 \cup \cdots \cup \Gamma_{n-i+1}$ but falsifying Γ_{n-i+2}, and
- S_m is the set of outcomes falsifying Γ_1.

If S_1 is empty then $\mathbb{T}$ is inconsistent.

Once $\mathcal{WOP}(\pi_{\mathbb{T}})$ is computed, the empty strata are removed and the S_i are renumbered in sequence.

Example 3.10. (Example 3.8 continued)
We have $\mathbb{T}_1 = \{(fish \vee white, 1), (fish, .8), (cake, .8), (red, .5)\}$. Then $\mathbb{T}_1 = (\{fish \vee white\}, \{fish, cake\}, \{red\})$ and $\mathcal{WOP}(\pi_{\mathbb{T}_1}) = (\{\omega_2\}, \{\omega_0\}, \{\omega_1, \omega_3, \omega_4, \omega_5\}, \{\omega_6, \omega_7\})$. $\mathbb{T}_1$ being consistent, the number of strata in $\mathcal{WOP}(\pi_{\mathbb{T}_1})$ is equal to $4 = 3 + 1$ where 3 is the number of strata in $\mathbb{T}_1$.

Let us now consider the possibilistic logic base given in Example 3.9. We have $\mathbb{T}_2 = \{(fish \vee white, 1), (fish, .8), (red, .7), (meat, .6), (cake, .4)\}$. Then, $\mathbb{T}_2 = (\{fish \vee white\}, \{fish\}, \{red\}, \{meat\}, \{cake\})$. We have $\mathcal{WOP}(\pi_{\mathbb{T}_2}) = (\{\}, \{\}, \{\omega_2, \omega_3\}, \{\omega_0, \omega_1\}, \{\omega_4, \omega_5\}, \{\omega_6, \omega_7\})$. The first two strata are empty because they correspond to the sets of outcomes which satisfy $\{fish \vee white, fish, red, meat, cake\}$ and $\{fish \vee white, fish, red, meat\}$, respectively. In fact, these two sets are inconsistent. We remove empty strata and get $\mathcal{WOP}(\pi_{\mathbb{T}_2}) = (\{\omega_2, \omega_3\}, \{\omega_0, \omega_1\}, \{\omega_4, \omega_5\}, \{\omega_6, \omega_7\})$. $\mathbb{T}_2$ being inconsistent, the number of strata in $\mathscr{WOP}(\pi_{\mathbb{T}_2})$ is different from $6 = 5 + 1$, where 5 is the number of strata in $\mathbb{T}_2$.

It is worth noticing that given a possibilistic logic base $\mathbb{T} = (\Gamma_1, \cdots, \Gamma_n)$, referring to the number of strata in $\mathscr{WOP}(\pi_{\mathbb{T}})$ to check the consistency of $\mathbb{T}$ is valid only when no strata $\mathbb{T}_i$ in $\mathbb{T}$ can be removed because it contains subsumed formulas. For example, let us consider $\mathbb{T} = (\{fish \vee white\}, \{fish\}, \{cake\}, \{cake \vee meat\}, \{red\})$. The qualitative tolerance distribution associated with $\mathbb{T}$ is $(\{\omega_2\}, \{\omega_0\}, \{\omega_1, \omega_3\}, \{\omega_4, \omega_5\}, \{\omega_6, \omega_7\})$. The number of its strata is 5 (< 6) because the stratum $\{cake \vee meat\}$ can be removed. In fact $cake \vee meat$ is subsumed by $cake$. Therefore, $\mathbb{T}$ is equivalent to $(\{fish \vee white\}, \{fish\}, \{cake\}, \{red\})$, whose associated tolerance distribution is $(\{\omega_2\}, \{\omega_0\}, \{\omega_1, \omega_3\}, \{\omega_4, \omega_5\}, \{\omega_6, \omega_7\})$.

3.3.4 Discrimin and Lexicographical Orderings

In penalty logic, the penalty distribution is an additive function of penalties induced by falsified formulas. Therefore, the weights associated with formulas are important, since the penalty distribution allows compensation between weights. On the other hand, possibilistic logic is a qualitative framework since outcomes are evaluated on the basis of the weights associated with the most important formulas they falsify without considering less important formulas. Therefore, two outcomes may have equal tolerance degrees, although one outcome also falsifies less important formulas, but not the other. This is the drowning problem explained in Subsection 3.3.3.

Discrimin and lexicographical orderings lie in between penalty logic and possibilistic logic. They gather the advantages of both logics. Like penalty logic, they consider all falsified formulas and like possibilistic logic, they are qualitative so weights associated with formulas are symbolic. No compensation is allowed.

Definition 3.2 (Discrimin ordering). [2, 3, 23, 37, 56]
Let Σ be a set of weighted formulas. Let $\mathscr{F}_{\geq \alpha}(\omega) = \{\varphi_i \mid (\varphi_i, \alpha_i) \in \Sigma, \alpha_i \geq \alpha, \omega \not\models \varphi_i\}$ and $\mathscr{F}_{=\alpha}(\omega) = \{\varphi_i \mid (\varphi_i, \alpha_i) \in \Sigma, \alpha_i = \alpha, \omega \not\models \varphi_i\}$. The discrimin ordering relation, denoted by $\succeq_{\Sigma}^{discrimin}$, is defined by $\forall \omega, \omega' \in \Omega$, $\omega \succeq_{\Sigma}^{discrimin} \omega'$ if and only if $\exists \beta$ such that both of the following conditions hold:

* $\forall \alpha > \beta, \mathscr{F}_{\geq \alpha}(\omega) = \mathscr{F}_{\geq \alpha}(\omega')$,
* $\mathscr{F}_{=\beta}(\omega) \subseteq \mathscr{F}_{=\beta}(\omega')$.

$\omega \succ_{\Sigma}^{discrimin} \omega'$ if and only if $\omega \succeq_{\Sigma}^{discrimin} \omega'$ holds but $\omega' \succeq_{\Sigma}^{discrimin} \omega$ does not.

Intuitively, the discrimin ordering means that ω is preferred to ω' when there exists a weight β such that ω and ω' falsify the same formulas whose weight is greater than β and the set of formulas with weight β falsified by ω is included in the set of formulas with weight β falsified by ω'.

The preference relation $\succeq_{\Sigma}^{discrimin}$ is a partial preorder.

Example 3.11.
Let $\Sigma_1 = \{(fish \vee white, 1), (fish, .8), (cake, .8), (red, .5)\}$. In Table 3.6 we give the set of formulas falsified by each outcome. We have

Table 3.6 Falsified formulas in Σ_1

Outcomes	Falsified formulas in Σ_1
$\omega_0 = fish - white - cake$	$\{(red, .5)\}$
$\omega_1 = fish - white - ice\_cream$	$\{(cake, .8), (red, .5)\}$
$\omega_2 = fish - red - cake$	$\emptyset$
$\omega_3 = fish - red - ice\_cream$	$\{(cake, .8)\}$
$\omega_4 = meat - white - cake$	$\{(fish, .8), (red, .5)\}$
$\omega_5 = meat - white - ice\_cream$	$\{(fish, .8), (cake, .8), (red, .5)\}$
$\omega_6 = meat - red - cake$	$\{(fish \vee white, 1), (fish, .8)\}$
$\omega_7 = meat - red - ice\_cream$	$\{(fish \vee white, 1), (fish, .8), (cake, .8)\}$

$$\omega_2 \succ_{\Sigma_1}^{discrimin} \omega_0 \succ_{\Sigma_1}^{discrimin} \omega_3 \succ_{\Sigma_1}^{discrimin} \omega_1 \succ_{\Sigma_1}^{discrimin} \omega_5 \succ_{\Sigma_1}^{discrimin} \omega_6 \succ_{\Sigma_1}^{discrimin} \omega_7$$
and $\omega_2 \succ_{\Sigma_1}^{discrimin} \omega_0 \succ_{\Sigma_1}^{discrimin} \omega_4 \succ_{\Sigma_1}^{discrimin} \omega_5 \succ_{\Sigma_1}^{discrimin} \omega_6 \succ_{\Sigma_1}^{discrimin} \omega_7$.

The preference relation $\succ_{\Sigma_1}^{discrimin}$ is partial due to the fact that ω_4 is incomparable to both ω_1 and ω_3. In fact, ω_4 falsifies $(fish, .8)$ while ω_1 and ω_3 falsify $(cake, .8)$.

The lexicographical ordering has the same principle as discrimin ordering. In contrast to the latter, it looks at the number of falsified formulas and not at the formulas themselves. Formally, we write:

Definition 3.3 (Lexicographical ordering). [3, 29, 30, 52]
Let Σ be a set of weighted formulas. Let $\mathcal{F}_{\geq \alpha}(\omega) = \{\varphi_i \mid (\varphi_i, \alpha_i) \in \Sigma, \alpha_i \geq \alpha, \omega \not\models \varphi_i\}$ and $\mathcal{F}_{=\alpha}(\omega) = \{\varphi_i \mid (\varphi_i, \alpha_i) \in \Sigma, \alpha_i = \alpha, \omega \not\models \varphi_i\}$. The lexicographical ordering relation, denoted by $\succeq_{\Sigma}^{lex}$, is defined by $\forall \omega, \omega' \in \Omega$, $\omega \succeq_{\Sigma}^{lex} \omega'$ if and only if $\exists \beta$ such that both of the following conditions hold:

- $\forall \alpha > \beta, |\mathcal{F}_{\geq \alpha}(\omega)| = |\mathcal{F}_{\geq \alpha}(\omega')|$,
- $|\mathcal{F}_{=\beta}(\omega)| \leq |\mathcal{F}_{=\beta}(\omega')|$,
  where $|\Gamma|$ is the number of formulas in Γ.

$\omega \succ_{\Sigma}^{lex} \omega'$ if and only if $\omega \succeq_{\Sigma}^{lex} \omega'$ holds but $\omega' \succeq_{\Sigma}^{lex} \omega$ does not.

The preference relation $\succeq_{\Sigma}^{lex}$ is a complete preorder.

Example 3.12. (Example 3.11 continued)
We have $\omega_2 \succ_{\Sigma_1}^{lex} \omega_0 \succ_{\Sigma_1}^{lex} \omega_3 \succ_{\Sigma_1}^{lex} \omega_1 \approx_{\Sigma_1}^{lex} \omega_4 \succ_{\Sigma_1}^{lex} \omega_5 \succ_{\Sigma_1}^{lex} \omega_6 \succ_{\Sigma_1}^{lex} \omega_7$.

3.3.5 Guaranteed Possibilistic Logic

In guaranteed possibilistic logic, a user's preferences are also represented by means of a set of weighted formulas of the form $\mathcal{G} = \{(\varphi_j, \beta_j) \mid i = 1, \cdots, n\}$. In contrast to possibilistic logic, this logic does not penalize outcomes falsifying a formula but rewards outcomes which satisfy it. More specifically, the weight β_j associated with a formula φ_j represents the minimal satisfaction degree guaranteed by the satisfaction of φ_j. Therefore, each outcome which satisfies φ_j is satisfactory to a degree at least equal to β_j. The higher β_j is, the more satisfactory are the outcomes satisfying φ_j. A guaranteed possibilistic logic base is a compact representation of a function δ from Ω to $[0,1]$ such that $\delta(\omega)$ represents the satisfaction degree of ω. The interval $[0,1]$ is a positive scale in the sense that $\delta_{\mathcal{G}}(\omega) = 1$ means that ω is fully satisfactory while $\delta_{\mathcal{G}}(\omega) = 0$ means that no information is available about the satisfaction of ω. The user is rather indifferent w.r.t. ω. The higher $\delta_{\mathcal{G}}(\omega)$ is, the more satisfactory is ω.

The satisfaction distribution associated with a preference formula (φ_j, β_j) is computed as follows [4]:

$$\delta_{(\varphi_j, \beta_j)}(\omega) = \begin{cases} \beta_j & \text{if } \omega \models \varphi_j \\ 0 & \text{otherwise} \end{cases}.$$

As stated above, each outcome satisfying a preference formula (φ_j, β_j) in $\mathcal{G}$ is satisfactory to a degree at least equal to β_j. Therefore, $\delta_{\mathcal{G}}$ associated with $\mathcal{G}$ is computed as follows:

$$\forall \omega \in \Omega, \delta_{\mathcal{G}}(\omega) = \max\{\beta_j \mid (\varphi_j, \beta_j) \in \mathcal{G}, \omega \models \varphi_j\}, \tag{3.7}$$

with $\max\{\emptyset\} = 0$.

In some situations, the satisfaction distribution δ is not computed from a guaranteed possibilistic logic but directly provided by the user (although this is generally not the case due to elicitation problems). In such a case, it is important to know some properties regarding sets of outcomes that can be considered as preference formulas. Given a satisfaction distribution δ, a guaranteed satisfaction measure associated with a formula φ can be computed. It is equal to

$$\Delta(\varphi_j) = \min\{\delta_{\mathcal{G}}(\omega) \mid \omega \in \Omega, \omega \models \varphi_j\}. \tag{3.8}$$

Given a guaranteed possibilistic base $\mathcal{G} = \{(\varphi_j, \beta_j) \mid i = 1, \cdots, n\}$ and its associated satisfaction distribution, the weight associated with a formula in $\mathcal{G}$ represents the lower bound of its guaranteed satisfaction measure. Formally, we have $\Delta(\varphi_j) \geq \beta_j$. Notice that the inequality $\Delta(\varphi_j) = \min\{\delta_{\mathcal{G}}(\omega) \mid \omega \in \Omega, \omega \models \varphi_j, (\varphi_j, \beta_j) \in \mathcal{G}\} \geq \beta_j$ suggests that a family of satisfaction distributions that satisfy the inequalities can be associated with $\mathcal{G}$. However, the computation of $\delta_{\mathcal{G}}$ as given in Equation (3.7) is the unique smallest satisfaction distribution that satisfies the inequalities [4].

Let us now analyze how a user's preferences are handled in guaranteed possibilistic logic. First, note that $\delta_{\mathscr{G}}(\omega) = 1$ is more informative than $\delta_{\mathscr{G}}(\omega) = 0$ since $\delta_{\mathscr{G}}(\omega) = 1$ means that ω is fully satisfactory while $\delta_{\mathscr{G}}(\omega) = 0$ only means that no information is available about the satisfaction of ω. Therefore, preferences behave as wishes that should be satisfied as much as possible. Lastly, $\delta_{\mathscr{G}}(\omega)$ is computed w.r.t. only formulas satisfied by ω. Indeed, guaranteed possibilistic logic is a logic of rewards. It offers a positive reading of a user's preferences. This is also confirmed by noticing that the addition of new user preferences to $\mathscr{G}$ may only increase the satisfaction degree of outcomes. In the worst case their satisfaction degree remains unchanged. See Equation (3.7). Also notice that preference formulas in guaranteed possibilistic logic are disjunctively combined. In fact, we have

$$\forall \phi, \varphi, \Delta(\phi \vee \varphi) = \min(\Delta(\phi), \Delta(\varphi)).$$

Example 3.13. Let $\mathscr{G} = \{(\textit{fish} \vee \textit{white}, 1), (\textit{fish}, .8), (\textit{cake}, .8), (\textit{red}, .5)\}$. In Table 3.7, we give the local and global satisfaction degrees.

Table 3.7 The satisfaction distribution associated with $\mathscr{G}$

Outcomes	$\delta_{(\textit{fish} \vee \textit{white}, 1)}(\omega)$	$\delta_{(\textit{fish}, .8)}(\omega)$	$\delta_{(\textit{cake}, .8)}(\omega)$	$\delta_{(\textit{red}, .5)}(\omega)$	$\delta_{\mathscr{G}}(\omega)$
$\omega_0 = \textit{fish} - \textit{white} - \textit{cake}$	1	.8	.8	0	1
$\omega_1 = \textit{fish} - \textit{white} - \textit{ice\_cream}$	1	.8	0	0	1
$\omega_2 = \textit{fish} - \textit{red} - \textit{cake}$	1	.8	.8	.5	1
$\omega_3 = \textit{fish} - \textit{red} - \textit{ice\_cream}$	1	.8	0	.5	1
$\omega_4 = \textit{meat} - \textit{white} - \textit{cake}$	1	0	.8	0	1
$\omega_5 = \textit{meat} - \textit{white} - \textit{ice\_cream}$	1	0	0	0	1
$\omega_6 = \textit{meat} - \textit{red} - \textit{cake}$	0	0	.8	.5	.8
$\omega_7 = \textit{meat} - \textit{red} - \textit{ice\_cream}$	0	0	0	.5	.5

User preferences can also be represented in a qualitative way by means of a set of ordered formulas of the form $\mathscr{G} = \mathscr{G}_1 \cup \cdots \cup \mathscr{G}_n$. The higher i is, the less preferred are formulas in $\mathscr{G}_i$. Since formulas are disjunctively combined in guaranteed possibilistic logic, an outcome satisfies $\mathscr{G}_i$ if and only if it satisfies at least one formula in $\mathscr{G}_i$. The satisfaction distribution associated with $\mathscr{G}$ is $\mathscr{WOP}(\pi_{\mathscr{G}}) = S_1 \cup \cdots \cup S_{n+1}$, computed as follows:

- S_i is the set of outcomes which satisfy $\mathscr{G}_i$ but falsify all formulas in $\mathscr{G}_1 \cup \cdots \cup \mathscr{G}_{i-1}$,
- S_{n+1} is the set of outcomes which falsify all formulas in $\mathscr{G}_1 \cup \cdots \cup \mathscr{G}_n$.

In contrast to possibilistic logic, inconsistency is not relevant in guaranteed possibilistic logic since preference formulas are considered as wishes which are disjunctively combined. Clearly, the case where all preference formulas are individually inconsistent is not interesting.

3.3.6 Qualitative Choice Logic

In the spirit of guaranteed possibilistic logic, qualitative choice logic (*QCL* for short) is also a logic of rewards [24]. *QCL* extends propositional logic with a new connector, denoted by $\widehat{\times}$, called *ordered disjunction*. A user's preferences are represented by formulas (called basic) of the form $a_1 \widehat{\times} a_2 \widehat{\times} \cdots \widehat{\times} a_n$, which are interpreted as follows: prefer a_1 but if a_1 is not possible then prefer a_2; if neither a_1 nor a_2 are possible then prefer a_3; and so on.

More complex formulas (called general) can also be expressed in this logic using standard logical connectors. Therefore, we can have $\phi \wedge \varphi$, $\neg \psi$, $\phi \vee \psi$ and $\phi \widehat{\times} \psi$, where ϕ and ψ are basic formulas. It has been shown in [24] that general choice formulas can be reduced to basic choice formulas using a normalization function. Therefore, we focus on basic choice formulas in the rest of this subsection.

Outcomes are rank-ordered in this logic w.r.t. their satisfaction level. Let $\phi = a_1 \widehat{\times} \cdots \widehat{\times} a_n$ be a basic formula. We say that ω satisfies ϕ to a degree k, denoted by $\omega \models_k \phi$, if and only if $\omega \models a_1 \vee \cdots \vee a_n$ and $k = \min\{j \mid \omega \models a_j\}$. Therefore, we have that $\omega \models_1 \phi$ if and only if $\omega \models \phi$, where ϕ is a propositional logic formula. If an outcome does not satisfy a formula, i.e., $\omega \not\models a_1 \vee \cdots \vee a_n$, then it is excluded.

Given a set of basic choice formulas $\{\phi_1, \cdots, \phi_m\}$, a vector of satisfaction degrees is associated with each outcome. Then outcomes are rank-ordered w.r.t. the lexicographical order of their satisfaction degrees.

Example 3.14. Suppose a user would prefer *white wine* with *fish* and *red wine* with *meat*; however, she would prefer *fish* and *white wine*. This preference is written as $\phi_1 = fish \wedge white \widehat{\times} meat \wedge red$. The user would also prefer *cake* to *ice cream*. This is written as $\phi_2 = cake \widehat{\times} ice\_cream$. Consider the outcome $meat - red - cake$. We have $meat - red - cake \models_2 \phi_1$ since $meat - red - cake$ falsifies $fish \wedge white$ and satisfies $meat \wedge red$. Now $meat - red - cake \models_1 \phi_2$ since the outcome satisfies *cake* but not *ice cream*.

Let us now consider the outcome $fish - red - cake$. This outcome is excluded by ϕ_1 since it falsifies both $fish \wedge white$ and $meat \wedge red$. Table 3.8 summarizes the satisfaction degree of each outcome. The symbol "_" means that the outcome is excluded by the corresponding formula. $fish - white - cake$ is the most preferred outcome as it satisfies both ϕ_1 and ϕ_2 with degree 1. The outcomes $fish - white - ice\_cream$, $meat - red - cake$ and $meat - red - ice\_cream$ are rank-ordered w.r.t. the lexicographical order. For example, if ϕ_1 is given priority over ϕ_2 then $fish - white - ice\_cream$ is preferred to $meat - red - cake$, which is in turn preferred to $meat - red - ice\_cream$. The remaining outcomes are not rank-ordered since they are excluded by at least one formula, namely, ϕ_1.

Different extensions of *QCL* have been proposed. We refer the reader to [11, 12] for further details.

Table 3.8 The satisfaction degrees w.r.t. ϕ_1 and ϕ_2

	$\phi_1 = fish \wedge white \widetilde{\times} meat \wedge red$	$\phi_2 = cake \widetilde{\times} ice\_cream$	(ϕ_1, ϕ_2)
$\omega_0 = fish - white - cake$	1	1	$(1,1)$
$\omega_1 = fish - white - ice\_cream$	1	2	$(1,2)$
$\omega_2 = fish - red - cake$	–	1	–
$\omega_3 = fish - red - ice\_cream$	–	2	–
$\omega_4 = meat - white - cake$	–	1	–
$\omega_5 = meat - white - ice\_cream$	–	2	–
$\omega_6 = meat - red - cake$	2	1	$(2,1)$
$\omega_7 = meat - red - ice\_cream$	2	2	$(2,2)$

3.3.7 Partially Ordered Formulas

Users may not wish to compare all preference formulas. In such a situation, we need to rank-order them (e.g., qualitative possibilistic logic) or to associate a weight with them (e.g., penalty logic). Therefore, we need to handle a set of partially ordered preference formulas. Formally, we have a pair $(\Sigma, \succeq_\Sigma)$, where Σ is a set of propositional logic formulas representing a user's preferences and $\succeq_\Sigma$ is a partial preorder over $\Sigma \times \Sigma$. Given $\varphi, \varphi' \in \Sigma$, $\varphi \succeq_\Sigma \varphi'$ (or $\varphi \succ_\Sigma \varphi'$) means that φ is at least as important as (or strictly more important than) φ'. Different ways have been proposed to define a preference relation over $\Omega \times \Omega$ from $(\Sigma, \succeq_\Sigma)$. Some of them are generalizations of those proposed in the case of totally ordered formulas. The following preference relation generalizes the possibilistic logic-based preference relation. Let $\omega, \omega' \in \Omega$ and $\mathscr{F}_\omega = \max(\{\varphi \mid \varphi \in \Sigma, \omega \not\models \varphi\}, \succeq_\Sigma)$, $\mathscr{F}_{\omega'} = \max(\{\varphi \mid \varphi \in \Sigma, \omega' \not\models \varphi\}, \succeq_\Sigma)$. Then, ω is strictly preferred to ω' if and only if one of the following conditions holds:

- $\mathscr{F}_\omega \subset \mathscr{F}_{\omega'}$,
- $\forall \varphi \in \mathscr{F}_\omega, \exists \varphi' \in \mathscr{F}_{\omega'}$ such that $\varphi' \succ \varphi$.

Example 3.15. Let $(\Sigma, \succeq_\Sigma)$ be a set of partially ordered preference formulas with $\Sigma = \{fish \vee white, fish, cake, red\}$ and $\succeq_\Sigma$ defined as $fish \vee white \succ_\Sigma fish$ and $cake \succ_\Sigma red$. Let us compare the outcomes $\omega_4 = meat - white - cake$ and $\omega_7 = meat - red - ice\_cream$. We have $\mathscr{F}_{\omega_4} = \{fish, red\}$ and $\mathscr{F}_{\omega_7} = \{fish \vee white, cake\}$. Then, $\omega_4 \succ \omega_7$.

The preference relation given in Definition 3.2 following the *discrimin* criterion does not need to be generalized. Indeed, it is defined for the most general case of weighted formulas, where the weights are symbolic and thus may be partially ordered.

3.4 Conditional Logics

Users may also express their partial preferences in term of comparative statements, e.g., "I like London more than Paris" and "I prefer tea to coffee". Comparative preference statements offer an intuitive and natural way to express preferences. Most of the preferences we express seem to be of this type. Users may also wish to consider some factors to express their comparative preference statements, e.g., "If fish is served, then I prefer white wine to red wine", allowing then to express general preferences (e.g., "I prefer fish to meat") and specific preferences in particular contexts (e.g., "If red wine is served, I prefer meat to fish").

The above statements have been studied in two communities: in the philosophical community in terms of preference logics which aim at understanding and reasoning with those statements, and in artificial intelligence community in terms of conditional logics. We do not present these logics as distinct languages since although artificial intelligence researchers are more concerned with representation issues, some conditional logics are based on philosophical interpretation of comparative preference statements.

The ultimate goal is to derive a preference relation over $\Omega \times \Omega$ given a set of comparative preference statements. To this end, we need to fix and understand some crucial points. Expressing a preference over p and q intuitively means having to choose from among p and q. Following Halldén [41] and von Wright [67], we interpret such a preference as a preference of p and not q (i.e., $p \wedge \neg q$) over q and not p (i.e., $q \wedge \neg p$). It is worth noticing that the problem here is not whether having both p and q is better than having only one or none of them. Instead, reducing p (or q) to $p \wedge \neg q$ (or $q \wedge \neg p$) should be understood as a way of rendering p (or q) more specific or precise in the statement "prefer p to q" (possibly w.r.t. some context or condition). However, this is a general interpretation that leaves room for some exceptions [42]. In particular, if the reduction results in a contradiction, i.e., $p \wedge \neg q$ (or $q \wedge \neg p$) is a contradiction, then it cannot replace p (or q). This is also true when $p \wedge \neg q$ (or $q \wedge \neg p$) is not a contradiction but is not feasible w.r.t. Ω, i.e., the set of outcomes satisfying $p \wedge \neg q$ (or $q \wedge \neg p$) has an empty intersection with Ω. To summarize, $p \wedge \neg q$ (or $q \wedge \neg p$) replaces p (or q) in the statement "prefer p to q" only when the set of outcomes satisfying $p \wedge \neg q$ (or $q \wedge \neg p$) has a nonempty intersection with Ω, i.e., $p \wedge \neg q$ (or $q \wedge \neg p$) is feasible and logically consistent.

3.4.1 Preference Semantics

As we previously stated, the comparative preference statement "prefer p to q", denoted by $p > q$, is interpreted as "prefer $p \wedge \neg q$ to $q \wedge \neg p$". If the preference is expressed w.r.t. a context "given r, prefer p to q", denoted by $r : p > q$, then it is equivalent to "prefer $r \wedge p$ to $r \wedge q$". Following the Halldén and von Wright translation, it is interpreted as "prefer $r \wedge p \wedge \neg q$ to $r \wedge q \wedge \neg p$". Indeed, without loss of generality and for simplicity, we suppose that all preference statements are expressed in the form "prefer p to q". We do not explicitly state whether the preference is contextual or not. We will explicitly refer to contexts when necessary for illustration. Also, for simplicity we suppose that both p and q can be reduced to $p \wedge \neg q$ and $q \wedge \neg p$, respectively.

Readers may be familiar with another representation of contextual preferences, that is, $r : p$ (or $D(r|p)$) standing for "if r is true then prefer p", interpreted as "if r is true then prefer p to $\neg p$". This is a particular case of our representation when $q = \neg p$. The statement $r : p$ only allows us to express a preference over p and its complement $\neg p$, while "$r : p > q$" allows to compare two different objects, e.g., "if white wine is served then I prefer fish to ice cream". Suppose that the choice is made between fish and meat on the one hand, and between cake and ice cream on the other hand. Then, the previous statement means that when white wine is served, the meal composed of fish and cake is preferred to the meal composed of meat and ice cream.

Let us now go back to our ultimate goal, that is, to construct the preference relation associated with a set of comparative preference statements. For this purpose, we first need to construct the preference relation w.r.t. a single comparative preference statement, let us say "prefer p to q", denoted by $p > q$. Let $\succeq$ be the preference relation we intend to construct. At the semantic level, $p > q$ means that $(p \wedge \neg q)$-outcomes are preferred to $(q \wedge \neg p)$-outcomes. This simple interpretation, however, creates difficulties in how the preference over the two sets of outcomes is implemented: is any $(p \wedge \neg q)$-outcome preferred to any $(q \wedge \neg p)$-outcome? Is at least one $(p \wedge \neg q)$-outcome preferred to at least $(q \wedge \neg p)$-outcome? Different preference semantics have been proposed in the literature. We recall the most well-known and used semantics:

Definition 3.4 (Preference semantics).
Let $\succeq$ be a preference relation and $p > q$ be a comparative preference statement.

- **Strong semantics** [10, 69]
  Any $(p \wedge \neg q)$-outcome is preferred w.r.t. $\succeq$ to any $(q \wedge \neg p)$-outcome.

- **Ceteris paribus[2] semantics** [67, 42, 19, 20, 69]
  Any $(p \wedge \neg q)$-outcome is preferred w.r.t. $\succeq$ to any $(q \wedge \neg p)$-outcome if the two outcomes have the same valuation over variables not appearing in $p \wedge \neg q$ and $q \wedge \neg p$.

- **Optimistic semantics** [58, 7, 17]
  Any best-ranked $(p \wedge \neg q)$-outcome w.r.t. $\succeq$ is preferred (also w.r.t. $\succ$) to any best-ranked $(q \wedge \neg p)$-outcome w.r.t. $\succeq$.

- **Pessimistic semantics** [4]
  Any worst-ranked $(p \wedge \neg q)$-outcome w.r.t. $\succeq$ is preferred (also w.r.t. $\succ$) to any

---

[2] The Latin term for "all else being equal".

worst-ranked $(q \wedge \neg p)$-outcome w.r.t. $\succeq$.

- **Opportunistic semantics** [65]
  Any best-ranked $(p \wedge \neg q)$-outcome w.r.t. $\succeq$ is preferred (also w.r.t. $\succeq$) to any
  worst-ranked $(q \wedge \neg p)$-outcome w.r.t. $\succeq$.

The notation $p >_{st} q$ (or $p >_{cp} q$, $p >_{opt} q$, $p >_{pes} q$, $p >_{opp} q$) stands for "prefer p
to q", following strong (or ceteris paribus, optimistic, pessimistic, opportunistic) semantics.
The definition of ceteris paribus given in the above definition is the most well-known
and used in the literature. It has been originally proposed by von Wright [67]. Other
definitions have also been proposed in the literature. See [27, 28, 63, 43]. For example in [43], an outcome ω is preferred to an outcome ω' given $p >_{cp} q$ if and only
if $\omega \models p \wedge \neg q$, $\omega' \models q \wedge \neg p$ and ω and ω' are similar w.r.t. variables that do not
appear in $p \wedge \neg q$ and $q \wedge \neg p$. The similarity condition is to be defined depending on
the application at hand.

The different semantics have requirements that a preference relation should fulfill in order to be admissible for representing a user's preferences. We say that the
preference relation $\succeq$ satisfies the comparative preference statement at hand. Let us
consider the comparative preference statement "prefer *fish* to *meat*" over two propositional variables M and W, which respectively stand for *main dish* and *wine*. Let
$Dom(M) = \{fish, meat\}$ and $Dom(W) = \{white, red\}$. We have four outcomes, i.e.,
$\Omega = \{fish - white, fish - red, meat - white, meat - red\}$. Let $\succeq_1$ be a preference relation defined as

$$fish - white \succ_1 meat - red \succ_1 meat - white \approx_1 fish - red.$$

$\succeq_1$ does not satisfy $fish >_{st} meat$ since $fish - red \succ_1 meat - red$ does not hold. It
does not satisfy $fish >_{cp} meat$ since $fish - red \succ_1 meat - red$ does not hold. It satisfies $fish >_{opt} meat$ since the best-ranked *fish*-based menu w.r.t. $\succeq_1$ is $fish - white$
and the best-ranked *meat*-based menu w.r.t. $\succeq_1$ is $meat - red$, and $fish - white \succ_1$
$meat - red$ holds. $\succeq_1$ does not satisfy $fish >_{pes} meat$ since the worst-ranked *fish*-
based menu w.r.t. $\succeq_1$ is $fish - red$ and the worst-ranked *meat*-based menu w.r.t. $\succeq_1$
is $meat - white$, but $fish - red \succ_1 meat - white$ does not hold. Lastly, $\succeq_1$ satisfies
$fish >_{opp} meat$ since $fish - white \succ_1 meat - white$.
  Consider now the preference relation $\succeq_2$ defined as

$$fish - white \approx_2 fish - red \succ_2 meat - white \approx_2 meat - red.$$

Then, $\succeq_2$ satisfies $fish >_{st} meat$, $fish >_{cp} meat$, $fish >_{opt} meat$, $fish >_{pes} meat$ and
$fish >_{opp} meat$. The following proposition gives the mathematical expression of Definition 3.4:

Proposition 3.1. *[45]*
*Let $\succeq$ be a preference relation. Let $p \triangleright q$ be a comparative preference statement
with $\triangleright \in \{ >_{st}, >_{cp}, >_{opt}, >_{pes}, >_{opp} \}$.*

- $\succeq$ satisfies $p >_{st} q$, denoted by $\succeq \models p >_{st} q$, iff $\forall \omega \in \min(p \wedge \neg q, \succeq)$, $\forall \omega' \in \max(q \wedge \neg p, \succeq)$, $\omega \succ \omega'$.
- $\succeq$ satisfies $p >_{cp} q$, denoted by $\succeq \models p >_{cp} q$, iff $\forall \omega \in \min(p \wedge \neg q, \succeq)$, $\forall \omega' \in \max(q \wedge \neg p, \succeq)$, $\omega \succ \omega'$ if ω and ω' have the same valuation over variables that do not appear in $p \wedge \neg q$ and $q \wedge \neg p$.
- $\succeq$ satisfies $p >_{opt} q$, denoted by $\succeq \models p >_{opt} q$, iff $\forall \omega \in \max(p \wedge \neg q, \succeq)$, $\forall \omega' \in \max(q \wedge \neg p, \succeq)$, $\omega \succ \omega'$.
- $\succeq$ satisfies $p >_{pes} q$, denoted by $\succeq \models p >_{pes} q$, iff $\forall \omega \in \min(p \wedge \neg q, \succeq)$, $\forall \omega' \in \min(q \wedge \neg p, \succeq)$, $\omega \succ \omega'$.
- $\succeq$ satisfies $p >_{opp} q$, denoted by $\succeq \models p >_{opp} q$, iff $\forall \omega \in \max(p \wedge \neg q, \succeq)$, $\forall \omega' \in \min(q \wedge \neg p, \succeq)$, $\omega \succ \omega'$.

We call a set of comparative preference statements a *preference set*, which we denote by $\mathscr{P}_{\triangleright} = \{p_i \triangleright q_i \mid \triangleright \in \{>_{st}, >_{cp}, >_{opt}, >_{pes}, >_{opp}\}\}$. A preference relation is a *model* of $\mathscr{P}_{\triangleright}$ if and only if it satisfies each comparative preference statement $p_i \triangleright q_i$ in $\mathscr{P}_{\triangleright}$. A preference set $\mathscr{P}_{\triangleright}$ is consistent if and only if it has a model. By abuse of language, given a comparative preference statement $p \triangleright q$, we say that $(p \wedge \neg q)$-outcomes satisfy $p \triangleright q$ and $(q \wedge \neg p)$-outcomes falsify $p \triangleright q$, since the former are preferred to the latter w.r.t. a given semantics.

3.4.2 From a Preference Set to a Preference Relation

Several preference relations may satisfy a preference set $\mathscr{P}_{\triangleright}$. An important problem in this case is how to answer the query "is ω preferred to ω'?" We can ambitiously approach this issue and check if the preference holds w.r.t. all models of $\mathscr{P}_{\triangleright}$. We can also approach this issue from the worst-case perspective and check if the preference holds w.r.t. some model of $\mathscr{P}_{\triangleright}$. The first way to answer the query is drastic as it generally results in an incomparability between ω and ω', which is not helpful from a decision viewpoint. Let us consider again our example given in the previous subsection, with $\Omega = \{fish - white, fish - red, meat - white, meat - red\}$. Let $\mathscr{P} >_{opt} = \{fish >_{opt} meat\}$. The following preference relations are some models of $\mathscr{P} >_{opt}$:

$\succeq_1 = (\{fish - red, fish - white\}, \{meat - red, meat - white\})$,
$\succeq_2 = (\{fish - red\}, \{fish - white, meat - red, meat - white\})$,
$\succeq_3 = (\{fish - white\}, \{fish - red, meat - red, meat - white\})$,
$\succeq_4 = (\{fish - red, fish - white\}, \{meat - red\}, \{meat - white\})$,
$\succeq_5 = (\{fish - red, fish - white\}, \{meat - white\}, \{meat - red\})$.

Suppose now that we want to compare all pairs of menus. If we require that the strict preference over two outcomes should hold w.r.t. all models of $\mathscr{P} >_{opt}$, then the four menus are incomparable. Namely, we have $fish - red \sim meat - red$, $fish - red \sim meat - white$, $fish - white \sim meat - red$ and $fish - white \sim meat - white$. Clearly, this is not a desirable result since we would expect that at least one *fish*-based menu is preferred to one *meat*-based menu given the preference statement "prefer *fish* to *meat*", whatever the semantics. In contrast, the second way is more informative but should be carefully used. In fact, ω may be preferred to ω' w.r.t. some model of $\mathscr{P}_{\rhd}$ while ω' is preferred to ω w.r.t. another model. In order to get a consistent result, we need to consider only one model of $\mathscr{P}_{\rhd}$. Clearly, it would be better if such a model could be uniquely characterized. In the following subsections, we characterize and construct a unique model of $\mathscr{P}_{\rhd}$ for each semantics.

3.4.3 Strong and Ceteris Paribus Semantics

Strong and ceteris paribus semantics are the easiest cases as they both induce a unique partial order over $\Omega \times \Omega$.

Example 3.16. Let M, W and D be three variables which respectively stand for *main dish*, *wine* and *dessert*, with $Dom(M) = \{fish, meat\}$, $Dom(W) = \{white, red\}$ and $Dom(D) = \{cake, ice\_cream\}$. We have

$$\Omega = \{\omega_0 : fish - white - cake,$$
$$\omega_1 : fish - white - ice\_cream,$$
$$\omega_2 : fish - red - cake,$$
$$\omega_3 : fish - red - ice\_cream,$$
$$\omega_4 : meat - white - cake,$$
$$\omega_5 : meat - white - ice\_cream,$$
$$\omega_6 : meat - red - cake,$$
$$\omega_7 : meat - red - ice\_cream\}.$$

Let $\mathscr{P}_{\rhd} = \{fish \rhd meat, red \wedge meat \rhd red \wedge fish, white \wedge cake \rhd white \wedge ice\_cream\}$. These preferences mean that the user would prefer *fish* to *meat*. Moreover, if *red wine* is served then she would prefer *meat* to *fish*. Lastly, if *white wine* is served then she would prefer *cake* to *ice cream*. Let $\succeq$ and $\succeq'$ be the preference relations associated with $\mathscr{P}_{>_{st}}$ and $\mathscr{P}_{>_{cp}}$, respectively. The preference relation $\succeq$ is cyclic since $\omega_2 = fish - red - cake$ is preferred to $\omega_7 = meat - red - ice\_cream$ according to $fish >_{st} meat$ while $\omega_7 = meat - red - ice\_cream$ is preferred to $\omega_2 = fish - red - cake$ according to $red \wedge meat >_{st} red \wedge fish$. The preference relation $\succeq'$ is also cyclic since $\omega_3 = fish - red - ice\_cream$ is preferred to $\omega_7 = meat - red - ice\_cream$ according to $fish >_{cp} meat$ while $\omega_7 = meat - red - ice\_cream$ is preferred to $\omega_3 = fish - red - ice\_cream$ according to $red \wedge meat >_{cp} red \wedge fish$.

The preference relation $\succeq$ (or $\succeq'$) being cyclic in the above example means that $\mathscr{P}_{>_{st}}$ (or $\mathscr{P}_{>_{cp}}$) is inconsistent, i.e., preference formulas in $\mathscr{P}_{>_{st}}$ (or $\mathscr{P}_{>_{cp}}$) cannot be fulfilled together.

Example 3.17. (Example 3.16 continued)
Let $\mathscr{P}_{\rhd} = \{$*fish* $\wedge$ *white* $\rhd$ *fish* $\wedge$ *red*,*meat* $\wedge$ *red* $\rhd$ *meat* $\wedge$ *white*, *red* $\wedge$ *cake* $\rhd$ *red* $\wedge$ *ice_cream*$\}$. So, the user would prefer *white wine* to *red wine* when *fish* is served. Her preference is reversed when *meat* is served. Lastly, she would prefer *cake* to *ice cream* when *red wine* is served.

Let $\succeq$ and $\succeq'$ be the preference relations associated with $\mathscr{P}_{>st}$ and $\mathscr{P}_{>cp}$, respectively. We have $\omega_0 \succ \omega_2 \succ \omega_3$, $\omega_0 \succ \omega_2 \succ \omega_7$, $\omega_1 \succ \omega_2 \succ \omega_3$, $\omega_1 \succ \omega_2 \succ \omega_7$, $\omega_1 \succ \omega_3$, $\omega_6 \succ \omega_4$, $\omega_6 \succ \omega_5$, $\omega_7 \succ \omega_4$, $\omega_7 \succ \omega_5$, $\omega_6 \succ \omega_3$, $\omega_6 \succ \omega_7$, and $\omega_0 \succ' \omega_2 \succ'$ ω_3, $\omega_1 \succ' \omega_3$, $\omega_6 \succ' \omega_4$, $\omega_6 \succ' \omega_7 \succ' \omega_5$.

In some applications, we do not need to explicitly compare pairs of outcomes but to know their rank if they were totally rank-ordered. This turns out to associate a total preorder with the partial order associated with $\mathscr{P}_{>st}$ (or $\mathscr{P}_{>cp}$).
Different complete preorders may be consistent with the unique partial order associated with $\mathscr{P}_{>st}$ (or $\mathscr{P}_{>cp}$). However, a unique complete preorder can be characterized following specificity principles [70]. More precisely, a unique least-specific preorder exists and a unique most-specific preorder exist. In order to compute the least-specific model of $\mathscr{P}_{\rhd}$, we first compute the set of the best outcomes. They are outcomes which are not dominated at all, that is no outcome is preferred to them. Let us consider the partial order $\succeq$ associated with $\mathscr{P}_{>st}$ in Example 3.17. These outcomes are ω_0, ω_1 and ω_6. Now if we ignore ω_0, ω_1 and ω_6, the outcome which is not dominated is ω_2. In fact, ω_2 is dominated by ω_0 and ω_1 only. Following a similar reasoning, we compute ω_3 and ω_7; then ω_4 and ω_5. So the least-specific model of $\mathscr{P}_{>st}$ is $(\{\omega_0, \omega_1, \omega_6\}, \{\omega_2\}, \{\omega_3, \omega_7\}, \{\omega_4, \omega_5\})$.
The computation of the most-specific model of $\mathscr{P}_{>st}$ works in a dual way. We first compute the set of the worst outcomes. They are outcomes which do not dominate any other outcome. Consider again the partial order $\succeq$ associated with $\mathscr{P}_{>st}$ in Example 3.17. These outcomes are ω_3, ω_4 and ω_5. Now if we ignore these outcomes, the worst outcome is ω_7. In fact, ω_7 dominates ω_4 and ω_5 only. Following a similar reasoning, the next worst outcomes are ω_2 and ω_6; then ω_0 and ω_1. So the most-specific model of $\mathscr{P}_{>st}$ is $(\{\omega_0, \omega_1\}, \{\omega_2, \omega_6\}, \{\omega_7\}, \{\omega_3, \omega_4, \omega_5\})$. Algorithm 3.1 (or 3.2) computes the unique least- (or most-) specific model of $\mathscr{P}_{>st}$.

Example 3.18. (Example 3.17 continued)
Let $\mathscr{P}_{>st} = \{s_1 :$ *fish* $\wedge$ *white* $>_{st}$*fish* $\wedge$ *red*,$s_2 :$ *meat* $\wedge$ *red* $>_{st}$*meat* $\wedge$ *white*, $s_3 :$ *red* $\wedge$ *cake* $>_{st}$*red* $\wedge$ *ice_cream*$\}$. We have $\mathscr{C}(\mathscr{P}_{>st}) = \{\mathscr{C}_1 = (L(s_1),R(s_1)),$ $\mathscr{C}_2 = (L(s_2),R(s_2)),\mathscr{C}_3 = (L(s_3),R(s_3))\} = \{\mathscr{C}_1 = (\{\omega_0,\omega_1\},\{\omega_2,\omega_3\}),$ $\mathscr{C}_2 = (\{\omega_6,\omega_7\},\{\omega_4,\omega_5\}),\mathscr{C}_3 = (\{\omega_2,\omega_6\},\{\omega_3,\omega_7\})\}$. We put in E_1 outcomes which do not appear in $R(s_1)$, $R(s_2)$ and $R(s_3)$. We get $E_1 = \{\omega_0,\omega_1,\omega_6\}$. We remove $(L(s_1),R(s_1))$ since $L(s_1) \subseteq E_1$ and update $(L(s_2),R(s_2))$ and $(L(s_3),R(s_3))$. We get $\mathscr{C}(\mathscr{P}_{>st}) = \{\mathscr{C}_2 = (\{\omega_7\},\{\omega_4,\omega_5\}),$ $\mathscr{C}_3 = (\{\omega_2\},\{\omega_3,\omega_7\})\}$. We repeat this process and get $E_2 = \{\omega_2\}$, $E_3 = \{\omega_3,\omega_7\}$ and $E_4 = \{\omega_4,\omega_5\}$. Therefore, the least-specific model of $\mathscr{P}_{>st}$ is $(\{\omega_0,\omega_1,\omega_6\},$ $\{\omega_2\},\{\omega_3,\omega_7\},\{\omega_4,\omega_5\})$.

Algorithm 3.1: Strong semantics and minimal specificity principle

Data: A preference set $\mathscr{P}_{>st} = \{s_i : p_i >_{st} q_i\}$.

Result: A complete preorder $\succeq$ over $\Omega \times \Omega$.

begin

    $l = 0$;

    $\mathscr{C}(\mathscr{P}_{>st}) = \{\mathscr{C}_i = (L(s_i), R(s_i)) = (Mod(p_i \wedge \neg q_i), Mod(q_i \wedge \neg p_i)) \mid$
    $s_i : p_i >_{st} q_i \in \mathscr{P}_{>st}\}$;

    while $\Omega \neq \emptyset$ **do**

        $- l = l + 1$;

        $- E_l = \{\omega \mid \forall \mathscr{C}_i \in \mathscr{C}(\mathscr{P}_{>st}), \omega \notin R(s_i)\}$;

        if $E_l = \emptyset$ **then** Stop (inconsistent preference statements);

        $-$ from Ω remove elements of E_l ;

        /** update preference statements $p_i >_{st} q_i$ **/

        $-$ replace $\mathscr{C}_i = (L(s_i), R(s_i))$ with $\mathscr{C}_i = (L(s_i) \setminus E_l, R(s_i))$;

        /** remove satisfied preference statements $p_i >_{st} q_i$ **/

        $-$ from $\mathscr{C}(\mathscr{P}_{>st})$ remove constraints $\mathscr{C}_i$ with empty $L(s_i)$;

    return $(E_1, \cdots, E_l)$

end

Algorithm 3.2: Strong semantics and maximal specificity principle

Data: A preference set $\mathscr{P}_{>st} = \{s_i : p_i >_{st} q_i\}$.

Result: A complete preorder $\succeq$ over $\Omega \times \Omega$.

begin

    $l = 0$;

    $\mathscr{C}(\mathscr{P}_{>st}) = \{\mathscr{C}_i = (L(s_i), R(s_i)) = (Mod(p_i \wedge \neg q_i), Mod(q_i \wedge \neg p_i)) \mid$
    $s_i : p_i >_{st} q_i \in \mathscr{P}_{>st}\}$;

    while $\Omega \neq \emptyset$ **do**

        $l = l + 1$;

        $E_l = \{\omega \mid \forall \mathscr{C}_i \in \mathscr{C}(\mathscr{P}_{>st}), \omega \notin L(s_i)\}$;

        if $E_l = \emptyset$ **then** Stop (inconsistent preference statements);

        $-$ From Ω remove elements of E_l;

        /** update preference statements $p_i >_{st} q_i$ **/

        $-$ replace $\mathscr{C}_i = (L(s_i), R(s_i))$ with $\mathscr{C}_i = (L(s_i), R(s_i) \setminus E_l)$;

        /** remove satisfied preference statements $p_i >_{st} q_i$ **/

        $-$ From $\mathscr{C}(\mathscr{P}_{>st})$ remove constraints $\mathscr{C}_i$ with empty $R(s_i)$;

    return $(E'_1, \cdots, E'_l)$ such that $\forall 1 \leq h \leq l, E'_h = E_{l-h+1}$

end

Let us now compute the most-specific model of $\mathscr{P}_{>st}$. We have $\mathscr{C}(\mathscr{P}_{>st}) = \{\mathscr{C}_1 = (L(s_1), R(s_1)), \mathscr{C}_2 = (L(s_2), R(s_2)), \mathscr{C}_3 = (L(s_3), R(s_3))\} = \{\mathscr{C}_1 = (\{\omega_0, \omega_1\}, \{\omega_2, \omega_3\}), \mathscr{C}_2 = (\{\omega_6, \omega_7\}, \{\omega_4, \omega_5\}), \mathscr{C}_3 = (\{\omega_2, \omega_6\}, \{\omega_3, \omega_7\})\}$. We put in E_1 outcomes which do not belong to $L(s_1)$, $L(s_2)$ and $L(s_3)$. We get $E_1 = \{\omega_3, \omega_4, \omega_5\}$. We remove $(L(s_2), R(s_2))$ since $R(s_2) \subseteq E_1$ and update $(L(s_1), R(s_1))$ and $(L(s_3), R(s_3))$. We get $\mathscr{C}(\mathscr{P}_{>st}) = \{\mathscr{C}_1 = (\{\omega_0, \omega_1\}, \{\omega_2\}), \mathscr{C}_3 = (\{\omega_2, \omega_6\}, \{\omega_7\})\}$. We repeat this process and get $E_2 = \{\omega_7\}$, $E_3 = \{\omega_2, \omega_6\}$ and $E_4 = \{\omega_0, \omega_1\}$. So, the most-specific model of $\mathscr{P}_{>st}$ is $(\{\omega_0, \omega_1\}, \{\omega_2, \omega_6\}, \{\omega_7\}, \{\omega_3, \omega_4, \omega_5\})$.

The algorithms associated with $\mathscr{P}_{>cp}$ are structurally similar to Algorithms 3.1 and 3.2. They differ on the update of preference statements. More details will be given later in the chapter.

3.4.4 Optimistic Semantics

Given a comparative preference statement $p > q$, ordering outcomes following optimistic semantics consists of preferring any $\neg(q \wedge \neg p)$-outcome to any $(q \wedge \neg p)$-outcome [58, 7]. This results in a complete preorder $\succeq = (E_1, E_2)$ where E_2 are the $(q \wedge \neg p)$-outcomes and $E_1 = \Omega \backslash E_2$. Therefore, E_1 is the set of the $(p \vee \neg q)$-outcomes, that is, outcomes which do not satisfy $q \wedge \neg p$. The latter are also outcomes which do not falsify $p > q$. In other words, an outcome is preferred w.r.t. $p >_{opt} q$ as soon as it does not falsify $p > q$. This reasoning process is generalized to the case where several comparative preference statements are handled. Let $\mathscr{P}_{>opt} = \{p_i >_{opt} q_i \mid i = 1, \cdots, n\}$ and let $\succeq = (E_1, \cdots, E_m)$ be its associated complete preorder. The preferred outcomes w.r.t. $\succeq$, i.e., the set E_1, are obtained by an AND-aggregation of the preferred outcomes associated with each $p_i >_{opt} q_i$ in $\mathscr{P}_{>opt}$. In other words, E_1 is the set of outcomes which satisfy $p_i \vee \neg q_i, i = 1, \cdots, n$. Therefore, E_1 is the set of outcomes which do not falsify any statement $p_i >_{opt} q_i$. Regarding the remaining outcomes, i.e., $\Omega \backslash E_1$, some of them are better than the others. In order to refine the ordering over these outcomes, let us recall the interpretation of optimistic semantics. Following Definition 3.4, a preference relation $\succeq$ satisfies $p >_{opt} q$ if and only if the best rank-ordered $(p \wedge \neg q)$-outcomes are preferred to the best rank-ordered $(q \wedge \neg p)$-outcomes w.r.t. $\succeq$. So, once E_1 is computed, we can know which preference statements in $\mathscr{P}_{>opt}$ are already satisfied. Consider $p_i >_{opt} q_i$ in $\mathscr{P}_{>opt}$. By construction, we know that the $(q_i \wedge \neg p_i)$-outcomes are not in E_1. Therefore, if some $(p_i \wedge \neg q_i)$-outcomes are in E_1 then they are the preferred $(p_i \wedge \neg q_i)$-outcomes w.r.t. $\succeq$ and they are necessarily preferred to the $(q_i \wedge \neg p_i)$-outcomes. So, $p_i >_{opt} q_i$ is satisfied w.r.t. $\succeq$ we are constructing. This permits us to remove satisfied preference statements from $\mathscr{P}_{>opt}$ and repeat the above reasoning over the new set of preferences. Therefore, the most preferred outcomes in $\Omega \backslash E_1$ are those which are not in any $(q_i \wedge \neg p_i)$-outcome of the current set of preferences.

At some step of the process, if E_i is empty then comparative preference statements at hand cannot be fulfilled all together. We say that the set $\mathscr{P}_{>opt}$ is inconsistent. The above process is summarized in Algorithm 3.3.

Example 3.19. (Example 3.16 continued)
Let $\mathscr{P}_{>opt} = \{s_1 : fish >_{opt} meat, s_2 : red \wedge meat >_{opt} red \wedge fish, s_3 : white \wedge cake >_{opt} white \wedge ice\_cream\}$. We have $\mathscr{C}(\mathscr{P}_{>opt}) = \{\mathscr{C}_1 = (L(s_1), R(s_1)) = (\{\omega_0, \omega_1, \omega_2, \omega_3\}, \{\omega_4, \omega_5, \omega_6, \omega_7\}), \mathscr{C}_2 = (L(s_2), R(s_2)) = (\{\omega_6, \omega_7\}, \{\omega_2, \omega_3\}), \mathscr{C}_3 = (L(s_3), R(s_3)) = (\{\omega_0, \omega_4\}, \{\omega_1, \omega_5\})\}$. E_1 is the set of outcomes which do not belong to any $R(s_1)$, $R(s_2)$ and $R(s_3)$, namely, $\{\omega_4, \omega_5, \omega_6, \omega_7\}$, $\{\omega_2, \omega_3\}$ and $\{\omega_1, \omega_5\}$. So $E_1 = \{\omega_0\}$. We remove $\mathscr{C}_1$ and $\mathscr{C}_3$ since $E_1 \cap L(s_1) \neq \emptyset$

Algorithm 3.3: Optimistic semantics

Data: A preference set $\mathscr{P}_{>opt} = \{s_i : p_i >_{opt} q_i\}$.

Result: A complete preorder $\succeq$ over $\Omega \times \Omega$.

begin

> $l = 0$;
> $\mathscr{C}(\mathscr{P}_{>opt}) = \{\mathscr{C}_i = (L(s_i), R(s_i)) = (Mod(p_i \wedge \neg q_i), Mod(q_i \wedge \neg p_i)) \mid$
> $s_i : p_i >_{opt} q_i \in \mathscr{P}_{>opt}\}$;
> **while** $\Omega \neq \emptyset$ **do**
>> $- l = l + 1$;
>> $- E_l = \{\omega \mid \forall \mathscr{C}_i \in \mathscr{C}(\mathscr{P}_{>opt}), \omega \notin R(s_i)\}$;
>> **if** $E_l = \emptyset$ **then** Stop (inconsistent preference statements);
>> $-$ from Ω remove elements of E_l ;
>> /** remove satisfied preference statements $p_i >_{opt} q_i$ **/
>> $-$ from $\mathscr{C}(\mathscr{P}_{>opt})$ remove constraints $\mathscr{C}_i$ such that $L(s_i) \cap E_l \neq \emptyset$;
>
> **return** $(E_1, \cdots, E_l)$

end

and $E_1 \cap L(s_3) \neq \emptyset$. This means that $s_1 : fish >_{opt} meat$ and $s_3 : white \wedge cake >_{opt} white \wedge ice\_cream$ are satisfied. Then, $\mathscr{C}(\mathscr{P}_{>opt}) = \{\mathscr{C}_2 = (L(s_2), R(s_2)) = (\{\omega_6, \omega_7\}, \{\omega_2, \omega_3\})\}$. We repeat this process and get $E_2 = \{\omega_1, \omega_4, \omega_5, \omega_6, \omega_7\}$ and $E_3 = \{\omega_2, \omega_3\}$. The model of $\mathscr{P}_{>opt}$ is $\succeq = (\{\omega_0\}, \{\omega_1, \omega_4, \omega_5, \omega_6, \omega_7\}, \{\omega_2, \omega_3\})$.

It has been shown that the complete preorder associated with $\mathscr{P}_{>opt}$ and constructed following Algorithm 3.3 is the unique least-specific model of $\mathscr{P}_{>opt}$.

Theorem 3.1. *[58, 7]*
Let $\mathscr{P}_{>opt} = \{p_i >_{opt} q_i \mid i = 1, \cdots, n\}$ *be a consistent set of preferences. Algorithm 3.3 computes the unique least-specific model of* $\mathscr{P}_{>opt}$.

Without sketching the proof of Theorem 3.1 in detail, the theorem can be checked on the construction of the preorder. At each step of the algorithm, E_i is composed of the maximal (for set inclusion) set of outcomes which do not falsify any preference statement in $\mathscr{P}_{>opt}$. Therefore, each outcome gets the most preferred possible rank in the preorder. In our example, if we move, for example, ω_5 to the first stratum, we get $\succeq' = (\{\omega_0, \omega_5\}, \{\omega_1, \omega_4, \omega_6, \omega_7\}, \{\omega_2, \omega_3\})$, which falsifies at least one preference statement in $\mathscr{P}_{>opt}$. In fact s_1 and s_3 are not satisfied. The property of maximal (for set inclusion) set of outcomes also guarantees the compactness of the constructed complete preorder.

3.4.5 Pessimistic Semantics

Pessimistic semantics behaves in a dual way, in contrast to optimistic semantics. Given a comparative preference statement $p >_{pes} q$, any outcome outside $Mod(p \wedge \neg q)$ is less preferred to any $(p \wedge \neg q)$-outcome. Indeed, a complete preorder $\succeq = (E_1, E_2)$ is associated with $p >_{pes} q$, where E_1 is the set of $(p \wedge \neg q)$-outcomes and

$E_2 = \Omega \backslash E_1$. In other words, the preferred outcomes are those which satisfy $p > q$. Generalizing this reasoning to a set of preference statements consists in computing a complete preorder $\succeq = (E_1, \cdots, E_m) = (E'_m, \cdots, E'_1)$ such that E'_1 is the result of an AND-aggregation of less preferred outcomes w.r.t. each preference statement $p_i >_{pes} q_i$ in $\mathcal{P}_{>pes}$. So, E'_1 is the set of outcomes which are in any $Mod(p_i \wedge \neg q_i)$, i.e., these outcomes do not satisfy any preference $p_i >_{pes} q_i$ in $\mathcal{P}_{>pes}$. As for the optimistic semantics, in order to rank-order the remaining outcomes, i.e., $\Omega \backslash E'_1$, we need to remove satisfied preferences. Recall that from Definition 3.4, a preference relation $\succeq$ satisfies $p >_{pes} q$ if the least preferred $(p \wedge \neg q)$-outcomes are preferred to the least preferred $(q \wedge \neg p)$-outcomes w.r.t. $\succeq$. Now once E'_1 is computed, if some or all $(q_i \wedge \neg p_i)$-outcomes are in E'_1 then $p_i >_{pes} q_i$ is necessarily satisfied since none of the $(p_i \wedge \neg q_i)$-outcomes belongs to E'_1 by construction. Algorithm 3.4 summarizes the above process.

Algorithm 3.4: Pessimistic semantics

Data: A preference set $\mathcal{P}_{>pes} = \{s_i : p_i >_{pes} q_i\}$.

Result: A complete preorder $\succeq$ over $\Omega \times \Omega$.

begin

$\quad l = 0;$

$\quad \mathcal{C}(\mathcal{P}_{>pes}) = \{\mathcal{C}_i = (L(s_i), R(s_i)) = (Mod(p_i \wedge \neg q_i), Mod(q_i \wedge \neg p_i)) \mid$
$\quad s_i : p_i >_{pes} q_i \in \mathcal{P}_{>pes}\};$

$\quad$ **while** $\Omega \neq \emptyset$ **do**

$\quad\quad l = l + 1;$

$\quad\quad E_l = \{\omega \mid \forall \mathcal{C}_i \in \mathcal{C}(\mathcal{P}_{>pes}), \omega \notin L(s_i)\};$

$\quad\quad$ **if** $E_l = \emptyset$ **then** Stop (inconsistent preference statements);

$\quad\quad$ – From Ω remove elements of E_l;

$\quad\quad$ /** remove satisfied preference statements $p_i >_{pes} q_i$ **/

$\quad\quad$ – From $\mathcal{C}(\mathcal{P}_{>pes})$ remove constraints $\mathcal{C}_i$ such that $E_l \cap R(s_i) \neq \emptyset$;

$\quad$ **return** $(E'_1, \cdots, E'_l)$ such that $\forall 1 \leq h \leq l, E'_h = E_{l-h+1}$

end

Example 3.20. (Example 3.16 continued)

Let $\mathcal{P}_{>pes} = \{s_1 : fish >_{pes} meat, s_2 : red \wedge meat >_{pes} red \wedge fish,$ $s_3 : white \wedge cake >_{pes} white \wedge ice\_cream\}$. We have $\mathcal{C}(\mathcal{P}_{>pes}) = \{\mathcal{C}_1 = (L(s_1),$ $R(s_1)) = (\{\omega_0, \omega_1, \omega_2, \omega_3\}, \{\omega_4, \omega_5, \omega_6, \omega_7\}), \mathcal{C}_2 = (L(s_2), R(s_2)) = (\{\omega_6, \omega_7\},$ $\{\omega_2, \omega_3\}), \mathcal{C}_3 = (L(s_3), R(s_3)) = (\{\omega_0, \omega_4\}, \{\omega_1, \omega_5\})\}$. E_1 is the set of outcomes which do not appear in $L(s_1)$, $L(s_2)$ and $L(s_3)$, namely, $\{\omega_0, \omega_1, \omega_2, \omega_3\}, \{\omega_6, \omega_7\}$ and $\{\omega_0, \omega_4\}$. So $E_1 = \{\omega_5\}$. We remove $\mathcal{C}_1$ and $\mathcal{C}_3$ since $E_1 \cap R(s_1) \neq \emptyset$ and $E_1 \cap R(s_3) \neq \emptyset$. This means that $s_1 : fish >_{pes} meat$ and $s_3 : white \wedge cake >_{pes} white \wedge ice\_cream$ are satisfied. Then, $\mathcal{C}(\mathcal{P}_{>pes}) = \{\mathcal{C}_2 = (L(s_2), R(s_2)) = (\{\omega_6, \omega_7\},$ $\{\omega_2, \omega_3\})\}$. We repeat this process and get $E_2 = \{\omega_0, \omega_1, \omega_2, \omega_3, \omega_4\}$ and $E_3 = \{\omega_6, \omega_7\}$. The model of $\mathcal{P}_{>pes}$ is $\succeq = (\{\omega_6, \omega_7\}, \{\omega_0, \omega_1, \omega_2, \omega_3, \omega_4\}, \{\omega_5\})$.

It has been shown that Algorithm 3.4 computes the unique most-specific model of
$\mathcal{P}>_{pes}$.

Theorem 3.2. *[5]*
Let $\mathcal{P}>_{pes} = \{p_i >_{pes}q_i \mid i = 1, \cdots, n\}$ be a consistent set of preferences. Algorithm 3.4 computes the unique most-specific model of $\mathcal{P}>_{pes}$.

This theorem can be checked from the construction of the preorder following Algorithm 3.4 by observing that each outcome is put in the least preferred possible rank in the preorder.

3.4.6 Opportunistic Semantics

Opportunistic semantics has not been investigated in the literature from an algorithmic perspective. This is because the aim has always been the computation of a unique model following specificity principles while opportunistic semantics does not obey these principles. Consider the preference statement *fish > meat* interpreted following opportunistic semantics. Let $\Omega = \{fish - white, fish - red, meat - white, meat - red\}$. The less specific models of $\{fish >_{opp}meat\}$ are $(\{fish - white, fish - red, meat - white\}, \{meat - red\})$ and $(\{fish - white, fish - red, meat - red\}, \{meat - white\})$. The more specific models of $\{fish >_{opp}meat\}$ are $(\{fish - white\}, \{fish - red, meat - white, meat - red\})$ and $(\{fish - red\}, \{fish - white, meat - white, meat - red\})$.

3.4.7 Beyond Semantics

Four main semantics have been studied in the literature, namely, strong, ceteris paribus, optimistic and pessimistic. Each corresponds to a different more or less strong requirement on how outcomes should be rank-ordered. Let $p \rhd q$ be a comparative preference statement and $\succeq$ be a preference relation. Strong semantics has the most requirements, as any $(p \wedge \neg q)$-outcome should be preferred to any $(q \wedge \neg p)$-outcome w.r.t. $\succeq$. This semantics has been weakened in different ways. Following ceteris paribus semantics, the preference is true only between $(p \wedge \neg q)$-outcomes and $(q \wedge \neg p)$-outcomes, which have the same valuation over variables that do not appear in $p \wedge \neg q$ and $q \wedge \neg p$. Following Definition 3.4, $\succeq$ satisfies $p >_{opt}q$ if and only if the best rank-ordered $(p \wedge \neg q)$-outcomes are preferred to the best rank-ordered $(q \wedge \neg p)$-outcomes. Technically speaking, this means that $\succeq$ satisfies $p >_{opt}q$ if and only if at least one $(p \wedge \neg q)$-outcome is preferred to all $(q \wedge \neg p)$-outcomes. Therefore, optimistic semantics is a left-hand side weakening of strong semantics. Lastly, following Definition 3.4, $\succeq$ satisfies $p >_{pes}q$ if and only if the worst rank-ordered $(p \wedge \neg q)$-outcomes are preferred to the worst rank-ordered $(q \wedge \neg p)$-outcomes. Technically speaking, this means that $\succeq$ satisfies $p >_{pes}q$ if and only if at least one $(q \wedge \neg p)$-outcome is less preferred to all $(p \wedge \neg q)$-outcomes. Therefore, pessimistic semantics is a right-hand side weakening of strong semantics.

Proposition 3.2. *[45]*
Let p and q be two propositional formulas. Let $\succeq$ be a complete preference relation over $\Omega \times \Omega$. If $\succeq \models p >_{st} q$, then $\succeq \models p >_{cp} q$, $\succeq \models p >_{opt} q$ and $\succeq \models p >_{pes} q$.

Observe that optimistic and pessimistic adjectives adequately reflect the behavior of their associated semantics since the former compares the best rank-ordered $(p \wedge \neg q)$-outcomes and $(q \wedge \neg p)$-outcomes while the latter compares the worst rank-ordered $(p \wedge \neg q)$-outcomes and $(q \wedge \neg p)$-outcomes.

Besides the above observations on the behavior of the different semantics, optimistic and pessimistic semantics focusing on at least one $(p \wedge \neg q)$-outcome and $(q \wedge \neg p)$-outcome, respectively, are important properties as they allow flexibility in the expression of preferences. Let us consider a user expressing two preferences, *fish > meat* and *red ∧ meat > red ∧ fish*. So, the user would prefer *fish* to *meat* and her preference is reversed when *red wine* is served. Strong semantics induces the following preference relation: *fish − red* ≻ *meat − red, fish − red* ≻ *meat − white*, *fish − white* ≻ *meat − red, fish − white* ≻ *meat − white* and *meat − red* ≻ *fish − red*, which is cyclic since both *fish − red* ≻ *meat − red* and *meat − red* ≻ *fish − red* hold. Ceteris paribus semantics induces fewer preferences; we have *fish − red* ≻ *meat − red, fish − white* ≻ *meat − white* and *meat − red* ≻ *fish − red*. However, again we have both *fish − red* ≻ *meat − red* and *meat − red* ≻ *fish − red*. This is rather an unwanted result since the user does not express here a "strict" preference in favor of *fish*-based meals. Instead, *fish > meat* and *red ∧ meat > red ∧ fish* should be interpreted as a default preference for *fish* (represented by *fish > meat*) and a preference for *meat* in the case where *red wine* is served (represented by *red ∧ meat > red ∧ fish*). This is a defeasible reasoning about preferences. We say that *red ∧ meat > red ∧ fish* is more specific than *fish > meat*. Here, specificity means that some preferences are expressed in a general context (for example, "prefer *fish* to *meat*"). Being expressed in a general context, such preferences are intended to leave room for exceptions. Therefore, they can be contradicted by other preferences expressed in a specific context (for example, "when *red wine* is served, prefer *meat* to *fish*"). Boutilier [17] represents these preferences using optimistic semantics. They are read as follows: ideally *fish* but if *red* wine is served then ideally *meat*. The associated preference relation is $\succeq = (\{fish - white\}, \{meat - white, meat - red\}, \{fish - red\})$.

Pessimistic semantics also allows us to reason about defeasible preferences. The preference relation associated with the above preferences is $\succeq' = (\{meat - red\}, \{fish - white, fish - red\}, \{meat - white\})$.

Both optimistic and pessimistic semantics give priority to the specific preference *red ∧ meat > red ∧ white*. Indeed, in the context of *red* wine, *meat* is preferred to *fish* w.r.t. both $\succeq$ and $\succeq'$. But the two semantics rank-order the outcomes in different ways. Following optimistic semantics, the preferred outcomes are those which do not falsify any preference, namely, *fish − white*. The following preferred outcomes are those which falsify *fish > meat* but not *red ∧ meat > red ∧ fish*, namely, *meat − white* and *meat − red*. Lastly, the least preferred outcomes are those which falsify the

most prioritized preference statement (i.e., $red \wedge meat > red \wedge fish$), namely, $fish -$
red.

On the other hand, outcomes are rank-ordered following pessimistic semantics in
the following way. The best outcomes are those which satisfy
$red \wedge meat > red \wedge fish$, namely, $meat - red$. The following preferred outcomes
are those which falsify $red \wedge meat > red \wedge fish$ but satisfy $fish > meat$, namely,
$fish - white$ and $fish - red$. Lastly, the least preferred outcomes are those which do
not satisfy any preference, namely, $meat - white$.

In sum, optimistic semantics looks for outcomes that *do not falsify* preferences
at hand while pessimistic semantics looks for outcomes that *satisfy* the preferences.
The former is called a "negative" reading of preferences and the latter is called a
"positive" reading of preferences [5]. These two readings will be further discussed
in Section 3.6.

3.4.8 Related Work

3.4.8.1 Optimistic Semantics + Utility

Lang [49] offers a quantitative counterpart of optimistic semantics. Each comparative preference statement is associated with a symbolic weight which measures the
loss of utility when the statement is not satisfied. Let $\mathscr{P}_u = \{(p_i > q_i, \alpha_i) \mid i = 1, \cdots, n\}$ be a set of weighted comparative preference statements. A local utility
function is associated with each statement $p_i > q_i$. An outcome gets the value $-\alpha_i$
($\alpha_i > 0$) if it does not satisfy $p_i > q_i$ and 0 if it does not falsify it. Formally, we have

$$\forall \omega \in \Omega, u_{p_i > q_i}(\omega) = \begin{cases} -\alpha_i & \text{if } \omega \models q_i \wedge \neg p_i \\ 0 & \text{otherwise} \end{cases}.$$

The global utility associated with ω w.r.t. $\mathscr{P}_u$ is the sum of its local utilities
$u_{p_i > q_i}(\omega)$.

Example 3.21. We associate symbolic weights with the preference statements given
in Example 3.16. Let $\mathscr{P}_u = \{(fish > meat, \alpha_1), (red \wedge meat > red \wedge fish, \alpha_2),$
$(white \wedge cake > white \wedge ice\_cream, \alpha_3)\}$. In Table 3.9, we give local utilities and
the global utility associated with each outcome in Ω.

Comparative preference statements in Lang's framework are interpreted follow-
ing optimistic semantics. Therefore, each statement $(p_i > q_i, \alpha_i)$ in $\mathscr{P}_u$ induces a
constraint on u in the following way:

$$\max\{u(\omega) \mid \omega \models p_i \wedge \neg q_i\} > \max\{u(\omega) \mid \omega \models q_i \wedge \neg p_i\}. \tag{3.9}$$

Then, a utility function u satisfies $\mathscr{P}_u$ if and only if it satisfies each constraint induced by a preference statement $(p_i > q_i, \alpha_i)$ in $\mathscr{P}_u$. A set $\mathscr{P}_u$ is consistent if and
only if there is a utility function u satisfying $\mathscr{P}_u$.

Table 3.9 The utility function associated to $\mathscr{P}_u$

	$(fish >$ $meat, \alpha_1)$	$(red \wedge meat >$ $red \wedge fish, \alpha_2)$	$(white \wedge cake >$ $white \wedge ice\_cream, \alpha_3)$	$u(\omega)$
$\omega_0 = fish - white - cake$	0	0	0	0
$\omega_1 = fish - white - ice\_cream$	0	0	$-\alpha_3$	$-\alpha_3$
$\omega_2 = fish - red - cake$	0	$-\alpha_2$	0	$-\alpha_2$
$\omega_3 = fish - red - ice\_cream$	0	$-\alpha_2$	0	$-\alpha_2$
$\omega_4 = meat - white - cake$	$-\alpha_1$	0	0	$-\alpha_1$
$\omega_5 = meat - white - ice\_cream$	$-\alpha_1$	0	$-\alpha_3$	$-\alpha_1 - \alpha_3$
$\omega_6 = meat - red - cake$	$-\alpha_1$	0	0	$-\alpha_1$
$\omega_7 = meat - red - ice\_cream$	$-\alpha_1$	0	0	$-\alpha_1$

Example 3.22. (Example 3.21 continued)

- Given $(fish > meat, \alpha_1) \in \mathscr{P}_u$ we have
  $\max\{u(\omega_0), u(\omega_1), u(\omega_2), u(\omega_3)\} > \max\{u(\omega_4), u(\omega_5), u(\omega_6), u(\omega_7)\}$ iff
  $\max\{0, -\alpha_3, -\alpha_2, -\alpha_2\} > \max\{-\alpha_1, -\alpha_1 - \alpha_3, -\alpha_1, -\alpha_1\}$ iff $\alpha_1 > 0$.
- Given $(red \wedge meat > red \wedge fish, \alpha_2) \in \mathscr{P}_u$ we have
  $\max\{u(\omega_6), u(\omega_7)\} > \max\{u(\omega_2), u(\omega_3)\}$ iff
  $\max\{-\alpha_1, -\alpha_1\} > \max\{-\alpha_2, -\alpha_2\}$ iff $\alpha_1 < \alpha_2$.
- Given $(white \wedge cake > white \wedge ice\_cream, \alpha_3) \in \mathscr{P}_u$ we have
  $\max\{u(\omega_0), u(\omega_4)\} > \max\{u(\omega_1), u(\omega_5)\}$ iff
  $\max\{0, -\alpha_1\} > \max\{-\alpha_3, -\alpha_1 - \alpha_3\}$ iff $\alpha_3 > 0$.

Therefore, there is only one constraint relating α_1 and α_2, namely, $\alpha_1 < \alpha_2$. The weight α_3 can take any strict positive value.

The preference relation $\succeq_u$ associated with $\mathscr{P}_u$ is defined as follows:

- $\omega \succeq_u \omega'$ iff $u(\omega) \geq u(\omega')$ for each u satisfying $\mathscr{P}_u$,
- $\omega \succ_u \omega'$ iff $\omega \succeq_u \omega'$ and $not(\omega' \succeq_u \omega)$,
- $\omega \approx_u \omega'$ iff $\omega \succeq_u \omega'$ and $\omega' \succeq_u \omega$.

So, $\succeq_u$ is a partial or complete preorder.

Example 3.23. (Example 3.21 continued)
Figure 3.1 shows the order over the weights α_1, α_2 and α_3. An edge from a weight to another weight means that the latter is strictly greater than the former. Therefore, the partial preorder associated with $\mathscr{P}_u$ is

$\omega_0 \succ_u \omega_1 \succ_u \omega_5$,
$\omega_0 \succ_u \omega_4 \approx_u \omega_6 \approx_u \omega_7 \succ_u \omega_5$,
$\omega_0 \succ_u \omega_4 \approx_u \omega_6 \approx_u \omega_7 \succ_u \omega_2 \succ_u \omega_3$.

Lang's framework resembles the optimistic semantics and minimal specificity principle (see Subsection 3.4.4) in different ways. First, Lang's framework also gives precedence to more specific comparative preference statements [49]. Second, when the set $\mathscr{P}_{>_{opt}} = \{p_i >_{opt} q_i \mid i = 1, \cdots, n\}$ is consistent, we have that

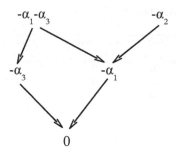

Fig. 3.1 The order over the weights

the model of $\mathscr{P} >_{opt}$ following Algorithm 3.3 is consistent with the partial pre-order associated with $\mathscr{P}_u = \{(p_i > q_i, \alpha_i) \mid p_i >_{opt} q_i \in \mathscr{P} >_{opt}\}$. Note, however, that the least-specific complete preorder consistent with the partial preorder $\succeq_u$ is not necessarily equivalent to the model of $\mathscr{P} >_{opt}$ constructed following Algo-rithm 3.3. In our example, the least-specific complete preorder consistent with $\succeq_u$ is $\succeq' = (\{\omega_0\}, \{\omega_1, \omega_4, \omega_6, \omega_7\}, \{\omega_2, \omega_3, \omega_5\})$. On the other hand, the model of $\mathscr{P} >_{opt}$ following Algorithm 3.3 is $\succeq = (\{\omega_0\}, \{\omega_1, \omega_5, \omega_6, \omega_7\}, \{\omega_2, \omega_3\})$. Lang's frame-work returns a more refined preference relation thanks to the additive utility func-tion. In fact, ω_5 is less preferred to $\omega_1, \omega_4, \omega_6$ and ω_7 w.r.t. $\succeq'$ since it falsi-fies two preference statements, namely, *fish > meat* and *white $\wedge$ cake > white $\wedge$ ice_cream*, while $\omega_1, \omega_4, \omega_6$ and ω_7 falsify only one preference statement, namely, *white $\wedge$ cake > white $\wedge$ ice_cream* for ω_1 and *fish > meat* for ω_4, ω_6 and ω_7. Lastly, despite the fact that Lang's approach makes use of weights, they are symbolic, mak-ing redundant preferences ignored [49].

Note that unlike the optimistic semantics handled following Algorithm 3.3, Lang's framework does not suffer from the drowning effect [49].

3.4.8.2 Ceteris Paribus Semantics + Specificity

Tan and Pearl overcome the non-defeasible behavior of ceteris paribus semantics by using the notion of specificity [63]. Their approach is a three-step process:

1. Given a set of comparative preference statements $\mathscr{P} = \{p_i > q_i \mid i = 1, \cdots, n\}$, they define a preorder over $\mathscr{P} \times \mathscr{P}$ following a specificity notion between the statements in $\mathscr{P}$. Note that this preorder is partial.

2. Comparative preference statements $p_i > q_i$ in $\mathscr{P}$ are interpreted following ceteris paribus semantics. Specifically, let $p_i > q_i$ be a statement in $\mathscr{P}$ and ω and ω' be two outcomes such that $\omega \models p_i \wedge \neg q_i$, $\omega \models q_i \wedge \neg p_i$ and ω and ω' have the same valuation over variables that do not appear in $p_i \wedge \neg q_i$ and $q_i \wedge \neg p_i$. Then, ω is preferred to ω' w.r.t. $p_i > q_i$.

3. The preference relation associated with $\mathscr{P}$ is the deductive closure of all local preferences obtained in item 2. If a contradiction occurs, i.e., given two outcomes ω and ω', ω is preferred to ω' w.r.t. $p_i > q_i \in \mathscr{P}$ and ω' is preferred to ω w.r.t. $p_j > q_j \in \mathscr{P}$, then the most-specific preference from among $p_i > q_i$ and $p_j > q_j$ overrides the least-specific one.

Example 3.24. (Example 3.16 continued)
We have $\mathscr{P} = \{s_1 : fish > meat, s_2 : red \wedge meat > red \wedge fish,$ $s_3 : white \wedge cake > white \wedge ice\_cream\}$. From Example 3.16, s_1, s_2 and s_3 interpreted following ceteris paribus semantics induce a cyclic preference relation. This is due to s_1 and s_2. In fact, s_1 expresses a preference for *fish* over *meat* and s_2 expresses a reversed preference when *red wine* is served. Therefore, s_2 is more specific than s_1. s_3 does not contradict either s_1 or s_2. The preference relation, let us say $\succeq$, associated with $\mathscr{P}$ following Tan and Pearl's approach is composed of strict preferences induced by s_2 and s_3 interpreted following ceteris paribus semantics and strict preferences induced by s_1 interpreted following ceteris paribus semantics provided that the latter preferences do not contradict those induced by s_2. Indeed, we have $\omega_6 \succ \omega_2$ and $\omega_7 \succ \omega_3$ (following s_2), and $\omega_0 \succ \omega_1$ and $\omega_4 \succ \omega_5$ (following s_3). s_1 induces the following preferences: $\omega_0 \succ \omega_4$, $\omega_1 \succ \omega_5$, $\omega_2 \succ \omega_6$ and $\omega_3 \succ \omega_7$ but $\omega_2 \succ \omega_6$ and $\omega_3 \succ \omega_7$ are discarded since they contradict s_2.

A utility function $u : \Omega \to \mathbb{N}$ is then constructed such that $u(\omega)$ evaluates how satisfactory ω is. The greater $u(\omega)$ is, the more satisfactory is ω.

Given the partial order, let us say $\succeq$, constructed in item 3, the utility function u should satisfy the following constraints:

$$\forall \omega, \omega' \in \Omega, \text{ if } \omega \succ \omega' \text{ then } u(\omega) \geq u(\omega') + \varepsilon,$$

where ε is a positive integer. We say that u is admissible to represent the user's preference set $\mathscr{P}$. From among admissible utility functions, Tan and Pearl select those which ensure a maximal indifference. These functions minimize the difference between outcomes. Formally, u^* belongs to the set of distinguished utility functions if and only if for each admissible utility function u we have

$$\sum_{\omega, \omega' \in \Omega} |u^*(\omega) - u^*(\omega')| \leq \sum_{\omega, \omega' \in \Omega} |u(\omega) - u(\omega')|.$$

Example 3.25. (Example 3.16 continued)
$u^{*,1}$ and $u^{*,2}$ are two distinguished utility functions associated with $\mathscr{P}$ (m is an integer):

- $u^{*,1}(\omega_0) = m,\ u^{*,1}(\omega_1) = u^{*,1}(\omega_4) = u^{*,1}(\omega_5) = u^{*,1}(\omega_6) = u^{*,1}(\omega_7) = m+\varepsilon,$
  $u^{*,1}(\omega_2) = u^{*,1}(\omega_3) = m+2\varepsilon,$
- $u^{*,2}(\omega_6) = u^{*,2}(\omega_7) = m,\ u^{*,2}(\omega_0) = u^{*,2}(\omega_1) = u^{*,2}(\omega_2) = u^{*,2}(\omega_3) = u^{*,2}(\omega_4) =$
  $m+\varepsilon,\ u^{*,2}(\omega_5) = m+2\varepsilon.$

3.4.9 Advanced Logics for Comparative Preference Statements

As stated in the previous subsections, we distinguish between different natural semantics, each corresponding to a particular reasoning line. Existing logics imple-
menting these semantics argue for the use of a unique semantics. However, this is
rather unfortunate since a user's preferences may require the simultaneous use of
different semantics. For example, a vegetarian person would prefer any *soup*-based
meal to any *meat*-based meal. At the same time, she may also prefer a meal composed of *cake* to a meal composed of *ice cream* if the two meals are exactly the same
otherwise. The former preference refers to strong semantics while the latter refers
to ceteris paribus semantics. Each of these semantics cannot adequately represent
both of the above preference statements.

3.4.9.1 Strong and Ceteris Paribus Semantics

Aware of the necessity of using different semantics simultaneously, Wilson [69] developed a logic for conditional preferences in which both strong and ceteris paribus
semantics are used. Preference statements have the form $r : x > x'[W]$, where x and
x' are values of a variable X, r is an assignment of a (possibly empty) set of variables
R and $W \subseteq S = V\backslash(R \cup \{X\})$. The statement $r : x > x'[W]$ is interpreted as "given
r and any assignment t of $T = S\backslash W$, prefer x to x' irrespective of the values of W".
Formally, this statement defines an order over $\Omega \times \Omega$ in which $trxw$ is preferred
to $trx'w'$. Comparative preference statements interpreted following ceteris paribus
semantics are represented by the above statement with $W = \emptyset$. Strong semantics is
represented by $r : x > x'[V\backslash(R \cup \{X\})]$, with R possibly empty.

   Given a set of preference statements, the logic of preferences derives a partial order which corresponds to the deductive closure of pairwise preference comparisons
between pairs of outcomes for each comparative preference statement.

Example 3.26. (Example 3.16 continued)
Suppose a user expresses the following preferences: All else being equal, she would
prefer *fish* to *meat*. All else being equal, she would prefer *meat* to *fish* when *red
wine* is served and she would prefer *cake* to *ice cream* when *white wine* is served
irrespective of the choice of the main dish. In Wilson's framework, these prefer-
ence statements are respectively written as $\top : fish > meat[\emptyset]$, $red : meat > fish[\emptyset]$
and $white : cake > ice\_cream[dish]$. They induce the following partial order over
$\Omega \times \Omega$: $\omega_0 \succ \omega_4 \succ \omega_1 \succ_5, \omega_2 \succ \omega_6, \omega_3 \succ \omega_7$.

Note that the above preference statements are written in our framework as $fish >_{cp} meat$, $red \wedge meat >_{cp} red \wedge fish$ and $white \wedge cake >_{st} white \wedge ice\_cream$.

3.4.9.2 Two Categories of Semantics

Using the same line of reasoning, Kaci and van der Torre [44, 45] developed a logic for comparative preference statements. They consider the four preference semantics (strong, ceteris paribus, optimistic, pessimistic) and distinguish between two categories: a set of semantics for which a unique least-specific model exists and a set of semantics for which a unique most-specific model exists. Recall that a unique least- (or most-) specific model exists given a set of comparative preference statements interpreted following optimistic (or pessimistic) semantics. Kaci and van der Torre's logic is based on the fact that both strong and ceteris paribus semantics induce a unique partial order over $\Omega \times \Omega$ and a unique complete preorder is consistent with that partial order following both minimal and maximal specificity principles. Therefore, strong, ceteris paribus and optimistic (or strong, ceteris paribus and pessimistic) semantics have the same behavior. Given these facts, two natural questions arise:

(1) is a least-specific model of a set of strong, ceteris paribus and optimistic preference statements unique?

(2) is a most-specific model of a set of strong, ceteris paribus and pessimistic preference statements unique?

In their logic, preference statements are expressed in a strict ($>$) or non-strict ($\geq$) form. Formally, we have the following definition:

Definition 3.5 (Preference specification). [44, 45]
A preference specification is a tuple of preference sets $\langle \mathscr{P}_{\triangleright} \mid \triangleright \in \{ >_x, \geq_x \mid x \in \{st, cp, opt, pes\}\}\rangle$. A complete preorder $\succeq$ is a model of a preference specification if and only if $\succeq$ is a model of each preference set in the specification. A preference specification is consistent if it has a model.

The following proposition states that the answer to questions (1) and (2) is positive.

Proposition 3.3. *[44, 45]*

- *The least-specific model of $\mathscr{P}_{>_{st}} \cup \mathscr{P}_{\geq_{st}} \cup \mathscr{P}_{>_{cp}} \cup \mathscr{P}_{\geq_{cp}} \cup \mathscr{P}_{>_{opt}} \cup \mathscr{P}_{\geq_{opt}}$ is unique.*
- *The most-specific model of $\mathscr{P}_{>_{st}} \cup \mathscr{P}_{\geq_{st}} \cup \mathscr{P}_{>_{cp}} \cup \mathscr{P}_{\geq_{cp}} \cup \mathscr{P}_{>_{pes}} \cup \mathscr{P}_{\geq_{pes}}$ is unique.*

It is worth noticing that for non-strict preference statements both least and most-specific models exist and they are the trivial preference relation in which all outcomes are equivalent. Thus, the notion of least and most-specific models for preference sets consisting only of non-strict preference statements is not useful.

Construction of the least-specific model for strong, ceteris paribus and optimistic preferences

We consider the following preference specification:

$$\mathscr{P} = \langle \mathscr{P}_\rhd \mid \rhd \in \{\ >_x,\ \geq_x \mid x \in \{st, cp, opt\}\}\rangle.$$

So, we consider the following six sets of preferences:

$$\mathscr{P}_{>_{opt}} = \{s_{i_1} : p_{i_1} >_{opt} q_{i_1}\},$$

$$\mathscr{P}_{\geq_{opt}} = \{s_{i_2} : p_{i_2} \geq_{opt} q_{i_2}\},$$

$$\mathscr{P}_{>_{st}} = \{s_{i_3} : p_{i_3} >_{st} q_{i_3}\},$$

$$\mathscr{P}_{\geq_{st}} = \{s_{i_4} : p_{i_4} \geq_{st} q_{i_4}\},$$

$$\mathscr{P}_{>_{cp}} = \{s_{i_5} : p_{i_5} >_{cp} q_{i_5}\},$$

$$\mathscr{P}_{\geq_{cp}} = \{s_{i_6} : p_{i_6} \geq_{cp} q_{i_6}\}.$$

Given $\mathscr{P}$, we define a set of constraints induced by the preferences by

$$\mathscr{C} = \bigcup_{k=1,\cdots,6} \{\mathscr{C}_{i_k} = (L(s_{i_k}), R(s_{i_k}))\},$$

where the left- and right-hand sides of these constraints are, respectively, $L(s_{i_k}) = \{\omega \mid \omega \in \Omega, \omega \models p_{i_k} \wedge \neg q_{i_k}\}$ and $R(s_{i_k}) = \{\omega \mid \omega \in \Omega, \omega \models q_{i_k} \wedge \neg p_{i_k}\}$.

Constraints induced by ceteris paribus semantics need to be preprocessed. These constraints are based on one-to-one correspondence between outcomes. More precisely, they state that any outcome in the left-hand side of the constraint is preferred to any outcome in the right-hand side of the constraint following ceteris paribus semantics. Therefore, when an outcome in the left- (or right-) hand side of a constraint does not have its associated outcome in the right- (or left-) hand side of the constraint following ceteris paribus semantics, it should be removed from the constraint. This situation occurs when the set of outcomes is incomplete or when given $p > q$, p (or q) does not reduce to $p \wedge \neg q$ (or $q \wedge \neg p$). Although we supposed in Chapter 2 that all possible outcomes are feasible and that both p and q reduce to $p \wedge \neg q$ and $q \wedge \neg p$, respectively, we believe that it is important to point this out again. In the following, we suppose that ceteris paribus preferences are processed before the algorithms are applied.

Let $s : p >_{cp} q$ (or $p \geq_{cp} q$). Let ω and ω' be two outcomes such that $\omega \in L(s)$ and $\omega' \in R(s)$. We write $\omega >>_{cp}^s \omega'$ when ω is strictly (at least as) preferred to ω' w.r.t. s and ceteris paribus semantics.

Algorithm 3.5 computes the least-specific model of strong, ceteris paribus and optimistic semantics of the preference specification previously described. The basic idea of the algorithm is to construct the preorder by calculating the sets of outcomes of the ordered partition, going from the best to the worst outcomes.

Algorithm 3.5: Handling strong, ceteris paribus and optimistic preferences

Data: A preference specification $\mathcal{P} = \langle \mathcal{P}_\triangleright \mid \triangleright \in \{ >_x, \geq_x \mid x \in \{st, cp, opt\} \rangle$
Result: A complete preorder $\succeq$ over $\Omega \times \Omega$.

begin

    $l = 0$;

    while $\Omega \neq \emptyset$ **do**

        $- l = l+1, j = 1$;

        /** strict constraints **/

        $- E_l = \{ \omega \mid \forall \mathcal{C}_{i_1}, \mathcal{C}_{i_3}, \mathcal{C}_{i_5} \in \mathcal{C}, \omega \notin (R(s_{i_1}) \cup R(s_{i_3}) \cup R(s_{i_5})) \}$;

        while $j = 1$ **do**

            $j = 0$;

            for *each $\mathcal{C}_{i_2}$, $\mathcal{C}_{i_4}$ and $\mathcal{C}_{i_6}$ in $\mathcal{C}$* **do**

                /** constraints induced by non-strict preferences **/

                if $(L(s_{i_2}) \cap E_l = \emptyset$ and $R(s_{i_2}) \cap E_l \neq \emptyset)$ or

                $(L(s_{i_4}) \not\subseteq E_l$ and $R(s_{i_4}) \cap E_l \neq \emptyset)$ or

                $(L(s_{i_6}) \cap E_l = \emptyset$ and $R(s_{i_6}) \cap E_l \neq \emptyset)$ **then**

                    $E_l = E_l \setminus (R(s_{i_2}) \cup R(s_{i_4}) \cup R(s_{i_6}))$;

                    $j = 1$

        if $E_l = \emptyset$ **then** Stop (inconsistent preference statements);

        $-$ from Ω remove elements of E_l ;

        /** remove satisfied constraints induced by $>_{opt}, \geq_{opt}$ preferences **/

        $-$ from $\mathcal{C}$ remove constraints $\mathcal{C}_{i_k} k \in \{1,2\}$ such that $L(s_{i_k}) \cap E_l \neq \emptyset$;

        /** update constraints induced by $>_{st}$ and $\geq_{st}$ preferences **/

        $-$ replace constraints $\mathcal{C}_{i_k}$ ($k \in \{3,4\}$) with $(L(s_{i_k}) \setminus E_l, R(s_{i_k}))$;

        /** update constraints induced by $>_{cp}$ and $\geq_{cp}$ preferences **/

        $-$ **for** *each $\omega \in E_l$* **do**

            for *each $(L(s_{i_k}), R(s_{i_k}))$ ($k \in \{5,6\}$) in $\mathcal{C}$* **do**

                if $\omega \in L(s_{i_k})$ **then**

                    - replace $(L(s_{i_k}), R(s_{i_k}))$ with $(L(s_{i_k}) \setminus \{\omega\}, R(s_{i_k}) \setminus \{\omega'\})$, where $\omega >>_{cp}^{s_{i_k}} \omega'$

        /** remove satisfied constraints induced by $>_{st}, \geq_{st}, >_{cp}$ and $\geq_{cp}$ preferences **/

        $-$ from $\mathcal{C}$ remove constraints $\mathcal{C}_{i_k}$ ($k \in \{3,4,5,6\}$) with empty $L(s_{i_k})$.

    return $(E_1, \cdots, E_l)$

end

At each step of the algorithm, we look for outcomes which can have the current best ranking in the preference relation. This corresponds to the current minimal value l. These outcomes are those which do not falsify any strict preference in $\mathcal{P}$. We first put in E_l outcomes which do not falsify any constraint induced by a strict preference. These outcomes are those which do not appear in the right-hand side of the constraints $\mathcal{C}_{i_1}$, $\mathcal{C}_{i_3}$ and $\mathcal{C}_{i_5}$. Now, we remove from E_l outcomes which falsify constraints induced by the non-strict preferences $\mathcal{C}_{i_2}$, $\mathcal{C}_{i_4}$ and $\mathcal{C}_{i_6}$. Constraints $\mathcal{C}_{i_2}$

(or $\mathscr{C}_{i_6}$) are violated if $L(s_{i_2}) \cap E_l = \emptyset$ and $R(s_{i_2}) \cap E_l \neq \emptyset$ (or $L(s_{i_6}) \cap E_l = \emptyset$ and $R(s_{i_6}) \cap E_l \neq \emptyset$), while the constraints $\mathscr{C}_{i_4}$ are violated if $L(s_{i_4}) \not\subseteq E_l$ and $R(s_{i_4}) \cap E_l \neq \emptyset$. Once E_l is fixed, satisfied constraints are removed. Note that constraints $\mathscr{C}_{i_k}$ s.t. $k \in \{1, 2\}$ are satisfied if $L(s_{i_k}) \cap E_l \neq \emptyset$ while constraints $\mathscr{C}_{i_k}$ for $k \in \{3, 4, 5, 6\}$ are satisfied only when $L(s_{i_k}) \subseteq E_l$; otherwise they should be updated.

Example 3.27. Let $\mathscr{P} = \{s_1 : fish >_{opt}meat, s_2 : red \wedge meat >_{st}red \wedge fish,$ $s_3 : white \wedge cake >_{cp}white \wedge ice\_cream\}$. We have $\mathscr{C}(\mathscr{P}) = \{\mathscr{C}_1 = (L(s_1), R(s_1)) = (\{\omega_0, \omega_1, \omega_2, \omega_3\}, \{\omega_4, \omega_5, \omega_6, \omega_7\}), \mathscr{C}_2 = (L(s_2), R(s_2)) = (\{\omega_6, \omega_7\}, \{\omega_2, \omega_3\}),$ $\mathscr{C}_3 = (L(s_3), R(s_3)) = (\{\omega_0, \omega_4\}, \{\omega_1, \omega_5\})\}$. E_1 is the set of outcomes which do not appear in the right-hand side of any constraint $\mathscr{C}_i$; so, $E_1 = \{\omega_0\}$. We remove $\mathscr{C}_1$ since $fish >_{opt}meat$ is satisfied and update $\mathscr{C}_3$. Indeed, we get $\mathscr{C}(\mathscr{P}) = \{\mathscr{C}_2 = (\{\omega_6, \omega_7\}, \{\omega_2, \omega_3\}), \mathscr{C}_3 = (\{\omega_4\}, \{\omega_5\})\}$. We repeat this process and get $E_2 = \{\omega_1, \omega_4, \omega_6, \omega_7\}$ and $E_3 = \{\omega_2, \omega_3, \omega_5\}$. So, the preference relation associated with $\mathscr{P}$ is $\succeq = (\{\omega_0\}, \{\omega_1, \omega_4, \omega_6, \omega_7\}, \{\omega_2, \omega_3, \omega_5\})$.

The following theorem states that Algorithm 3.5 computes the least-specific model of a preference specification composed of strong, ceteris paribus and optimistic preferences.

Theorem 3.3. *[45]*
Let $\mathscr{P} = \langle \mathscr{P}_\triangleright \mid \triangleright \in \{ >_x, \geq_x \mid x \in \{st, cp, opt\}\}\rangle$ be a consistent preference specification. Let $\succeq$ be the preference relation associated with $\mathscr{P}$ following Algorithm 3.5. Then, $\succeq$ is the least-specific model of $\mathscr{P}$.

When the preference specification is $\mathscr{P} = \langle \mathscr{P} >_{opt}\rangle$, Algorithm 3.5 reduces to Algorithm 3.3. When $\mathscr{P} = \langle \mathscr{P} >_{st}\rangle$, it reduces to Algorithm 3.1. Lastly, when $\mathscr{P} = \langle \mathscr{P} >_{cp}\rangle$, the complete preorder induced by Algorithm 3.5 is the least-specific complete preorder consistent with the partial order induced by $\mathscr{P} >_{cp}$.

The authors of [9] deal with equal preferences, denoted by $p =_{opt} q$, which stand for "all best p-outcomes are q-outcomes and all best q-outcomes are p-outcomes". These equivalences can be represented in our framework by two non-strict preferences, $p \geq_{opt}q$ and $q \geq_{opt}p$. They propose an algorithm which returns the least-specific model of a set of strict optimistic preferences $\{p_i >_{opt}q_i\}$ together with a set of equal optimistic preferences $\{p_j =_{opt} q_j\}$. Algorithm 3.5 reduces to their algorithm when applied to $\{p_i >_{opt}q_i\} \cup \{p_j \geq_{opt}q_j\} \cup \{q_j \geq_{opt}p_j\}$. Booth and Paris [16] propose an algorithm for $>_{opt}$ and $\geq_{opt}$ preferences, which is also generalized by Algorithm 3.5. Moreover, their algorithm does not contain a consistency check and seems to be based on the construction of all preorders as an intermediate step. Strict and non-strict preference statements together with different semantics have also been recently used in [64, 13].

Construction of the most-specific model for strong, ceteris paribus and pessimistic preferences

Algorithm 3.6 is structurally similar to Algorithm 3.5. Let

$$\mathscr{P} = \langle \mathscr{P}_\rhd \mid \rhd \in \{ >_x, \geq_x \mid x \in \{st, cp, pes\}\}\rangle.$$

We consider the following six sets of preferences:

$$\mathscr{P} >_{pes} = \{(s_{i_1}) : p_{i_1} >_{pes} q_{i_1}\},$$

$$\mathscr{P} \geq_{pes} = \{(s_{i_2}) : p_{i_2} \geq_{pes} q_{i_2}\},$$

$$\mathscr{P} >_{st} = \{(s_{i_3}) : p_{i_3} >_{st} q_{i_3}\},$$

$$\mathscr{P} \geq_{st} = \{(s_{i_4}) : p_{i_4} \geq_{st} q_{i_4}\},$$

$$\mathscr{P} >_{cp} = \{(s_{i_5}) : p_{i_5} >_{cp} q_{i_5}\},$$

$$\mathscr{P} \geq_{cp} = \{(s_{i_6}) : p_{i_6} \geq_{cp} q_{i_6}\}.$$

Let $\mathscr{C} = \bigcup_{k=1,\cdots,6}\{\mathscr{C}_{i_k} = (L(s_{i_k}),R(s_{i_k}))\}$, where $L(s_{i_k}) = \{\omega \mid \omega \in \Omega, \omega \models p_{i_k} \wedge \neg q_{i_k}\}$ and $R(s_{i_k}) = \{\omega \mid \omega \in \Omega, \omega \models q_{i_k} \wedge \neg p_{i_k}\}$.

Example 3.28. Let $\mathscr{P} = \{s_1 : fish >_{pes} meat, s_2 : red \wedge meat >_{st} red \wedge fish,$ $s_3 : white \wedge cake >_{cp} white \wedge ice\_cream\}$. We have $\mathscr{C}(\mathscr{P}) = \{\mathscr{C}_1 = (L(s_1),R(s_1)) = (\{\omega_0,\omega_1,\omega_2,\omega_3\},\{\omega_4,\omega_5,\omega_6,\omega_7\}), \mathscr{C}_2 = (L(s_2),R(s_2)) = (\{\omega_6,\omega_7\},\{\omega_2,\omega_3\}),$ $\mathscr{C}_3 = (L(s_3),R(s_3)) = (\{\omega_0,\omega_4\},\{\omega_1,\omega_5\})\}$. E_1 is the set of outcomes which do not appear in the left-hand side of any constraint $\mathscr{C}_i$; so, $E_1 = \{\omega_5\}$. We remove $\mathscr{C}_1$ since $fish >_{pes} meat$ is satisfied and update $\mathscr{C}_3$. Indeed, we get $\mathscr{C}(\mathscr{P}) = \{\mathscr{C}_2 = (\{\omega_6,\omega_7\},\{\omega_2,\omega_3\}),\mathscr{C}_3 = (\{\omega_0\},\{\omega_1\})\}$. We repeat this process and get $E_2 = \{\omega_1,\omega_2,\omega_3,\omega_4\}$ and $E_3 = \{\omega_0,\omega_6,\omega_7\}$. So, the preference relation associated with $\mathscr{P}$ is $\succeq = (\{\omega_0,\omega_6,\omega_7\},\{\omega_1,\omega_2,\omega_3,\omega_4\},\{\omega_5\})$.

The following theorem states that Algorithm 3.6 computes the most-specific model of a set of strong, ceteris paribus and pessimistic preferences.

Theorem 3.4. *[45]*
Let $\mathscr{P} = \langle \mathscr{P}_\rhd \mid \rhd \in \{ >_x, \geq_x \mid x \in \{st, cp, pes\}\}\rangle$ be a consistent preference specification. Then, Algorithm 3.6 computes the most-specific model of $\mathscr{P}$.

When the preference specification is $\mathscr{P} = \langle \mathscr{P} >_{pes}\rangle$, Algorithm 3.6 reduces to Algorithm 3.4. When $\mathscr{P} = \langle \mathscr{P} >_{st}\rangle$, it reduces to Algorithm 3.2. Lastly, when $\mathscr{P} = \langle \mathscr{P} >_{cp}\rangle$, the complete preorder induced by Algorithm 3.6 is the most-specific complete preorder consistent with the partial order induced by $\mathscr{P} >_{cp}$.

Following Algorithm 3.6 we can notice that given a set of preferences $\mathscr{P}$ composed of strong, ceteris paribus and pessimistic preferences, the most-specific model

Algorithm 3.6: Handling strong, ceteris paribus and pessimistic preferences

Data: A preference specification $\mathscr{P} = \langle \mathscr{P}_{\rhd} \mid \rhd \in \{ >_x, \geq_x \mid x \in \{st, cp, pes\} \} \rangle$

Result: A complete preorder $\succeq$ over $\Omega \times \Omega$.

begin

$\quad l = 0$;

$\quad$ **while** $\Omega \neq \emptyset$ **do**

$\qquad l = l+1, j = 1$;

$\qquad E_l = \{ \omega \mid \forall \mathscr{C}_{i_1}, \mathscr{C}_{i_3}, \mathscr{C}_{i_5} \in \mathscr{C}, \omega \notin (L(s_{i_1}) \cup L(s_{i_3}) \cup L(s_{i_5})) \}$;

$\qquad$ **while** $j = 1$ **do**

$\qquad\quad j = 0$;

$\qquad\quad$ **for** each $\mathscr{C}_{i_2}$, $\mathscr{C}_{i_4}$ and $\mathscr{C}_{i_6}$ in $\mathscr{C}$ **do**

$\qquad\qquad$ /** constraints induced by non-strict preferences **/

$\qquad\qquad$ **if** $(L(s_{i_2}) \cap E_l \neq \emptyset$ and $R(s_{i_2}) \cap E_l = \emptyset)$ or

$\qquad\qquad$ $(L(s_{i_4}) \cap E_l \neq \emptyset$ and $R(s_{i_4}) \not\subseteq E_l)$ or

$\qquad\qquad$ $(L(s_{i_6}) \cap E_l \neq \emptyset$ and $R(s_{i_6}) \cap E_l = \emptyset)$ **then**

$\qquad\qquad\quad E_l = E_l \backslash (L(s_{i_2}) \cup L(s_{i_4}) \cup L(s_{i_6}))$;

$\qquad\qquad\quad j = 1$

$\qquad$ **if** $E_l = \emptyset$ **then** Stop (inconsistent preference statements);

$\qquad$ – From Ω remove elements of E_l;

$\qquad$ /** remove satisfied constraints induced by $>_{pes}$ and $\geq_{pes}$ preferences **/

$\qquad$ – from $\mathscr{C}$ Remove constraints $\mathscr{C}_{i_k}$ (for $k \in \{1,2\}$) such that $E_l \cap R(s_{i_k}) \neq \emptyset$;

$\qquad$ /** update constraints induced by $>_{st}$ and $\geq_{st}$ preferences **/

$\qquad$ – Replace $\mathscr{C}_{i_k}$ (for $k \in \{3,4\}$) in $\mathscr{C}$ with $(L(s_{i_k}), R(s_{i_k}) \backslash E_l)$;

$\qquad$ /** update constraints induced by $>_{cp}$ and $\geq_{cp}$ preferences **/

$\qquad$ – **for** each $\omega \in E_l$ **do**

$\qquad\quad$ **for** each $(L(s_{i_k}), R(s_{i_k}))$ $(k \in \{5,6\})$ in $\mathscr{C}$ **do**

$\qquad\qquad$ **if** $\omega \in R(s_{i_k})$ **then**

$\qquad\qquad\quad$ - replace $(L(s_{i_k}), R(s_{i_k}))$ with $(L(s_{i_k}) \backslash \{\omega'\}, R(s_{i_k}) \backslash \{\omega\})$, where $\omega' >>_{cp}^{s_{i_k}} \omega$

$\qquad$ /** remove satisfied constraints induced by $>_{st}$, $\geq_{st}$, $>_{cp}$ and $\geq_{cp}$ preferences **/

$\qquad$ – From $\mathscr{C}$ remove constraints $\mathscr{C}_{i_k}$ $(k \in \{3,4,5,6\})$ with empty $R(s_{i_k})$;

$\quad$ **return** $(E'_1, \cdots, E'_l)$ such that $\forall 1 \leq h \leq l, E'_h = E_{l-h+1}$

end

of $\mathscr{P}$ is computed in the following way. First, all outcomes are considered having the same level of preference. They are put in the lowest stratum of the preorder. Then, an outcome is moved to a higher stratum when it is preferred to another outcome w.r.t. some preference statement in $\mathscr{P}$. Therefore, at each step of the algorithm, an outcome is considered worse unless there is a reason (i.e., a preference statement) which allows us to move it to a higher stratum. Similarly, following Algorithm 3.5, we can notice that given a set of strong, ceteris paribus and optimistic preferences, all outcomes are considered having the same preference. Then, an outcome is moved to a lower stratum when it is less preferred to another outcome w.r.t. some preference statement. This means that at each step of the algorithm, an outcome is considered good when there is no reason to move it to a lower stratum. Indeed, in the least-specific model, each outcome is put as preferred as possible in the preorder while in the most-specific model, each outcome is put as less preferred as possible in the preorder. Sometimes we refer to these lines of reasoning as optimistic and pessimistic, respectively.

3.5 Graphical Languages

The elicitation process of a utility function or preference relation becomes much easier when it exhibits a particular structure, namely, preferential independence between variables. Informally speaking, preference independence means that the preference over some variables can be stated given a fixed value of the other variables. Notice that preferential independence is not commutative in the sense that if a variable X is preferentially independent of a variable Y this does not necessarily mean that Y is preferentially independent of X. For example, a user's preference over the main dish may be independent of the wine. Therefore she prefers *fish* to *meat* given a fixed value of wine. We have that *fish* − *white* is preferred to *meat* − *white* and *fish* − *red* is preferred to *meat* − *red*. However, her preference over wine depends on the main dish. Therefore, she prefers *white wine* with *fish* and *red wine* with *meat*. There has been considerable work on exploiting the preference independence between variables in order to decompose utility functions, using notions from multiattribute utility theory [46]. Interestingly, such decomposability allows for a compact representation of the underlying utility function or preference relation by means of an annotated graph which captures preference independencies. In the following subsections we review the main graphical languages for preference representation.

3.5.1 Generalized Additive Independence Networks

The simplest and best-known form of independence among variables is called "mutual preferential independence", which means that any subset Y of V is independent of its complement $V \backslash Y$. This property allows the utility function to be an additive decomposition of a set of utility functions [47, 1]. In particular, it is equal to the sum of utility functions over single variables. Formally, we write

$$u(X_1 \cdots X_n) = \sum_{i=1}^{n} u_i(X_i).$$

Such a form of decomposability assumes complete independence among variables. Suppose a user is asked to express her preferences over a set of menus composed of a main dish (*fish* or *meat*) and wine (*red* or *white*). Assuming mutual preferential independence between the main dish and wine means that the user's preferences over values of the main dish depend on these values and only on them. Also, her preference over values of the wine depend on these values and only on them. Therefore, the user expresses two independent utility functions, $u_1(dish)$ and $u_2(wine)$; let us say $u_1(fish) = 5$, $u_1(meat) = 3$, $u_2(white) = 2$ and $u_2(red) = 1$. The utility function over the whole set of variables $u(dish, wine)$ is equal to $u_1(dish) + u_2(wine)$. Therefore, we have $u(fish - white) = 7$, $u(fish - red) = 6$, $u(meat - white) = 5$ and $u(meat - red) = 4$.

Such decomposability makes the elicitation process easy to perform as it requires the elicitation of n utility functions over single variables. Unfortunately, the mutual preferential independence between all variables appears to be a strong assumption. In fact, variables generally exhibit some form of dependence, namely, preferences over the values of a variable may be conditional on the values of other variables. For example, a user's preference over values of wine may depend on the values of the main dish. Therefore, the users may prefer *white wine* when *fish* is served and *red wine* when *meat* is served. In order to model this preference, the utility function should be such that $u(fish - white) > u(fish - red)$ and $u(meat - red) > u(meat - white)$. However, these constraints cannot be satisfied by a utility function u summing up two independent utility functions u_1 and u_2 because the independence assumption between main dish and wine means that if the user prefers *white wine* with *fish* then she prefers *white wine* with *meat*. Similarly, if the user prefers *meat* with *red wine* then she prefers *fish* with *red wine*.

To deal with this shortcoming, generalized additive independence, which preserves decomposability while allowing any kind of interaction between variables [34, 1], has been defined.

Definition 3.6 (Generalized additive independence GAI). [1]
Let u be a utility function over $V = \{X_1, \cdots, X_n\}$. Let $Z_1, \cdots, Z_k$ be k not necessarily disjoint subsets of variables such that $V = Z_1 \cup \cdots \cup Z_k$. $Z_1, \cdots, Z_k$ are generalized additively independent for u if and only if there exist utility functions $u_i : Z_i \mapsto \mathbb{R}$ such that

$$u(X_1 \cdots X_n) = \sum_{i=1}^{k} u_i(Z_i). \tag{3.10}$$

The subsets $Z_1, \cdots, Z_k$ are called "factors".

A generalized additive independent utility function is a utility function which can be additively decomposed following Equation (3.10). We say that u is GAI-decomposable over $Z_1, \cdots, Z_k$.

Example 3.29. (Borrowed from [39])
Let u be a utility function over $V = \{X_1, X_2, X_3, X_4, X_5, X_6, X_7\}$. Suppose that u is GAI-decomposable over $\{X_1, X_2\}$, $\{X_2, X_3, X_4\}$, $\{X_3, X_5\}$, $\{X_2, X_4, X_6\}$ and $\{X_2, X_7\}$. Then, $u(X_1X_2X_3X_4X_5X_6X_7) = u_1(X_1X_2) + u_2(X_2X_3X_4) + u_3(X_3X_5) + u_4(X_2X_4X_6) + u_5(X_2X_7)$. We can see from this example the benefit of u being GAI-decomposable. Suppose that $X_1, \cdots, X_n$ are binary variables. The elicitation of u requires the elicitation of $128 (= 2^7)$ values while the elicitation of u_1, u_2, u_3, u_4 and u_5 only requires

the elicitation of 28 $(= 2^2 + 2^3 + 2^2 + 2^3 + 2^2)$ values.

It is worth noticing that Definition 3.6 is general in the sense that any utility function is generalized additive independent by simply putting $k = 1$; therefore, $Z_1 = V$. Moreover, an additively independent utility function is generalized additive independent with $k = n$ and each Z_i is composed of a single variable.

Generalized additive independence networks (GAI-nets for short) [38, 39] are graphical languages which capture the structure of generalized additive independent utility functions. Let u be a generalized additive independent utility function over $Z_1, \cdots, Z_k$. A GAI-net representing u is an undirected graph whose nodes are factors Z_i. Factors are called cliques and represented by ellipses in the graph. A clique Z_i in the graph is annotated with the values of the utility function over the variables in Z_i. Every pair of cliques (Z_i, Z_j) with $Z_i \cap Z_j \neq \emptyset$ is connected by an edge, labelled $Z_i \cap Z_j$ and called a separator. The separators are represented by rectangles in the graph. Figure 3.2 shows the GAI-net associated with the utility function given in Example 3.29.

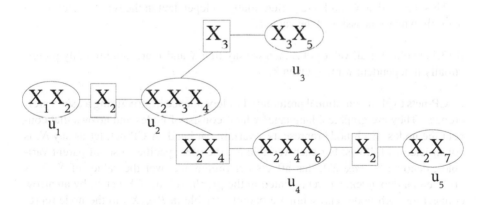

Fig. 3.2 A GAI-net

Comparing two alternatives in GAI-nets is straightforward as one only needs to compute the utility of each outcome. In contrast, optimization queries are less simple and require sophisticated techniques. For more details, we refer the reader to [38, 39].

3.5.2 Conditional Preference Networks

Conditional preference networks (CP-nets for short) [19, 20] are compact representations of preference relations; generally partial orders. The structure of the underlying preference relation exhibits preferential independence between disjoint subsets of variables.

Definition 3.7 (Preferential independence). [19]
Let $\succeq$ be a preference relation over $\Omega \times \Omega$. $X \subseteq V$ is *preferentially independent* of its complement $Y = V \setminus X$ w.r.t. $\succeq$ if and only if for all $x, x' \in Asst(X), y, y' \in Asst(Y)$, we have

$$xy \succeq x'y \text{ iff } xy' \succeq x'y'.$$

In other words, the preference relation over values of X, when all other variables get a fixed value, is the same regardless the values of these variables. This is the qualitative counterpart of the additive independence property of a utility function. We say that x is preferred to x' ceteris paribus.

Definition 3.8 (Conditional preferential independence). [19]
Let $\succeq$ be a preference relation over $\Omega \times \Omega$. Let X, Y and Z be a partition of V. X and Y are *conditionally preferentially independent* given $z \in Asst(Z)$ w.r.t. $\succeq$ if and only if for all $x, x' \in Asst(X), y, y' \in Asst(Y)$, we have

$$xyz \succeq x'yz \text{ iff } xy'z \succeq x'y'z. \tag{3.11}$$

This means that X and Y are preferentially independent in the sense of Definition 3.7 only when Z is assigned the value z.

If (3.11) holds for all values of Z then we say that X and Y are conditionally preferentially independent w.r.t. $\succeq$ given Z.

CP-nets exploit conditional preferential independence in structuring a user's preferences. They are graphical languages which consist of nodes and arrows that connect the nodes. Each node represents a variable at hand. A CP-net, let us say N, is constructed as follows. For each variable X_i, the user specifies a set of parent variables, denoted by $Pa_N(X_i)$, that affects her preference over the values of X_i. This preferential dependency is represented in the graph, i.e., the CP-net N, by an arrow connecting each node representing a parent variable in $Pa_N(X_i)$ to the node representing X_i. By abuse of language, we simply speak about the node X_i (instead of the node representing X_i) and the parent nodes. The set $Pa_N(X_i)$ may be empty, which is interpreted as the user specifying her preference over the values of X_i independently of the values of the remaining variables. In this case, X_i is called a root node. Then, the user specifies a preference order over the values of X_i for all instantiations of the variable set $Pa_N(X_i)$. Therefore, the node X_i in the graph is annotated with a conditional preference table $CPT(X_i)$ representing these preferences. More specifically,

- for root nodes X_i, the conditional preference table $CPT(X_i)$ provides the strict preference from among x_i and $\neg x_i$ (suppose that we act over binary variables), other things being equal, i.e., $\forall y \in Asst(Y)$, $x_i y \succ \neg x_i y$, where $Y = V \setminus \{X_i\}$; this is the ceteris paribus semantics; this means that X is preferentially independent of Y in the sense of Definition 3.7; in $CPT(X_i)$ this preference is written $x_i > \neg x_i$;

- for other nodes X_j, $CPT(X_j)$ describes the preferences from among x_j and $\neg x_j$, other things being equal, given any assignment of $Pa_N(X_j)$, i.e., $x_j z y \succ \neg x_j z y$, $\forall z \in Asst(Pa_N(X_j))$ and $\forall y \in Asst(Y)$, where $Y = V \setminus (\{X_j\} \cup Pa_N(X_j))$; this means that X is preferentially independent of Y given Z in the sense of Definition 3.8; in the preference table $CPT(X_j)$ we write $z : x_j > \neg x_j$ for each assignment z of $Pa_N(X_j)$.

The preference relation over $\Omega \times \Omega$ associated with a CP-net N, denoted by $\succeq_N$, is the deductive closure of all local preferences induced by the conditional preference tables of N between completely specified outcomes. Generally, $\succeq_N$ is a partial order and represented by its associated strict preference relation $\succ_N$. When the CP-net is acyclic, its associated preference relation is acyclic too.

Example 3.30 (How to be dressed for an evening party? (inspired from [26])).
Consider four binary variables $V(vest)$, $P(pants)$, $S(shirt)$ and $C(shoes)$ with $Dom(V) = \{V_b, V_w\}$, $Dom(P) = \{P_b, P_w\}$, $Dom(S) = \{S_r, S_w\}$ and $Dom(C) = \{C_r, C_w\}$. The subscripts b, w and r stand for *black*, *white* and *red* respectively. There is no constraint restricting the set of possible outfits; therefore, we have sixteen possible evening outfits (or outcomes):

$$\Omega = \{V_b P_b S_r C_r, V_b P_b S_w C_r, V_b P_w S_r C_r, V_b P_w S_w C_r,$$
$$V_w P_b S_r C_r, V_w P_b S_w C_r, V_w P_w S_r C_r, V_w P_w S_w C_r,$$
$$V_b P_b S_r C_w, V_b P_b S_w C_w, V_b P_w S_r C_w, V_b P_w S_w C_w,$$
$$V_w P_b S_r C_w, V_w P_b S_w C_w, V_w P_w S_r C_w, V_w P_w S_w C_w\}.$$

Assume that when choosing his evening outfit, Peter is not able to compare the sixteen outcomes but expresses the following preferences over partial descriptions of outcomes:

(P_1): he prefers a black vest to a white vest,

(P_2): he prefers black pants to white pants,

(P_3): when vest and pants have the same color, he prefers a red shirt to a white shirt; otherwise, he prefers a white shirt, and

(P_4): when the shirt is red, he prefers red shoes; otherwise, he prefers white shoes.

The problem now is how to rank-order the 16 possible outcomes according to Peter's preferences.

Assume that when Peter expresses a preference over partial specifications of outcomes, he refers to outcomes that are identical besides what is specified in his preference. For example (P_1) means that an outfit with a black vest is preferred to an outfit with a white vest if the two outfits are identical w.r.t. the color of pants, shirt and shoes. Therefore, $V_b P_w S_r C_r$ is preferred to $V_w P_w S_r C_r$ w.r.t. (P_1) but not to $V_w P_b S_r C_r$ w.r.t. (P_1) because the two outcomes have different colors of pants. This is the ceteris paribus semantics.

Peter's preferences exhibit a dependency between variables (which can also be seen as independence between variables) which, associated with ceteris paribus semantics, can be graphically represented by the CP-net, let us say N, depicted in Figure 3.3. Let $\succ_N$ be the preference relation over $\Omega \times \Omega$ associated with N. It is par-

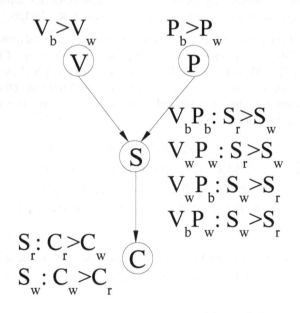

Fig. 3.3 A CP-net, N

tially described by each conditional preference table in the CP-net. Table 3.10 describes $\succ_N$ w.r.t. each conditional preference table in N. The preference relation $\succ_N$ is the transitive closure of all local preferences between complete outcomes

Table 3.10 Local preferences induced by the CP-net

Preference statements	Local preferences		
$V_b > V_w$	$V_b P_b S_r C_r$	$\succ_N$	$V_w P_b S_r C_r$
	$V_b P_b S_r C_w$	$\succ_N$	$V_w P_b S_r C_w$
	$V_b P_b S_w C_r$	$\succ_N$	$V_w P_b S_w C_r$
	$V_b P_b S_w C_w$	$\succ_N$	$V_w P_b S_w C_w$
	$V_b P_w S_r C_r$	$\succ_N$	$V_w P_w S_r C_r$
	$V_b P_w S_r C_w$	$\succ_N$	$V_w P_w S_r C_w$
	$V_b P_w S_w C_r$	$\succ_N$	$V_w P_w S_w C_r$
	$V_b P_w S_w C_w$	$\succ_N$	$V_w P_w S_w C_w$
$P_b > P_w$	$V_b P_b S_r C_r$	$\succ_N$	$V_b P_w S_r C_r$
	$V_b P_b S_r C_w$	$\succ_N$	$V_b P_w S_r C_w$
	$V_b P_b S_w C_r$	$\succ_N$	$V_b P_w S_w C_r$
	$V_b P_b S_w C_w$	$\succ_N$	$V_b P_w S_w C_w$
	$V_w P_b S_r C_r$	$\succ_N$	$V_w P_w S_r C_r$
	$V_w P_b S_r C_w$	$\succ_N$	$V_w P_w S_r C_w$
	$V_w P_b S_w C_r$	$\succ_N$	$V_w P_w S_w C_r$
	$V_w P_b S_w C_w$	$\succ_N$	$V_w P_w S_w C_w$
$V_b P_b : S_r > S_w$	$V_b P_b S_r C_r$	$\succ_N$	$V_b P_b S_w C_r$
	$V_b P_b S_r C_w$	$\succ_N$	$V_b P_b S_w C_w$
$V_w P_w : S_r > S_w$	$V_w P_w S_r C_r$	$\succ_N$	$V_w P_w S_w C_r$
	$V_w P_w S_r C_w$	$\succ_N$	$V_w P_w S_w C_w$
$V_w P_b : S_w > S_r$	$V_w P_b S_w C_r$	$\succ_N$	$V_w P_b S_r C_r$
	$V_w P_b S_w C_w$	$\succ_N$	$V_w P_b S_r C_w$
$V_b P_w : S_w > S_r$	$V_b P_w S_w C_r$	$\succ_N$	$V_b P_w S_r C_r$
	$V_b P_w S_w C_w$	$\succ_N$	$V_b P_w S_r C_w$
$S_r : C_r > C_w$	$V_b P_b S_r C_r$	$\succ_N$	$V_b P_b S_r C_w$
	$V_b P_w S_r C_r$	$\succ_N$	$V_b P_w S_r C_w$
	$V_w P_b S_r C_r$	$\succ_N$	$V_w P_b S_r C_w$
	$V_w P_w S_r C_r$	$\succ_N$	$V_w P_w S_r C_w$
$S_w : C_w > C_r$	$V_b P_b S_w C_w$	$\succ_N$	$V_b P_b S_w C_r$
	$V_b P_w S_w C_w$	$\succ_N$	$V_b P_w S_w C_r$
	$V_w P_b S_w C_w$	$\succ_N$	$V_w P_b S_w C_r$
	$V_w P_w S_w C_w$	$\succ_N$	$V_w P_w S_w C_r$

induced by the conditional preference tables. It is the partial order over $\Omega \times \Omega$ depicted in Figure 3.4. An arrow from ω to ω' is interpreted as "ω' is preferred to ω" w.r.t. N. For example, the following strict preferences between outcomes hold: $V_w P_b S_w C_w \succ_N V_w P_w S_r C_w$ and $V_w P_w S_r C_w \succ_N V_w P_w S_w C_w$. We also have that the three outcomes $V_w P_b S_r C_w$, $V_w P_w S_r C_r$ and $V_b P_w S_r C_w$ are incomparable.

We can observe that the ceteris paribus semantics implicitly gives priority to parent nodes. For example, $V_w P_w S_r C_w$ is preferred to $V_w P_w S_w C_w$. They both falsify the preferences associated with the nodes V and P. However, $V_w P_w S_r C_w$ falsifies the preference associated with the node C while $V_w P_w S_w C_w$ falsifies the preference associated with the node S. Note, however, that this priority does not hold for every

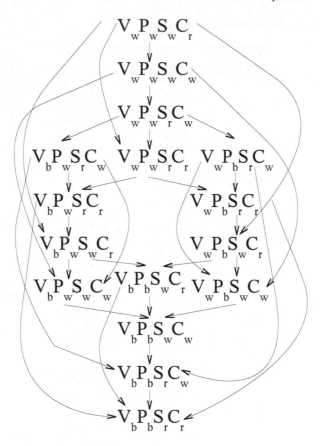

Fig. 3.4 The partial order associated with the CP-net N

outcome. For example, the two outcomes $V_w P_w S_r C_r$ and $V_w P_b S_r C_w$ are incomparable. They both falsify the preference associated with V; the former falsifies the preference associated with P while the latter falsifies the preferences associated with S
and C.

Note that due to the ceteris paribus semantics, strict preferences induced by conditional preference tables hold among outcomes which differ only in the value of
one variable. This is called "a worsening flip". On the other hand, recall that $\succ_N$
is the deductive closure of local preferences induced by the conditional preference
tables. Indeed, the preferential comparison of two outcomes w.r.t. $\succ_N$ is limited to
the pairs for which there exists a path between them through a sequence in which
two successive outcomes differ only in the value of one variable. For example,
$V_b P_b S_w C_w$ is preferred to $V_w P_b S_r C_w$ thanks to the following sequence of worsening

flips: $V_bP_bS_wC_w \succ_N V_wP_bS_wC_w \succ_N V_wP_bS_wC_r \succ_N V_wP_bS_rC_r \succ_N V_wP_bS_rC_w$. In fact, we have

- $V_bP_bS_wC_w \succ_N V_wP_bS_wC_w$ according to $CPT(V)$ $(V_b > V_w)$,
- $V_wP_bS_wC_w \succ_N V_wP_bS_wC_r$ according to $CPT(C)$ $(S_w : C_w > C_r)$,
- $V_wP_bS_wC_r \succ_N V_wP_bS_rC_r$ according to $CPT(S)$ $(V_wP_b : S_w > S_r)$,
- $V_wP_bS_rC_r \succ_N V_wP_bS_rC_w$ according to $CPT(C)$ $(S_r : C_r > C_w)$.

Technically speaking, we know that a partial order is the intersection of all complete preference relations that extend it. Therefore, an outcome dominates another outcome w.r.t. a CP-net N if and only if the strict preference holds w.r.t. to all complete preference relations extending (or consistent with) $\succ_N$. In our example, we distinguish between the following two complete preference relations (from among many others) extending $\succ_N$:

- $\succ_1$:
  $V_bP_bS_rC_r \succ_1 V_bP_bS_rC_w \succ_1 V_bP_bS_wC_w \succ_1 V_wP_bS_wC_w \succ_1 V_bP_bS_wC_r \succ_1 V_bP_wS_wC_w$
  $\succ_1 V_wP_bS_wC_r \succ_1 V_bP_wS_wC_r \succ_1 V_wP_bS_rC_r \succ_1 V_bP_wS_rC_r \succ_1 V_wP_bS_rC_w \succ_1 V_wP_wS_rC_r$
  $\succ_1 V_bP_wS_rC_w \succ_1 V_wP_wS_rC_w \succ_1 V_wP_wS_wC_w \succ_1 V_wP_wS_wC_r$
- $\succ_2$:
  $V_bP_bS_rC_r \succ_2 V_bP_bS_rC_w \succ_2 V_bP_bS_wC_w \succ_2 V_wP_bS_wC_w \succ_2 V_bP_bS_wC_r \succ_2 V_bP_wS_wC_w$
  $\succ_2 V_bP_wS_wC_r \succ_2 V_wP_bS_wC_r \succ_2 V_wP_bS_rC_r \succ_2 V_bP_wS_rC_r \succ_2 V_wP_bS_rC_w \succ_2 V_wP_wS_rC_r$
  $\succ_2 V_bP_wS_rC_w \succ_2 V_wP_wS_rC_w \succ_2 V_wP_wS_wC_w \succ_2 V_wP_wS_wC_r$

Given $\succ_1$ and $\succ_2$ we can state that $V_wP_bS_wC_r$ and $V_bP_wS_wC_r$ are incomparable w.r.t. $\succ_N$ because no strict preference holds in both $\succ_1$ and $\succ_2$. Dominance queries (i.e., checking whether an outcome dominates another outcome) are more complicated as they require us to check the strict preference w.r.t. "all" complete preference relations extending $\succ_N$. This makes these queries costly; they are NP-complete [20]. In order to overcome this complexity, dominance queries have been weakened into ordering queries. More specifically, instead of asking whether ω dominates ω', we ask whether the dominance relation does not hold. Accordingly, queries can be performed w.r.t. only one complete preference relation consistent with $\succ_N$. Considering $\succ_1$ in our example, we ensure that we do not have $V_bP_bS_wC_w \succ_N V_bP_bS_rC_w$ since we have $V_bP_bS_rC_w \succ_1 V_bP_bS_wC_w$. However, we cannot ensure that $V_bP_bS_rC_w$ is preferred to $V_bP_bS_wC_w$ w.r.t. N on the basis of $\succ_1$ only since the strict preference should hold w.r.t. all complete preference relations consistent with $\succ_N$. We can only say that the strict preference of $V_bP_bS_rC_w$ over $V_bP_bS_wC_w$ is consistent with the CP-net N in the sense that we certainly do not have $V_bP_bS_wC_w \succ_N V_bP_bS_rC_w$.

Note that due to the directionality of preferences in CP-nets and the use of ceteris paribus semantics, not all partial orders can be compactly represented by a CP-net.

Usually it is assumed that the values of each variable are totally ordered given each instantiation of its (possibly empty) parent set. This can be easily extended to a partial preorder in which the values of a variable can have an equal preference or remain unordered. It is worth noticing that equality in CP-nets may lead to a cyclic preference relation even if the graph is acyclic. Let N' be a CP-net over two variables X_1 and X_2 such that X_1 is a parent of X_2. Suppose that $x_1 = \neg x_1$, $x_1 : x_2 > \neg x_2$ and $\neg x_1 : \neg x_2 > x_2$ [20]. Then, we have $x_1 x_2 \succ_{N'} x_1 \neg x_2 \approx_{N'} \neg x_1 \neg x_2 \succ_{N'} \neg x_1 x_2 \approx_{N'} x_1 x_2$.

It is worth noticing that CP-nets make a particular use of ceteris paribus semantics. In fact, a contextual preference statement $r : p > q$ is equivalent to $r \wedge p \wedge \neg q > r \wedge q \wedge \neg p$ following Halldén and von Wright translation. According to Definition 3.4, interpreting $r \wedge p \wedge \neg q > r \wedge q \wedge \neg p$ following ceteris paribus means that $\forall \omega \models r \wedge p \wedge \neg q, \forall \omega' \models r \wedge q \wedge \neg p$ we have $\omega \succ \omega'$ if ω and ω' give the same valuation to variables that do not appear in $r \wedge p \wedge \neg q$ and $r \wedge q \wedge \neg p$. However in CP-net framework, ω and ω' should give the same valuation to variables that do not appear in $p \wedge \neg q$ and $q \wedge \neg p$. For example given $V_b \vee P_b : S_r > S_w$, we have the following strict preferences: $V_b P_b S_r C_r \succ V_b P_b S_w C_r$, $V_b P_b S_r C_w \succ V_b P_b S_w C_w$, $V_w P_b S_r C_r \succ V_w P_b S_w C_r$, $V_w P_b S_r C_w \succ V_w P_b S_w C_w$, $V_b P_w S_r C_r \succ V_b P_w S_w C_r$ and $V_b P_w S_r C_w \succ V_b P_w S_w C_w$. However $V_w P_b S_r C_w$ is not preferred to $V_b P_w S_w C_w$.

3.5.3 Conditional Preference Networks with Tradeoffs

In the preference relation $\succ_N$ associated with the CP-net N (depicted in Figure 3.4), we have the following incomparabilities:

$$V_b P_w S_r C_w \sim_N V_w P_b S_r C_w,$$
$$V_b P_w S_r C_r \sim_N V_w P_b S_r C_r,$$
$$V_b P_w S_w C_r \sim_N V_w P_b S_w C_r,$$
$$V_b P_w S_w C_w \sim_N V_w P_b S_w C_w.$$

This means that for fixed colors of shirt and shoes, the combination *black vest-white pants* is incomparable to the combination *white vest-black pants*. Nevertheless, the user may wish to give priority to her preference over the vest's color. More specifically, it is more important for the user to see the vest getting its preferred value (namely, black) than to see the pants getting its preferred value (namely, black). Therefore, the above incomparabilities turn into strict preferences, i.e.,

$$V_b P_w S_r C_w \succ_N V_w P_b S_r C_w,$$
$$V_b P_w S_r C_r \succ_N V_w P_b S_r C_r,$$
$$V_b P_w S_w C_r \succ_N V_w P_b S_w C_r,$$
$$V_b P_w S_w C_w \succ_N V_w P_b S_w C_w.$$

These strict preferences cannot be represented by a CP-net. They require additional information stating that preferences over values of V are more important than preferences over values of P.

Conditional preference networks with tradeoffs (TCP-nets for short) [22] are extensions of CP-nets which allow us to express relative importance between two variables. Figure 3.5 shows the TCP-net which extends N with "V is more important than P", represented by the dashed arrow from V to P. Its associated preference relation extends $\succ_N$ with four strict preferences induced by "V is more important than P" and represented by the bold arrows. The relative importance may also be conditional. For example, consider a CP-net N built on three binary variables X_1, X_2 and X_3 such that X_1 is a parent of both X_2 and X_3. Then, X_2 is more important than X_3 conditioned on X_1 can be expressed as follows: given x_1, X_2 is more important than X_3 and the importance is reversed when $\neg x_1$ holds.

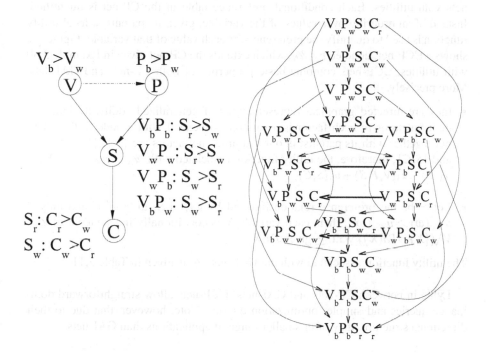

Fig. 3.5 A TCP-net and its associated order

3.5.4 Conditional Importance Networks

Inspired from TCP-nets, Bouveret et al. [21] developed conditional importance networks (CI-nets for short). A CI-net over a set of variables V is a set of conditional importance statements over V comparing sets of variables of arbitrary size (instead of single variables as in TCP-nets), ceteris paribus. The preference relation induced by a CI-net is a monotonic strict order over 2^V. That is, Σ_1 is preferred to Σ_2 when $\Sigma_2 \subset \Sigma_1$, with $\Sigma_1, \Sigma_2 \in 2^V$.

Let $V = \{a, b, c, d\}$. The statement "given d, b is more important than c" means that "everything else being equal, it is preferred to have $\{d, b\}$ rather than $\{d, c\}$". This turns out to have $\{b, d\}$ preferred to $\{c, d\}$, and $\{a, b, d\}$ preferred to $\{a, c, d\}$.

3.5.5 Conditional Preference Networks with Utilities

Conditional preference networks with utilities (UCP-nets for short) [18] extend CP-nets with utilities. Each conditional preference table in the CP-net is quantified. Instead of an ordering over values of the variable, given its parents, a local utility function is used to quantify the preference for each value of that variable. Figure 3.6 shows a UCP-net, denoted by $\mathcal{U}_N$, which extends the CP-net given in Example 3.30 with utilities. UCP-nets combine basic properties of both CP-nets and GAI-nets. More precisely,

- they are directed graphical representations of generalized additively independent functions u; each factor is a variable associated with a node in the UCP-net together with its parents; in our example, the factors are $\{V\}$, $\{P\}$, $\{V, P, S\}$ and $\{S, C\}$; therefore, the utility function associated with $\mathcal{U}_N$ is $u_{\mathcal{U}_N} = u_1(V) + u_2(P) + u_3(V, P, S) + u_4(S, C)$;

- Let $\succeq$ be the preference relation induced by $u_{\mathcal{U}_N}$, i.e., $\omega \succeq \omega'$ if and only if $u_{\mathcal{U}_N}(\omega) \geq u_{\mathcal{U}_N}(\omega')$; then, each variable X is conditionally independent of $Z = V \setminus (\{X\} \cup Pa(X))$ w.r.t. $\succeq$ given $Pa(X)$.

The utility function associated with the UCP-net $\mathcal{U}_N$ is given in Table 3.11.

Lying in between CP-nets and GAI-nets, UCP-nets allow straightforward dominance queries and simpler optimization queries. Note, however, that due to their directional structure, they offer smaller range of applications than GAI-nets.

3.5.6 Soft Constraint Satisfaction Problems

A constraint network is a triple (V, D, C), where $V = \{X_1, \cdots, X_n\}$ is the set of variables, $D = \{Dom(X_1), \cdots, Dom(X_n)\}$ and C is a set of constraints. A constraint over $V' \subseteq V$ specifies the values it allows for variables of V'. An outcome satisfies a constraint network (V, D, C) when it satisfies each constraint in the network. The search of such outcomes is known as a constraint satisfaction problem (CSP for short) [55, 54].

Soft constraint satisfaction problems (SCSPs for short) [14] generalize classical CSPs. A constraint over a set of variables V' in an SCSP associates with each in-

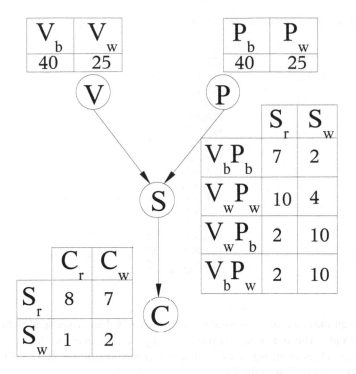

Fig. 3.6 A UCP-net $\mathscr{U}_N$

stantiation of variables in V' a value taken from a totally or partially ordered set. The mathematical formalization of SCSP is based on the concept of c-semiring, which is a tuple $S = (A, \oplus, \otimes, 0, 1)$, where

- A is a set with $0, 1 \in A$,
- $\oplus$ is a commutative, associative and idempotent function having 0 as a unit element and 1 as its absorbing element,
- $\otimes$ is a commutative and associative function which distributes over $\oplus$. 1 is its unit element and 0 is its absorbing element.

Given a c-semiring $S = (A, \oplus, \otimes, 0, 1)$ and a set of variables V, a soft constraint is a pair $\langle f, V' \rangle$, where $V' \subseteq V$ and f is a function which associates with each element in $Asst(V')$ a value in A. An SCSP is a set of soft constraints over a set of variables.

Table 3.11 The utility function associated with $\mathcal{U}_N$

ω	$u_{\mathcal{U}_N}(\omega)$
$V_b P_b S_r C_r$	95
$V_b P_b S_r C_w$	94
$V_b P_b S_w C_r$	83
$V_b P_b S_w C_w$	84
$V_b P_w S_r C_r$	75
$V_b P_w S_r C_w$	74
$V_b P_w S_w C_r$	76
$V_b P_w S_w C_w$	77
$V_w P_b S_r C_r$	75
$V_w P_b S_r C_w$	74
$V_w P_b S_w C_r$	76
$V_w P_b S_w C_w$	77
$V_w P_w S_r C_r$	68
$V_w P_w S_r C_w$	67
$V_w P_w S_w C_r$	55
$V_w P_w S_w C_w$	56

Given an outcome ω, $\otimes$ is used to combine the values associated with ω w.r.t. all constraints. The function $\oplus$ is used to compare outcomes on the basis of their aggregated values resulting from $\otimes$. The preference relation over $\Omega \times \Omega$ induced by $S = (A, \oplus, \otimes, 0, 1)$ is defined by

$$\forall \omega, \omega' \in \Omega, \omega \succ_S \omega' \text{ iff } \omega \oplus \omega' = \omega.$$

Thanks to the generality of the c-semiring $S = (A, \oplus, \otimes, 0, 1)$, SCSPs can capture classical CSPs and their extensions. More specifically, an SCSP reduces to a classical CSP when the c-semiring is equal to $(\{true, false\}, \vee, \wedge, false, true)$ [14]. Hence an outcome is accepted, i.e., preferred w.r.t. a constraint when its associated value is true; it is rejected if this value is false. Since the combination function is $\wedge$, outcomes are either accepted or rejected w.r.t. the SCSP. Clearly, optimal outcomes are accepted outcomes.

Fuzzy CSPs [61] are a special case of SCSPs where the c-semiring is equal to $([0,1], \max, \min, 0, 1)$. Weighted CSPs [51] are recovered by SCSPs when the c-semiring is equal to $(\mathbb{R}^+, \min, +, +\infty, 0)$. Probabilistic CSPs [33] are recovered when the c-semiring is equal to $([0,1], \max, \times, 0, 1)$. Lastly, valued CSPs [62] which are based on a unique operator, can also be encoded by SCSPs.

We refer the reader to [14] for a formal description of the above frameworks.

Example 3.31 (Weighted CSP).
Consider a weighted CSP over three variables, J_{VP}, S and C, with $Dom(J_{VP}) = \{(V_b, P_b), (V_b, P_w), (V_w, P_b), (V_w, P_w)\}$, $Dom(S) = \{S_r, S_w\}$ and $Dom(C) = \{C_r, C_w\}$. The CSP and its associated constraints are depicted in Figure 3.7. Each constraint in the graph expresses a local penalty of an outcome satisfying the values of the constraint. For example, the constraint $(((V_b, P_b), S_w), 2)$ expresses that any outcome

in which $V_b P_b S_w$ is true has a penalty 2 w.r.t. this constraint. The global penalty associated with an outcome is the sum of its local penalties.

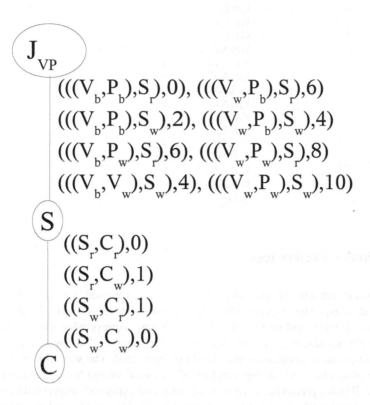

Fig. 3.7 A weighted CSP

In Table 3.12 we give the penalty associated with each outcome.

In the quest of overcoming the hard complexity of preference queries in CP-nets, Domshlak et al. [26] have proposed an approximation of CP-nets. The latter returns a complete preorder consistent with the partial order induced by the CP-net. The approximation consists in building a weighted CSP from a CP-net. We can check in the above example that the penalty distribution recovers all strict preferences of the partial order depicted in Figure 3.4.

Table 3.12 The penalty distribution associated with the weighted CSP

ω	Penalty degree
$V_b P_b S_r C_r$	0
$V_b P_b S_r C_w$	1
$V_b P_b S_w C_r$	3
$V_b P_b S_w C_w$	2
$V_b P_w S_r C_r$	6
$V_b P_w S_r C_w$	7
$V_b P_w S_w C_r$	5
$V_b P_w S_w C_w$	4
$V_w P_b S_r C_r$	6
$V_w P_b S_r C_w$	7
$V_w P_b S_w C_r$	5
$V_w P_b S_w C_w$	4
$V_w P_w S_r C_r$	8
$V_w P_w S_r C_w$	9
$V_w P_w S_w C_r$	11
$V_w P_w S_w C_w$	10

3.6 Bipolar Preferences

Preferences over a set of outcomes are sometimes expressed in two forms. On the one hand, a user may express what she considers (more or less) tolerable or unacceptable for her, and on the other hand she may express what she considers as being really satisfactory. The first form of preference is called negative preference and corresponds to constraints that should be respected. The second form is called positive preference and corresponds to wishes which should be satisfied as best as possible. Bipolar preferences can be conjointly and compactly expressed in various formats: weighted logics [4, 6], conditional logics [5, 65, 50] and graphical representations [15]. These are generally not new representation languages dedicated to bipolar preferences. Actually, it has been shown that existing preference representation languages are suitable for representing negative preferences or positive preferences. In the following subsections we give an overview of some of these representation languages.

3.6.1 Representing Bipolar Preferences in Weighted Logics

Negative preferences correspond to what is not tolerated, what is rejected by the user. They are expressed by a set of inequality constraints of the form $\mathbb{R} = \{\mathscr{R}(\phi_i) \geq \alpha_i \mid i = 1, \cdots, n\}$, where ϕ_i is a propositional logic formula which must be violated (since it represents what is rejected by the user). The weight α_i represents the priority level of rejecting ϕ_i; it lies in a finite totally ordered scale. By convention this scale is the unit interval $(0, 1]$. The constraint $\mathscr{R}(\phi_i) \geq \alpha_i$ expresses that all outcomes which satisfy ϕ_i are non-tolerated at least at level α_i. The higher α_i is, the more non-tolerated are the outcomes satisfying ϕ_i. $\mathcal{R}(\phi_i) = 1$ means that ϕ_i is fully rejected and no outcome satisfying ϕ_i is tolerated by the user. When an outcome does not satisfy any formula ϕ_i, nothing prevents it of being fully tolerated. Therefore, the intolerance function, denoted by $un(.)$, associated with a constraint $\mathcal{R}(\phi_i) \geq \alpha_i$ is constructed as follows:

$$\forall \omega \in \Omega, un_{\mathcal{R}(\phi_i) \geq \alpha_i}(\omega) = \begin{cases} 0 & \text{if } \omega \not\models \phi_i \\ \alpha_i & \text{otherwise} \end{cases}.$$

By complementation, a tolerance function, denoted by $t(.)$, associated with $\mathcal{R}(\phi_i) \geq \alpha_i$ is deduced:

$$\forall \omega \in \Omega, t_{\mathcal{R}(\phi_i) \geq \alpha_i}(\omega) = \begin{cases} 1 & \text{if } \omega \not\models \phi_i \\ 1 - \alpha_i & \text{otherwise} \end{cases}.$$

We can observe that this resembles the tolerance distribution associated with a possibilistic logic formula $(\neg\phi_i, \alpha_i)$. Let us now check whether this observation still holds when we consider two constraints, $\mathcal{R}(\phi_1) \geq \alpha_1$ and $\mathcal{R}(\phi_2) \geq \alpha_2$.

Let $\mathcal{R} = \{\mathcal{R}(\phi_1) \geq \alpha_1, \mathcal{R}(\phi_2) \geq \alpha_2\}$. We distinguish between three cases:

- If $\omega \not\models \phi_1$ and $\omega \not\models \phi_2$ then ω is fully tolerated. Hence $t_{\mathcal{R}}(\omega) = 1$.

- If $\omega \models \neg\phi_1 \wedge \phi_2$ (or $\omega \models \phi_1 \wedge \neg\phi_2$) then the higher α_2 (or α_1) is, the less tolerated is ω. So, $t_{\mathcal{R}}(\omega) = 1 - \alpha_2$ (or $1 - \alpha_1$).

- If $\omega \models \phi_1 \wedge \phi_2$ then the higher α_1 or α_2 are, the less tolerated is ω. So, $t_{\mathcal{R}}(\omega) = 1 - \max(\alpha_1, \alpha_2)$.

This also resembles a tolerance distribution associated with a possibilistic logic base $\mathbb{T} = \{(\neg\phi_1, \alpha_1), (\neg\phi_2, \alpha_2)\}$. Therefore, possibilistic logic is a suitable framework for the logical representation of negative preferences [4]. Thus, the weight associated with a formula corresponds to the necessity degree of that formula.

Positive preferences correspond to what is really described by the user. They are expressed by means of a set of inequalities of the form $\mathbb{S} = \{\mathscr{S}(\varphi_j) \geq \beta_j \mid j = 1, \cdots, m\}$, where φ_j is a propositional logic formula that brings satisfaction to the user if it is satisfied. The weight β_j represents the satisfaction level of φ_j. It lies in a finite totally ordered scale. By convention this scale is the unit interval $(0, 1]$. The inequality $\mathscr{S}(\varphi_j) \geq \beta_j$ means that any outcome satisfying φ_j is satisfactory at least at level β_j. The higher β_j is, the more satisfactory are the outcomes which satisfy φ_j. Unlike negative preferences, an outcome which does not satisfy φ_j is not excluded. We say that the user is indifferent w.r.t. that outcome given φ_j. The satisfaction function, denoted by $s(.)$, associated with $\mathscr{S}(\varphi_j) \geq \beta_j$ is computed as follows:

$$\forall \omega \in \Omega, s_{\mathscr{S}(\varphi_j) \geq \beta_j}(\omega) = \begin{cases} \beta_j & \text{if } \omega \models \varphi_j \\ 0 & \text{otherwise} \end{cases}.$$

Note that this satisfaction function coincides with the satisfaction distribution associated with a formula (φ_j, β_j) in a guaranteed possibilistic logic base. Let us now check whether this observation still holds when we consider two inequalities, $\mathscr{S}(\varphi_1) \geq \beta_1$ and $\mathscr{S}(\varphi_2) \geq \beta_2$. Let $\mathbb{S} = \{\mathscr{S}(\varphi_1) \geq \beta_1, \mathscr{S}(\varphi_2) \geq \beta_2\}$. We distinguish between three cases:

- If $\omega \not\models \varphi_1$ and $\omega \not\models \varphi_2$ then the user is indifferent w.r.t. ω given φ_1 and φ_2. Hence, $s_{\mathbb{S}}(\omega) = 0$.

- If $\omega \models \varphi_1 \wedge \neg\varphi_2$ (or $\omega \models \neg\varphi_1 \wedge \varphi_2$) then the higher β_1 (or β_2) is, the more satisfactory is ω. Hence, $s_{\mathbb{S}}(\omega) = \beta_1$ (or $s_{\mathbb{S}}(\omega) = \beta_2$).

- If $\omega \models \varphi_1$, $\omega \models \varphi_2$ then the higher is β_1 or β_2, the more satisfactory is ω. Hence, $s_{\mathbb{S}}(\omega) = \max(\beta_1, \beta_2)$.

This also coincides with the satisfaction distribution associated with the guaranteed possibilistic logic base $\mathscr{G} = \{(\varphi_1, \beta_1), (\varphi_2, \beta_2)\}$. Hence, guaranteed possibilistic logic is a suitable framework for representing positive preferences [4]. Thus, the weight associated with a formula corresponds to the guaranteed possibilistic measure of that formula.

To summarize, negative preferences and positive preferences are respectively represented by a possibilistic logic base $\mathbb{T} = \{(\phi_i, \alpha_i) \mid i = 1, \cdots, n\}$ and a guaranteed possibilistic logic base $\mathscr{G} = \{(\varphi_j, \beta_j) \mid j = 1, \cdots, m\}$. They respectively induce a tolerance distribution and a satisfaction distribution computed in the following way: $\forall \omega \in \Omega$,

$$\pi_{\mathbb{T}}(\omega) = \begin{cases} 1 & \text{if } \omega \models \phi_1 \wedge \cdots \wedge \phi_n \\ 1 - \max\{\alpha_i \mid (\phi_i, \alpha_i) \in \mathbb{T}, \omega \not\models \phi_i\} & \text{otherwise} \end{cases},$$

$$\delta_{\mathscr{G}}(\omega) = \begin{cases} \max\{\beta_j \mid (\varphi_j, \beta_j) \in \mathscr{G}, \omega \models \varphi_j\} & \text{if } \omega \models \varphi_1 \vee \cdots \vee \varphi_m \\ 0 & \text{otherwise} \end{cases}.$$

Negative preferences and positive preferences behave in a dual way. $\pi_{\mathbb{T}}(\omega) = 0$ is more informative than $\pi_{\mathbb{T}}(\omega) = 1$. Indeed, $\pi_{\mathbb{T}}(\omega) = 0$ means that ω is excluded as it falsifies a preference formula with an importance degree equal to 1, i.e., an absolute preference, while $\pi_{\mathbb{T}}(\omega) = 1$ only means that nothing prevents ω from being fully tolerated given $\mathbb{T}$. On the other hand, $\delta_{\mathscr{G}}(\omega) = 1$ is more informative than $\delta_{\mathscr{G}}(\omega) = 0$. Indeed, $\delta_{\mathscr{G}}(\omega) = 1$ means that ω is fully satisfactory as it satisfies a preference formula with a satisfaction level equal to 1 while $\delta_{\mathscr{G}}(\omega) = 0$ only means that the user is indifferent w.r.t. ω given $\mathscr{G}$. Notice also that an outcome is tolerated w.r.t. $\mathbb{T}$ as soon as it is not rejected by any formula and an outcome is satisfactory only when it is satisfactory w.r.t. at least one formula. Lastly, notice that additional negative preferences in $\mathbb{T}$ may only decrease the tolerance degree of outcomes while additional positive preferences may only increase the satisfaction degree of outcomes. So, negative preferences are conjunctively combined while positive preferences are disjunctively combined. This is faithful with what is intended by bipolar preferences since negative preferences are viewed as constraints while positive preferences are viewed as wishes.

Outcomes can be rank-ordered in different ways given bipolar preferences. One may select satisfactory outcomes from among tolerated ones or select tolerated outcomes from among satisfactory ones. We refer the reader to [6] for further details.

3.6.2 Representing Bipolar Preferences in Conditional Logics

As stated in the previous subsection, negative preferences can be represented by a possibilistic logic base $\mathbb{T} = \{(\phi_i, \alpha_i) \mid i = 1, \cdots, n\}$. The weight α_i corresponds to the minimal necessity measure of ϕ_i, i.e., $N(\phi_i) \geq \alpha_i$. We have that $\mathbb{T}$ is equivalent to $\mathbb{T}' = \{(\phi_i, N(\phi_i)) \mid i = 1, \cdots, n\}$ in the sense that the two bases induce the same tolerance distribution.

Let $\succeq_{\mathbb{T}}$ be a preference relation over $\phi_1, \cdots, \phi_n$ defined as $\phi_i \succ_{\mathbb{T}} \phi_k$ if and only if $N(\phi_i) > N(\phi_k)$. We have $\phi_i \succ_{\mathbb{T}} \phi_k$ if and only if $N(\phi_i) > N(\phi_k)$ iff $1 - \Pi(\neg\phi_i) > 1 - \Pi(\neg\phi_k)$ iff $\Pi(\neg\phi_i) < \Pi(\neg\phi_k)$. Therefore, negative preferences can be expressed by means of constraints on the tolerance measure.

A constraint $\Pi(\phi_i) > \Pi(\phi_k)$, which is equivalent to $\max\{\pi_{\mathbb{T}}(\omega) \mid \omega \models \phi_i\} > \max\{\pi_{\mathbb{T}}(\omega) \mid \omega \models \phi_k\}$, means that the maximal ϕ_i-outcomes w.r.t. $\pi_{\mathbb{T}}$ are preferred to the maximal ϕ_j-outcomes w.r.t. $\pi_{\mathbb{T}}$. From Subsection 3.4.1, a comparative preference statement $p > q$ interpreted following optimistic reasoning is mathematically expressed as

$$\forall \omega \in \max(p \wedge \neg q, \succeq), \forall \omega' \in \max(q \wedge \neg p, \succeq), \text{ we have } \omega \succ \omega',$$

where $\succeq$ is a preference relation over $\Omega \times \Omega$. By analogy we conclude that optimistic semantics is suitable for representing negative preferences. Following Algorithm 3.3, the preference relation associated with a comparative preference statement $p > q$ is $\succeq = (E_1, E_2)$, where E_1 is the set of outcomes falsifying $q \wedge \neg p$, i.e., it is the set of $(p \vee \neg q)$-outcomes. Recall that given $p > q$, $(p \wedge \neg q)$-outcomes are outcomes which satisfy $p > q$ while $(q \wedge \neg p)$-outcomes are outcomes which falsify $p > q$. Therefore, E_1 includes outcomes which do not falsify $p > q$ but do not satisfy it either. Consider a preference statement, "if *fish* is served then prefer *white wine* to *red wine*". Let $\Omega = \{fish - white, fish - red, meat - white, meat - red\}$. The preference statement is written as $fish \wedge white > fish \wedge red$. Then, $E_1 = \{fish - white, meat - red, meat - white\}$. Note that $fish - white$ satisfies the preference. On the other hand, $meat - red$ and $meat - white$ do not falsify the preference statement but do not satisfy it either. Not being excluded by the preference statement, such outcomes belong to the set of preferred outcomes. This is faithful to the intended meaning of negative preferences in the sense that what is not rejected or excluded is tolerated.

Again, as stated in the previous subsection, positive preferences are represented by means of a guaranteed possibilistic logic base $\mathcal{G} = \{(\varphi_j, \beta_j) \mid j = 1, \cdots, m\}$. The weight associated with a formula corresponds to its minimal satisfaction level, namely, $\Delta(\varphi_j) \geq \beta_j$. $\mathcal{G}$ is equivalent to $\mathcal{G}' = \{(\varphi_j, \Delta(\varphi_j)) \mid j = 1, \cdots, m\}$ in the sense that they induce the same satisfaction distribution. We define a preference relation over $\varphi_1, \cdots, \varphi_m$ as $\varphi_j \succ_{\mathcal{G}} \varphi_h$ iff $\Delta(\varphi_j) > \Delta(\varphi_h)$. This constraint is equivalent to $\min\{\delta_{\mathcal{G}}(\omega) \mid \omega \models \varphi_j\} > \min\{\delta_{\mathcal{G}}(\omega) \mid \omega \models \varphi_h\}$, which means that the minimal φ_j-outcomes w.r.t. $\delta_{\mathcal{G}}$ are preferred to the minimal φ_h-outcomes w.r.t. $\delta_{\mathcal{G}}$. From Subsection 3.4.1, a comparative preference statement $p > q$ interpreted following pessimistic semantics is mathematically expressed as

$$\forall \omega \in \min(p \wedge \neg q, \succeq), \forall \omega' \in \min(q \wedge \neg p, \succeq), \text{ we have } \omega \succ \omega',$$

where $\succeq$ is a preference relation over $\Omega \times \Omega$.

By analogy we conclude that pessimistic semantics represents positive preferences. Following Algorithm 3.4, the preference relation associated with $p > q$ interpreted following pessimistic semantics is $\succeq = (E_1, E_2)$, where E_1 is the set of $(p \wedge \neg q)$-outcomes and E_2 is the set of remaining outcomes. Therefore, only those outcomes which satisfy the preference statement are considered as preferred. This is the intended meaning of positive preferences. In the above example, we have $E_1 = \{fish - white\}$ and $E_2 = \{fish - red, meat - white, meat - red\}$.

The authors of [65, 50] also make use of bipolarity in preference representation but do not distinguish between two separate sets of preferences (i.e., a set of negative preferences and a set of positive preferences). In their framework, a preference is represented by a conditional desire, denoted by $D(p|q)$, which is interpreted as a constraint on a utility function to be constructed. The semantics underlying $D(p|q)$ is the one proposed by Boutilier [17], that is, "the q-outcomes with highest utility satisfy p" (this is the optimistic semantics). Desires in their framework are interpreted in a bipolar way: they induce a loss of utility when they are violated and a gain of utility when they are satisfied. The global utility function is additive, i.e., the utility of an outcome is the result of summing up losses and gains of that outcome induced by each conditional desire. Therefore, this framework for dealing with bipolar preferences does not offer a separate treatment of these preferences.

3.6.3 Representing Bipolar Preferences in Graphical Languages

Soft constraint satisfaction problems use a combination function $\otimes$ whose unit element is 1. Therefore, combining two values a and b with $\otimes$ results in a value at most equal to $\min(a, b)$. In fact, we have $a = a \otimes 1 = a \otimes (1 \oplus b) = (a \otimes 1) \oplus (a \otimes b) = a \oplus (a \otimes b)$. Thus, $a \geq a \oplus b$. Similarly, we get $b \geq a \oplus b$. Thus, $a \oplus b \leq \min(a, b)$. This means that considering additional constraints leads to a worse result. This is the behavior of negative preferences. Therefore, SCSPs are suitable for representing negative preferences. The authors of [15] defined SCSP to represent positive preferences. They are based on a c-semiring $S' = (A, \times_p, +_p, 0, 1)$ such that $\times_p$ has the same properties as $\otimes$ used in standard SCSP. The difference appears with the operator $+_p$ whose unit element is 0 and absorbing element is 1.

3.7 Conclusion

The chapter presents a panoramic view of different compact languages for preference representation. They correspond to different ways users express their preferences. While each of these languages has its merits, it does not adequately and naturally capture all forms of preferences. In fact, graphical languages are appealing when variables explicitly exhibit some form of independency. Therefore, the interaction between variables can be directly read from the graph. Conditional logics have the ability to naturally express default preferences that generally hold together with more specific ones that reverse them. Note, however, that when dealing with comparative preference statements, we do not necessarily have indications about their respective levels of importance. The logical representation of preferences using ordered propositional logic formulas allows for a graded representation of preferences w.r.t. their priority levels.

While researchers are still studying the properties of compact preference representation languages, mainly from computational point of view, it seems that we know relatively much less about the semantics underpinning these languages. In particular, compact preference representation languages have a common point, that is, they are based on priorities. While such information is explicitly perceived in weighted logics, it is implicit in conditional logics and graphical languages. It would be worth trying to understand these implicit priorities. This is the subject of the next chapter.

References

1. Bacchus, F., Grove, A.J.: Graphical models for preference and utility. In: Besnard, P., Hanks, S. (eds.), 11th International Conference on Uncertainty in Artificial Intelligence, pp. 3-10. Morgan Kaufmann, (1995)
2. Behringer, F.A.: On optimal decisions under complete ignorance: A new criterion stronger than both Pareto and maxmin. European Journal of Operational Research **1(5)**, 295–306 (1977)
3. Benferhat, S., Cayrol, C., Dubois, D., Lang, J., Prade, H.: Inconsistency management and prioritized syntax-based entailment. In: Bajcsy, R. (eds.), 13th International Joint Conference on Artificial Intelligence, pp. 640-645. Morgan Kaufmann, (1993)
4. Benferhat, S., Dubois, D., Kaci, S., Prade, H.: Bipolar representation and fusion of preferences in the possibilistic logic framework. In: Fensel, D., Giunchiglia, F., McGuinness, D.L.,

Williams, M.A. (eds.), 8th International Conference on Principle of Knowledge Representation and Reasoning, pp. 421-432. Morgan Kaufmann, (2002)

5. Benferhat, S., Dubois, D., Kaci, S., Prade, H.: Bipolar possibilistic representations. In: Darwiche, A., Friedman, N. (eds.), 18th International Conference on Uncertainty in Artificial Intelligence, pp. 45-52. Morgan Kaufmann, (2002)

6. Benferhat, S., Dubois, D., Kaci, S., Prade, H.: Bipolar possibility theory in preference modeling: Representation, fusion and optimal solutions. Information Fusion 7, 135–150 (2006)

7. Benferhat, S., Dubois, D., Prade, H.: Representing default rules in possibilistic logic. In: Nebel, B., Rich, C., Swartout, W.R. (eds.), 3rd International Conference of Principles of Knowledge Representation and Reasoning, pp. 673-684. Morgan Kaufmann, (1992)

8. Benferhat, S., Dubois, D., Prade, H.: Some syntactic approaches to the handling of inconsistent knowledge bases: A comparative study Part 2: The prioritized case. Logic at Work 24, 473–511 (1998)

9. Benferhat, S., Dubois, D., Prade, H.: Towards a possibilistic logic handling of preferences. Applied Intelligence 14(3), 303–317 (2001)

10. Benferhat, S., Kaci, S.: A possibilistic logic handling of strong preferences. In: Smith, M.H., Gruver, W.A. (eds.), International Fuzzy Systems Association, pp. 962-967. (2001)

11. Benferhat, S., Sedki, K.: A revised qualitative choice logic for handling prioritized preferences. In: Mellouli, K. (eds.), 9th European Conferences on Symbolic and Quantitative Approaches to Reasoning with Uncertainty, pp. 635-647. Springer, (2007)

12. Benferhat, S., Sedki, K.: Two alternatives for handling preferences in qualitative choice logic. Fuzzy Sets and Systems 159(15), 1889–1912 (2008)

13. Bienvenu, M., Lang, J., Wilson, N.: From preference logics to preference languages, and back. In: Lin, F., Sattler, U., Truszczynski, M. (eds.), 12th International Conference on Principles of Knowledge Representation and Reasoning. AAAI Press, Toronto (2010)

14. Bistarelli, S., Montanari, U., Rossi, F., Schiex, T., Verfaillie, G., Fargier, H.: Semiring-based CSPs and valued CSPs: Frameworks, Properties, and Comparison. Constraints 4(3), 199–240 (1999)

15. Bistarelli, S., Pini, M.S., Rossi, F., Venable, K.B.: From soft constraints to bipolar preferences: modelling framework and solving issues. Journal of Experimental and Theoretical Artificial Intelligence 22(2), 135–158 (2010)

16. Booth, R., Paris, J.: A note on the rational closure of knowledge bases with both positive and negative knowledge. Journal of Logic, Language and Information 7(2), 165–190 (1998)

17. Boutilier, C.: Toward a logic for qualitative decision theory. In: Doyle, J., Sandewall, E., Torasso, P. (eds.), 4th International Conference on Principles of Knowledge Representation, pp. 75-86. Morgan Kaufmann, (1994)

18. Boutilier, C., Bacchus, F., Brafman, R.I.: UCP-networks: A directed graphical representation of conditional utilities. In: Breese, J.S., Koller, D. (eds.), 17th International Conference on Uncertainty in Artificial Intelligence, pp. 56-64. Morgan Kaufmann, (2001)

19. Boutilier, C., Brafman, R.I., Hoos, H.H., Poole, D.: Reasoning with conditional ceteris paribus preference statements. In: Laskey, K.B., Prade, H. (eds.), 15th International Conference on Uncertainty in Artificial Intelligence, pp. 71-80. Morgan Kaufmann, (1999)

20. Boutilier, C., Brafman, R.I., Domshlak, C., Hoos, H.H., Poole, D.: CP-nets: A tool for representing and reasoning with conditional ceteris paribus preference statements. Journal of Artificial Intelligence Research 21, 135–191 (2004)

21. Bouveret, S., Endriss, U., Lang, J.: Conditional importance networks: A graphical language for representing ordinal, monotonic preferences over sets of goods. In: Boutilier, G. (eds.), 21st International Joint Conference on Artificial Intelligence, pp. 67-72. (2009)

22. Brafman, R.I., Domshlak, C.: Introducing variable importance tradeoffs into CP-nets. In: Darwiche, A., Friedman, N. (eds.), 18th International Conference on Uncertainty in Artificial Intelligence, pp. 69-76. Morgan Kaufmann, (2002)

23. Brewka, G.: Preferred subtheories: An extended logical framework for default reasoning. In: Sridharan, N.S. (eds.), 11th International Joint Conference on Artificial Intelligence, pp. 1043-1048. Morgan Kaufmann, (1989)

24. Brewka, G., Benferhat, S.,Le Berre, D.: Qualitative choice logic. Artificial Intelligence 157(1-2), 203–237 (2004)
25. Dalal, M.: Investigations into a theory of knowledge base revision: Preliminary report. In: Mitchel, T., Smith, R. (eds.), 7th National Conference on Artificial Intelligence, pp. 475-479. AAAI Press, (1988)
26. Domshlak, C., Rossi, F., Venable, K.B., Walsh, T.: Reasoning about soft constraints and conditional preferences: Complexity results and approximation techniques. In: Gottlob, G., Walsh, T. (eds.), 18th Joint Conference on Artificial Intelligence, pp. 215-220. Morgan Kaufmann, (2003)
27. Doyle, J., Shoham, Y., Wellman, M.P.: A Logic of Relative Desire (Preliminary Report). In: Ras, Z.W., Zemankova, M. (eds.), 6th International Symposium on Methodologies for Intelligent Systems, pp. 16-31. Springer, (1991)
28. Doyle, J., Wellman, M.P.: Representing preferences as ceteris paribus comparatives. AAAI Symposium on Decision-Theoretic Planning, Stanford (1994)
29. Dubois, D., Fargier, H., Prade, H.: Beyond min aggregation in multicriteria decision: (Ordered) weighted min, discrimin, leximin. In: Yager, R.R., Kacprzyk, J. (eds.), The Ordered Weighted Averaging Operators - Theory and Applications, pp. 181-192. Kluwer Academic (1997)
30. Dubois, D., Fortemps, P.: Leximin optimality and fuzzy set theoretic operations. European Journal of Operational Research 130, 20–28 (2001)
31. Dubois, D., Lang, J., Prade, H.: Possibilistic logic. In: D. Gabbay et al. (eds.), Handbook of Logic in Artificial Intelligence and Logic Programming, pp. 439-513. Oxford University Press (1994)
32. Dupin de Saint-Cyr, F., Lang, J., Schiex, T.: Penalty logic and its link with Dempster-Shafer theory. In: López de Mántaras, R., Poole, D. (eds.), 10th International Conference on Uncertainty in Artificial Intelligence, pp. 204-211. Morgan Kaufmann, (1994)
33. Fargier, H., Lang, J.: Uncertainty in constraint satisfaction problems: A probalistic approach. In: Clarke, M., Kruse, R., Moral, S. (eds.), 2nd European Conference on Symbolic and Quantitative Approaches to Reasoning with Uncertainty, pp. 97-104. Springer, (1993)
34. Fishburn, P.C.: Utility Theory for Decision Making. Huntington, NY. Robert E. Krieger Publishing Co. (1970)
35. Fishburn, P.C.: Interval Orders and Interval Graphs. Wiley, New York (1985)
36. Fishburn, P.C.: Generalisations of semiorders: A review note. Journal of Mathematical Psychology 41, 357–366 (1997)
37. Geffner, H.: Default reasoning: Causal and conditional theories. MIT Press (1992)
38. Gonzales, C., Perny, P.: GAI networks for utility elicitation. In: Dubois, D., Welty, Ch.A., Williams, M.A. (eds.), 9th International Conference on Principles of Knowledge Representation and Reasoning, pp. 224-234. AAAI Press, (2004)
39. Gonzales, C., Perny, P., Queiroz, S.: GAI-networks: Optimization, ranking and collective choice in combinatorial domains. Foundations of Computing and Decision Sciences 32(4), 3–24 (2008)
40. Haddawy, P., Hanks, St.: Representations for decision-theoretic planning: Utility functions for deadline goals. In: Nebel, B., Rich, C., Swartout, W.R. (eds.), 3rd International Conference on Principles of Knowledge Representation and Reasoning, pp. 71-82. Morgan Kaufmann, (1992)
41. Halldén, S.: On the Logic of "Better". Library of Theoria, Lund (1957)
42. Hansson, S.O.: What is ceteris paribus preference? Journal of Philosophical Logic 25, 307–332 (1996)
43. Hansson, S.O.: The structure of values and norms. Cambridge University Press (2001)
44. Kaci, S., van der Torre, L.: Algorithms for a nonmonotonic logic of preferences. In: Godo, L. (eds.), 8th European Conference on Symbolic and Quantitative Approaches to Reasoning with Uncertainty, pp. 281-292. Springer, (2005)
45. Kaci, S., van der Torre, L.: Reasoning with various kinds of preferences: Logic, non-monotonicity and algorithms. Annals of Operations Research 163(1), 89–114 (2008)

46. Keeney, R.L., Raiffa, H.: Decisions with Multiple Objectives: Preferences and Value Trade-offs. Wiley, New York (1976)
47. Krantz, D., Luce, R.D., Suppes, P. Tversky, A.: Foundations of Measurement: Additive and Polynomial Representations. Academic Press (1971)
48. Lafage, C., Lang, J.: Propositional distances and preference representation. In: Benferhat, S., Besnard, P. (eds.), 6th European Conference on Symbolic and Quantitative Approaches to Reasoning and Uncertainty, pp. 48-59. Springer, (2001)
49. Lang, J.: Conditional desires and utilities and alternative logical approach to qualitative decision theory. In: Wahlster, W. (eds.), 12th European Conference on Artificial Intelligence, pp. 318-322. John Wiley and Sons, (1996)
50. Lang, J., van der Torre, L., Weydert, E.: Utilitarian desires. Autonomous Agents and Multi-Agent Systems 5, 329–363 (2002)
51. Larrosa, J.: Node and arc consistency in weighted CSP. In: Dechter, R., Kearns, M., Sutton, R. (eds.), 18th National Conference on Artificial Intelligence, pp. 48-53. AAAI Press, (2002)
52. Lehmann, D.: Another perspective on default reasoning. Annals of Mathematics and Artificial Intelligence 15(1), 61–82 (1995)
53. Luce, R.D.: Semiorders and a theory of utility discrimination. Econometrica 24, 178–191 (1956)
54. Mackworth, A.K.: Constraint satisfaction. Encyclopedia of AI. pp. 205-211. Springer (1988)
55. Montanari, U.: Networks of constraints: Fundamental properties and application to picture processing. Information science 7, 95–132 (1974)
56. Nebel, B.: Belief revision and default reasoning: Syntax-based approaches. In: Allen, J.F., Fikes, R., Sandewall, E. (eds.), 2nd International Conference on Principles of Knowledge Representation and Reasoning, pp. 417-428. Morgan Kaufmann, (1991)
57. Öztürk, M., Tsoukiàs, A.: Preference representation with 3-points intervals. In: Brewka, G., Coradeschi, S., Perini, A., Traverso, P. (eds.), 17th European Conference on Artificial Intelligence, pp. 417-421. IOS Press, (2006)
58. Pearl, J.: System Z: A natural ordering of defaults with tractable applications to default reasoning. In: Parikh, R. (eds.), 3rd Conference on Theoretical Aspects of Reasoning about Knowledge, pp. 121-135. Morgan Kaufmann, (1990)
59. Pinkas, G.: Reasoning, nonmonotonicity and learning in connectionist networks that capture propositional knowledge. Artificial Intelligence 77, 203–247 (1995)
60. Pirlot, M., Vincke, P.: Semi Orders. Kluwer Academic, Dordrecht (1997)
61. Schiex, T.: Possibilistic constraint satisfaction problems or "how to handle soft constraints? In: Dubois, D., Wellman, M.P. (eds.), 8th Annual Conference on Uncertainty in Artificial Intelligence, pp. 268-275. Morgan Kaufmann, (1992)
62. Schiex, T., Fargier, H., Verfaillie, G.: Valued constraint satisfaction problems: Hard and easy Problems. In: Mellish, C.S. (eds.), 14th International Joint Conference on Artificial Intelligence, pp. 631-639. Morgan Kaufmann, (1995)
63. Tan, S.W., Pearl, J.: Specification and evaluation of preferences under uncertainty. In: Doyle, J., Sandewall, E., Torasso, P. (eds.), 4th International Conference on Principles of Knowledge Representation and Reasoning, pp. 530-539. Morgan Kaufmann, (1994)
64. van Benthem, J., Girard, P., Roy, O.: Everything else being equal: A modal logic for ceteris paribus preferences. Journal of Philosophical Logic 38(1), 83–125 (2009)
65. van der Torre, L., Weydert, E.: Parameters for utilitarian desires in a qualitative decision theory. Applied Intelligence 14(3), 285–301 (2001)
66. von Neumann, J., Morgenstern, O.: Theory of Games and Economic Behavior. Princeton University Press, Princeton (1944)
67. von Wright, G.H.: The Logic of Preference. University of Edinburgh Press (1963)
68. Wiener, N.: A contribution to the theory of relative position. Philosophical Society 17, 441–449 (1914)
69. Wilson, N.: Extending CP-nets with stronger conditional preference statements. In: Ferguson, G. (eds.), 19th Conference on Artificial Intelligence, pp. 735-741. AAAI Press, (2004)
70. Yager, R.R.: Entropy and specificity in a mathematical theory of evidence. International Journal of General Systems 9, 249–260 (1983)

71. Zadeh, L.: Fuzzy sets as a basis for a theory of possibility. Fuzzy Sets and Systems **1**, 3–28 (1978)

Chapter 4
Making Hidden Priorities Explicit

4.1 Introduction

Users' preferences show up in different formats: quantitative vs. qualitative, conditional vs. unconditional, prioritized vs. flat, etc. In fact, depending on the reason, it could be more natural to express preferences in one a format or another. Thus, it became a challenge for researchers to adequately capture many varieties of preference forms. To this end, artificial intelligence has seen a number of compact languages for preference representation (cf. Chapter 3). However, each language has not been conceived to explicitly and naturally capture all forms of preferences. Instead, it focuses on a particular specification of preferences. It induces a preference relation over the set of outcomes which is a partial or total (pre)order.

From a preference representation perspective, plurality of compact preference representation languages looks nice for adequately coping with all forms of preferences. It, however, creates a difficulty when choosing a language to use. Indeed, which is the best language? On which criteria can the languages be compared? Does a language represent any preference relation (e.g., total preorder, partial order) it is conceived for? One may tackle this difficulty by arguing for some language in a particular application or domain. Our interest here is purely theoretical; we suppose that the comparison of the languages is domain-independent.

The comparison of compact preference representation languages has been addressed from different angles. In particular, complexity, expressiveness, and succinctness (i.e., spatial efficiency) have been considered as the main criteria for demonstrating the superiority of one language over another [7, 9]. It has been shown that no language is the best w.r.t. all the criteria. Thus, the choice of a language should be based on the the criterion that one privileges.

In this chapter we come to the comparison problem from a different (but complementary) angle. More precisely, we are interested in establishing the bridges between the languages. To this end, we observe that the three categories presented in Chapter 3 can roughly be seen as two ways for expressing preferences: prioritized preference (quantitative or qualitative) and comparative preference statements (quantitative or qualitative). This categorization is motivated by our aim at confronting weighted languages and unweighted languages. The key advantage of weighted languages is that they permit a finer-grained level of analysis of preferences given that the latter are represented with explicit priorities. In particular, priorities are of interest in conflict resolution (e.g., preferences aggregation or revision) since they give indication about which preferences (generally the less important ones) can be ignored or weakened. In conditional logics and conditional preference networks some preferences are more important than others. However, this priority is implicit, that is, it does not explicitly appear in these languages. In the following subsections, we present procedures for the translation of conditional logics and conditional preference networks into weighted propositional logic formulas. Besides the above cited motivation, these bridges allow us to understand the principles underpinning the priority between the preferences.

4.2 Conditional Logics and Weighted Logics

As we have seen in Chapter 3, preferences are represented in conditional logics by means of comparative preference statements of the form $p > q$ for "prefer p to q". This preference may be context-dependent "in the context r, prefer p to q", which means that when r is true, p is preferred to q. We have also identified different more or less requiring semantics (strong, optimistic, pessimistic, ceteris paribus) to interpret comparative preference statements. Lastly, a set of comparative preference statements and a given semantics induce a total preorder over the set of outcomes. Thus, this suggests that some comparative preference statements are more important than others. In this section we aim at understanding which priority over the preference statements governs the computation of the associated preference relation over outcomes.

For simplicity we commit to the standard representation of comparative preference statements, i.e., we compare opposite statements. Formally, we have preference statements of the form "prefer p to $\neg p$", denoted by $(|p)$, and conditional or contextual preference statements of the form "if r is true then prefer p to $\neg p$", denoted by $(r|p)$. Clearly, $(|p)$ is a particular case of $(r|p)$ when r is a tautology.

We also focus on strong, optimistic and pessimistic semantics. Ceteris paribus semantics will be addressed later in the chapter.

4.2.1 Optimistic Semantics vs. Prioritized Preferences

Consider the preference statement "if r then prefer p to $\neg p$". This statement means that $(r \wedge p)$-outcomes are preferred to $(r \wedge \neg p)$-outcomes. Following optimistic semantics, the preference relation associated with $(r|p)$ is $\succeq = (E_1, E_2)$ such that E_1 is the of $(\neg r \vee p)$-outcomes and $E_2 = \Omega \backslash E_1$, i.e., the set of $(r \wedge \neg p)$-outcomes. The construction of $\succeq$ suggests that an outcome is preferred (i.e., it belongs to E_1) as soon as it complies with the preference. In this situation, an outcome complies with the preference when it does not falsify it, i.e., it does not satisfy $r \wedge \neg p$. Therefore, $(r|p)$ is interpreted as a default rule. It can be represented by a weighted propositional logic formula $(\neg r \vee p, \alpha)$ [1], which stands for "if r is true, one would prefer to have p". In order to get the above preference relation $\succeq$, we associate the weight 1 with $(\neg r \vee p)$-outcomes and the weight $1 - \alpha$ with $\neg(\neg r \vee p)$-outcomes, i.e., $(r \wedge \neg p)$-outcomes. So, we associate a numerical function f with $(\neg r \vee p, \alpha)$ such that

$$f(\omega) = \begin{cases} 1 & \text{if } \omega \models \neg r \vee p \\ 1 - \alpha & \text{if } \omega \models r \wedge \neg p. \end{cases}$$

Note that this is the possibilistic logic-based reasoning and f corresponds to the tolerance distribution π associated with $\{(\neg r \vee p, \alpha)\}$. $\pi = f$ provides a numerical counterpart of $\succeq$ given above. Note, however, that α is a symbolic weight. It should be such that $1 > 1 - \alpha$ with $\alpha \neq 0$.

According to the above encoding, a set of comparative preference statements $\mathscr{P} = \{(r_i|p_i)|i = 1, \cdots, n\}$ interpreted following optimistic semantics is represented by a possibilistic logic base $\mathbb{T} = \{(\neg r_i \vee p_i, \alpha_i) \mid i = 1, \cdots, n\}$. The question now is how to rank-order the weights α_i in such a way that the tolerance distribution associated with $\mathbb{T}$ and the preference relation associated with $\mathscr{P}$ return an identical ordering over outcomes? More precisely, let $\succeq_{\mathscr{P}}$ be the preference relation associated with $\mathscr{P}$ following Algorithm 3.3 (see Subsection 3.4.4). Let $\pi_{\mathbb{T}}$ be the tolerance distribution associated with $\mathbb{T}$ (see Subsection 3.3.3). We aim at constructing $\mathbb{T}$ from $\mathscr{P}$ such that

$$\forall \omega, \omega' \in \Omega, \omega \succeq_{\mathscr{P}} \omega' \text{ iff } \pi_{\mathbb{T}}(\omega) \geq \pi_{\mathbb{T}}(\omega').$$

Since preference statements are interpreted here as default rules, the ordering over the weights in $\mathbb{T}$ is induced by the specificity relation between the preferences. More specifically, the more specific a preference is, the more prioritized it is in $\mathbb{T}$. Intuitively, a more specific preference expresses a preference in a specific context. So, if two preference statements express preferences for two opposite propositions, the one which is expressed in a more specific context is prioritized. The construction of $\mathbb{T}$ associated with $\mathscr{P}$ is formally described in Algorithm 4.1 [1]. The basic idea of the algorithm is to first construct the least-prioritized formulas in $\mathbb{T}$. The latter are propositional formulas associated with the preference statements $(r_i|p_i)$ such that if applied (i.e., r_i is true), they do not cause inconsistency.

Example 4.1. Let M, W and D be three variables which respectively stand for *main dish*, *wine* and *dessert* with $Dom(M) = \{fish, meat\}$, $Dom(W) = \{white, red\}$ and $Dom(D) = \{cake, ice\_cream\}$. We have

Algorithm 4.1: From optimistic semantics to prioritized preferences

Data: A preference set $\mathcal{P} = \{(r_i | p_i)\}$.
Result: A possibilistic logic base $\mathbb{T}$.
begin

> $l = 1$;
> **while** $\mathcal{P} \neq \emptyset$ **do**
>> $- S = \{\neg r_i \vee p_i \mid (r_i | p_i) \in \mathcal{P}\}$;
>> $- K_l = \{\neg r_i \vee p_i \mid \neg r_i \vee p_i \in S \text{ and } S \cup \{r_i\} \text{ is consistent}\}$;
>> **if** $K_l = \emptyset$ **then** Stop (inconsistent preference statements);
>> $- \mathcal{P} = \mathcal{P} \backslash \{(r_i | p_i) \mid \neg r_i \vee p_i \in K_l\}$;
>> $- l = l + 1$;
>
> **return** $\mathbb{T} = \mathbb{T}_1 \cup \cdots \cup \mathbb{T}_{l-1}$, such that for $j = 1, \cdots, l-1$ $\mathbb{T}_j = \{(\neg r_i \vee p_i, \alpha_j) \mid \neg r_i \vee p_i \in K_j\}$ with $\alpha_j = \frac{j}{l}$

end

$$\Omega = \{\omega_0 = fish - white - cake,$$
$$\omega_1 = fish - white - ice\_cream,$$
$$\omega_2 = fish - red - cake,$$
$$\omega_3 = fish - red - ice\_cream,$$
$$\omega_4 = meat - white - cake,$$
$$\omega_5 = meat - white - ice\_cream,$$
$$\omega_6 = meat - red - cake,$$
$$\omega_7 = meat - red - ice\_cream\}.$$

Suppose that a user expresses three comparative preference statements $\mathcal{P} = \{(|fish), (red|meat), (white|cake)\}$. That is, the user has an unconditional preference for *fish* but she would prefer *meat* when *red wine* is served. Moreover, the user would prefer *cake* when *white wine* is served.

Let us first compute the preference relation $\succeq$ associated with $\mathcal{P}$ interpreted following optimistic semantics. We give an informal description of its construction. We refer the reader to Algorithm 3.3 for a formal description.

We first compute the best outcomes. They are outcomes which do not falsify any preference in $\mathcal{P}$; so they do not falsify $(|fish)$, $(red|meat)$ and $(white|cake)$. There is only one best outcome, $\omega_0 = fish - white - cake$. Let $E_1 = \{\omega_0\}$. Now, we remove satisfied preferences from $\mathcal{P}$. We remove $(|fish)$ and $(white|cake)$, so $\mathcal{P} = \{(red|meat)\}$. We repeat the above process. The best outcomes are the outcomes which do not falsify $(red|meat)$. These outcomes are $\omega_1, \omega_4, \omega_5, \omega_6$ and ω_7. Let $E_2 = \{\omega_1, \omega_4, \omega_5, \omega_6, \omega_7\}$. $(red|meat)$ is satisfied, so $\mathcal{P}$ is now empty. Let $E_3 = \{\omega_2, \omega_3\}$. The preference relation associated with $\mathcal{P}$ is $\succeq = (E_1, E_2, E_3) = (\{\omega_0\}, \{\omega_1, \omega_4, \omega_5, \omega_6, \omega_7\}, \{\omega_2, \omega_3\}) = (\{fish - white - cake\}, \{fish - white - ice\_cream, meat - white - cake, meat - white - ice\_cream, meat -$

$red - cake, meat - red - ice\_cream\}, \{fish - red - cake, fish - red - ice\_cream\})$.

Before we apply Algorithm 4.1 to construct $\mathbb{T}$, we conjuncture how the formulas *fish*, $\neg red \vee meat$ and $\neg white \vee cake$ respectively associated with $(|fish)$, $(red|meat)$ and $(white|cake)$ should be rank-ordered in $\mathbb{T}$. The two preference statements $(|fish)$ and $(red|meat)$ are conflicting because the first expresses a preference for *fish* while the second expresses a preference for *meat*. But the second preference is more specific because it only holds when *red wine* is served. The third preference $(white|cake)$ does not contradict any of the two other preferences. So, priority should be given to $\neg red \vee meat$. The formulas *fish* and $\neg white \vee cake$ have the same priority and are less prioritized than $\neg red \vee meat$.

Let us now apply Algorithm 4.1. We have $\mathscr{P} = \{(|fish), (red|meat), (white|cake)\}$. At the first iteration, we have $S = \{fish, \neg red \vee meat, \neg white \vee cake\}$. Both $S \cup \{\top\}$ and $S \cup \{white\}$ are consistent while $S \cup \{red\}$ is inconsistent. So $K_1 = \{fish, \neg white \vee cake\}$. We update $\mathscr{P}$ and get $\mathscr{P} = \{(red|meat)\}$.

At the second iteration, we have $S = \{\neg red \vee meat\}$. $S \cup \{red\}$ is consistent, so $K_2 = \{\neg red \vee meat\}$. Indeed, $\mathbb{T} = \{(\neg red \vee meat, \frac{2}{3}), (fish, \frac{1}{3}), (\neg white \vee cake, \frac{1}{3})\}$. The tolerance distribution associated with $\mathbb{T}$ is given in Table 4.1. We can check that

Table 4.1 The tolerance distribution associated with $\mathbb{T}$

ω	$\pi_{\mathbb{T}}(\omega)$
$\omega_0 = fish - white - cake$	1
$\omega_1 = fish - white - ice\ cream$	$\frac{2}{3}$
$\omega_2 = fish - red - cake$	$\frac{1}{3}$
$\omega_3 = fish - red - ice\_cream$	$\frac{1}{3}$
$\omega_4 = meat - white - cake$	$\frac{2}{3}$
$\omega_5 = meat - white - ice\_cream$	$\frac{2}{3}$
$\omega_6 = meat - red - cake$	$\frac{2}{3}$
$\omega_7 = meat - red - ice\_cream$	$\frac{2}{3}$

the outcomes are rank-ordered in the same way in $\succeq$ and $\pi_{\mathbb{T}}$.

Note that the weights are symbolic in $\mathbb{T}$. Only the order over the formulas should be preserved. Indeed, $\mathbb{T}$ can be equivalently written in a qualitative form,

$\mathbb{T} = (K_2, K_1) = (\{\neg red \vee meat\}, \{fish, \neg white \vee cake\})$. The possibilistic logic base returned by Algorithm 4.1 can be given in a qualitative form in the following way: $\mathbb{T} = (\mathbb{T}_1, \cdots, \mathbb{T}_{l-1})$ such that $\mathbb{T}_j = \{\neg r_i \vee p_i \mid \neg r_i \vee p_i \in K_{l-j}\}$ for $j = 1, \cdots, l-1$.

The translation given in this subsection shows that a comparative preference statement $(r|p)$ obeying optimistic semantics is encoded by a propositional logic formula $\neg r \vee p$. But this should not be understood as a material implication $r \Rightarrow p$ since $(r \wedge \neg p)$-outcomes (i.e., the outcomes which falsify the material implication) are not excluded. $(r|p)$ means that there is an *ideal* $(r \wedge p)$-outcome which is preferred to any $(r \wedge \neg p)$-outcome. This interpretation allows us to express general (or default) preferences and specific preferences. In our example, the user has a general preference for *fish* but she prefers *meat* when *red wine* is served. Following $\succeq$, $fish - white - cake$ is the ideal outcome for both $(|fish)$ and $(white|cake)$. The ideal outcomes for $(red|meat)$ are $meat - red - cake$ and $meat - red - ice\_cream$.

4.2.2 Strong Semantics vs. Prioritized Preferences

Strong semantics has more requirements than optimistic semantics. A preference statement $(r|p)$ interpreted following optimistic semantics means that there is at least one $(r \wedge p)$-outcome (considered as an ideal outcome) which should be preferred to any $(r \wedge \neg p)$-outcome. When strong semantics is employed, any $(r \wedge p)$-outcome should be preferred to any $(r \wedge \neg p)$-outcome. This semantics means that when r is true, p is always preferred to $\neg p$.

We have seen in Subsection 3.4.1 that a unique least-specific preorder and a unique most-specific preorder can be associated with a set of comparative preference statements obeying strong semantics. In this subsection we focus on the least-specific preorder. Recall that Algorithms 3.3 and 3.1 are structurally similar. They differ in the removal of satisfied preferences. Moreover, preference statements are updated when using strong semantics. Algorithm 4.2 constructs a possibilistic logic base associated with a set of preference statements interpreted following strong semantics [4].

Algorithms 4.1 and 4.2 are structurally similar. The block *"For each"* in Algorithm 4.2 corresponds to the removal of satisfied preferences and the update of the remaining ones. The notation $r_i \wedge p_i \models S$ means that $(r_i \wedge p_i)$-outcomes are included in the set of outcomes satisfying S. Note that at each step of Algorithm 3.1 E_l is the set of outcomes which do not falsify any preference statement $(r_i|p_i)$ in the current set $\mathscr{P}$. So, they satisfy all $\neg r_i \vee p_i$ in $\mathscr{P}$. Indeed, E_l is the set of outcomes which satisfy the set S. Given E_l, any preference statement $(r_i|p_i)$ in $\mathscr{P}$ such that all $(r_i \wedge p_i)$-outcomes are in E_l is satisfied and should be removed. This corresponds to the "If" condition $r_i \wedge p_i \models S$. The other preference statements are updated by removing $(r_i \wedge p_i)$-outcomes which are in E_l. This is captured by the last "If" condition in the algorithm.

Algorithm 4.2: From strong semantics to prioritized preferences

Data: A preference set $\mathscr{P} = \{(r_i|p_i)\}$.
Result: A possibilistic logic base $\mathbb{T}$.

begin

  $l = 1$;

  while $\mathscr{P} \neq \emptyset$ **do**

   $- S = \{\neg r_i \vee p_i \mid (r_i|p_i) \in \mathscr{P}\}$;

   $- K_l = \{\neg r_i \vee p_i \mid \neg r_i \vee p_i \in S \text{ and } S \cup \{r_i\} \text{ is consistent}\}$;

   if $K_l = \emptyset$ **then** Stop (inconsistent preference statements);

   for *each* $(r_i|p_i)$ *in* K_l **do**

    if $r_i \wedge p_i \models S$ **then** $\mathscr{P} = \mathscr{P} \backslash (r_i|p_i)$;

    if *there is no change in* $\mathscr{P}$ **then** Stop (inconsistent preference statements);

    if $r_i \wedge p_i \wedge S$ *is consistent and* $r_i \wedge p_i \not\models S$ **then** replace $(r_i|p_i)$ in $\mathscr{P}$ with $(r_i \wedge \neg S|p_i)$;

   $- l = l + 1$;

  return $\mathbb{T} = (\mathbb{T}_1, \cdots, \mathbb{T}_{l-1})$ *with* $\mathbb{T}_j = K_{l-j}$ *for* $j = 1, \cdots, l-1$

end

Example 4.2. (Example 4.1 continued)
We have $S = \{fish, \neg red \vee meat, \neg white \vee cake\}$. $K_1 = \{fish, \neg white \vee cake\}$ since $S \cup \{\top\}$ and $S \cup \{white\}$ are both consistent but $S \cup \{red\}$ is inconsistent.
Let us now see whether there are preference statements which are satisfied. None of $fish \models S$, $red \wedge meat \models S$ and $white \wedge cake \models S$ holds, so there are no satisfied preference statements. Indeed, the set of preferences is inconsistent. The algorithm stops.

The inconsistency of the set $\mathscr{P}$ in the above example is due to the fact that strong semantics does not allow for exceptions. The two preference statements $(|fish)$ and $(red|meat)$ interpreted following strong semantics mean that on the one hand any *fish*-based meal is preferred to any *meat*-based meal (according to $(|fish)$) and on the other hand any *red* and *meat*-based meal is preferred to any *red* and *fish*-based meal. Contradiction. In the following we give an example of a consistent set of preference statements interpreted following strong semantics.

Example 4.3.
Let $\mathscr{P} = \{(fish|white), (meat|red), (red|cake)\}$ be a user's preferences. That is, the user would prefer *white wine* with *fish*, would prefer *red wine* with *meat* and would prefer *cake* with *red wine*.

At the first iteration of the algorithm, we have $S = \{\neg fish \vee white, \neg meat \vee red, \neg red \vee cake\}$. $K_1 = \{\neg fish \vee white, \neg meat \vee red, \neg red \vee cake\}$ since $S \cup \{fish\}$, $S \cup \{meat\}$ and $S \cup \{red\}$ are consistent. We have $fish \wedge white \models S$ but $meat \wedge red \not\models S$ and $red \wedge cake \not\models S$. However, both $\{meat \wedge red\} \cup S$ and $\{red \wedge cake\} \cup S$ are consistent. We replace $(meat|red)$ and $(red|cake)$ with $(meat \wedge \neg S|red)$ and $(red \wedge \neg S|cake)$, respectively. We get $(meat \wedge (white \vee ice\_cream)|red)$ and $(red \wedge (fish \vee ice\_cream)|cake)$. So,

$\mathscr{P} = \{(meat \wedge (white \vee ice\_cream)|red), (red \wedge (fish \vee ice\_cream)|cake)\}$.

At the second iteration, we have $S = \{\neg meat \vee (\neg white \wedge \neg ice\_cream) \vee red,$ $\neg red \vee (\neg fish \wedge \neg ice\_cream) \vee cake\}$, which is equivalent to $\{fish \vee red,$ $white \vee cake\}$. $\{meat \wedge (white \vee ice\_cream) \wedge red\} \cup S$ is inconsistent but $\{red \wedge (fish \vee ice\_cream) \wedge cake\} \cup S$ is consistent. So, $K_2 = \{\neg red \vee (\neg fish \wedge$ $\neg ice\_cream) \vee cake\}$, which is equivalent to $\{white \vee cake\}$. $\{meat \wedge (white \vee$ $ice\_cream) \wedge red\} \cup S$ is inconsistent. $red \wedge (fish \vee ice\_cream) \wedge cake \models S$ so $(red \wedge$ $(fish \vee ice\_cream)|cake)$ is removed from $\mathscr{P}$. We have $\mathscr{P} = \{(meat \wedge (white \vee$ $ice\_cream)|red)\}$.

At the third iteration, $S = \{\neg meat \vee (\neg white \wedge \neg ice\_cream)\}$. $\{meat \wedge (white \vee$ $ice\_cream) \quad \wedge \quad red\} \quad \cup \quad S \qquad$ is $\qquad$ consistent. $\qquad$ So $K_3 = \{\neg meat \vee (\neg white \wedge \neg ice\_cream\}$, which is equivalent to $\{fish \vee red\}$.

The possibilistic logic base associated with $\mathscr{P}$ is $\mathbb{T} = (\{fish \vee red\}, \{white \vee cake\},$ $\{meat \vee white, fish \vee red, fish \vee cake\})$, which is equivalent to $\mathbb{T} = (\{fish \vee red\},$ $\{white \vee cake\}, \{meat \vee white, fish \vee cake\})$. The preference relation associated with $\mathbb{T}$ is $(\{\omega_0, \omega_1, \omega_6\}, \{\omega_2\}, \{\omega_3, \omega_7\}, \{\omega_4, \omega_5\}) = (\{fish - white - cake, fish - white -$ $ice\_cream, meat - red - cake\}, \{fish - red - cake\}, \{fish - red - ice\_cream, meat -$ $red - ice\_cream\}, \{meat - white - cake, meat - white - ice\_cream\})$.

Let us now compute the preference relation associated with $\mathscr{P}$ following strong semantics. We refer the reader to Algorithm 3.1 for a formal description. Let $\mathscr{C} = \{\mathscr{C}_1 = (\{\omega_0, \omega_1\}, \{\omega_2, \omega_3\}), \mathscr{C}_2 = (\{\omega_6, \omega_7\}, \{\omega_4, \omega_5\}), \mathscr{C}_3 = (\{\omega_2, \omega_6\}, \{\omega_3, \omega_7\})\}$. We put in E_1 the outcomes which are not in the right-hand side of any $\mathscr{C}_i$ in $\mathscr{C}$. So $E_1 = \{\omega_0, \omega_1, \omega_6\}$. We remove $\mathscr{C}_1$ from $\mathscr{C}$ since the preference statement $(fish|white)$ is satisfied. We update $\mathscr{C}_2$ and $\mathscr{C}_3$. We get $\mathscr{C} = \{\mathscr{C}_2 = (\{\omega_7\}, \{\omega_4, \omega_5\}),$ $\mathscr{C}_3 = (\{\omega_2\}, \{\omega_3, \omega_7\})\}$. Now, $E_2 = \{\omega_2\}$. We remove $\mathscr{C}_3$ so $\mathscr{C} = \{\mathscr{C}_2 = (\{\omega_7\},$ $\{\omega_4, \omega_5\})\}$. Now, $E_3 = \{\omega_3, \omega_7\}$. We remove $\mathscr{C}_2$. Lastly, $E_4 = \{\omega_4, \omega_5\}$. Indeed, the preference relation is $(\{\omega_0, \omega_1, \omega_6\}, \{\omega_2\}, \{\omega_3, \omega_7\}, \{\omega_4, \omega_5\})$.

$\mathscr{P}$ interpreted following strong semantics and $\mathbb{T}$ induces the same preference relation over outcomes.

Note that $\mathbb{T}$ contains more formulas than $\{\neg r_i \vee p_i\}$ in the above example due to the fact that the preference statements which are not satisfied need to be updated. Compared to optimistic semantics, strong semantics is hardly characterized in terms of prioritized preferences. This is, however, not surprising given that it does not allow default preferences, so it does not obey the defeasibility principle.

4.2.3 Pessimistic Semantics vs. Prioritized Preferences

Consider the preference statement "if r is true then prefer p to $\neg p$". Following pessimistic semantics, this statement means that $(r \wedge p)$-outcomes are preferred to both $(r \wedge \neg p)$-outcomes and $\neg r$-outcomes. The preference relation induced by this preference statement is $\succeq = (E_1, E_2)$, where E_1 is the set of $(r \wedge p)$-outcomes and $E_2 = \Omega \backslash E_1$. Pessimistic semantics applies the closed-world assumption, i.e., only outcomes which satisfy the preference statement are preferred. The weighted formula $(r \wedge p, \beta)$ represented in guaranteed possibilistic logic captures the above interpretation. It associates the satisfaction degree β with $(r \wedge p)$-outcomes and the satisfaction degree 0 with the remaining outcomes. Formally, we have

$$\delta_{(r \wedge p, \beta)}(\omega) = \begin{cases} \beta & \text{if } \omega \models r \wedge p \\ 0 & \text{otherwise} \end{cases} .$$

This satisfaction distribution is the numerical counterpart of the preference relation $\succeq$ given above. Note, however, that the weight β is symbolic. It should be such that $\beta > 0$.

According to the above encoding, a set of preference statements $\mathscr{P} = \{(r_i|p_i) \mid i = 1, \cdots, n\}$ interpreted following pessimistic semantics can be represented by a guaranteed possibilistic logic base $\mathscr{G} = \{(r_i \wedge p_i, \beta_i) \mid (r_i|p_i) \in \mathscr{P}\}$. The question now is how to rank-order the weights β_i in order to have the following result:

$$\forall \omega, \omega' \in \Omega, \omega \succeq \omega' \text{ iff } \delta_{\mathscr{G}}(\omega) \geq \delta_{\mathscr{G}}(\omega').$$

Here also, the preference statements are rank-ordered following the specificity principle. A preference statement $(r|p)$ is less prioritized w.r.t. the current set $\mathscr{P}$ if its application (i.e., r is true) does not lead to inconsistency. Algorithm 4.3 formally describes the computation of $\mathscr{G}$ [2]. Since the weights β_i are symbolic, the algorithm returns the qualitative counterpart of $\mathscr{G}$.

At each step of Algorithm 3.4, E_l is the set of outcomes which do not satisfy any preference $p_i > q_i$ in $\mathscr{P}$. So they are outcomes which satisfy all $\neg r_i \vee \neg p_i$ with $p_i > q_i \in \mathscr{P}$. This is the set S in Algorithm 4.3. Then we remove satisfied preference statements. A preference statement $r_i|p_i$ (i.e., $r_i \wedge p_i > r_i \wedge \neg p_i$ following the notation used in Chapter 3) is satisfied in Algorithm 3.4 if the intersection of E_l and the set of $(r_i \wedge \neg p_i)$-outcomes is not empty. At the syntactic level, this means that $S \cup \{r_i \wedge \neg p_i\}$ is consistent. This is the set K_l in Algorithm 4.3.

Example 4.4. (Example 4.1 continued)
At the first iteration, we have $S = \{\neg fish, \neg red \vee \neg meat, \neg white \vee \neg cake\}$. $S \cup \{\top\}$ and $S \cup \{white\}$ are consistent but $S \cup \{red\}$ is inconsistent, so $K_1 = \{fish, white \wedge cake\}$. We update $\mathscr{P}$ by removing $(|fish)$ and $(white|cake)$, so $\mathscr{P} = \{(red|meat)\}$. At the second iteration, $S = \{\neg red \vee \neg meat\}$ and $K_2 = \{red \wedge meat\}$. Therefore, $\mathscr{G} = (\mathscr{G}_1, \mathscr{G}_2) = (\{red \wedge meat\}, \{fish, white \wedge cake\})$. The preference relation associated with the guaranteed possibilistic logic base $\mathscr{G}$ is

Algorithm 4.3: From pessimistic semantics to prioritized preferences

Data: A preference set $\mathcal{P} = \{(r_i|p_i)\}$.
Result: A guaranteed possibilistic logic base $\mathcal{G}$.

begin

$\quad l = 1$;

$\quad$ **while** $\mathcal{P} \neq \emptyset$ **do**

$\quad\quad - S = \{\neg r_i \vee \neg p_i \mid (r_i|p_i) \in \mathcal{P}\}$;

$\quad\quad - K_l = \{r_i \wedge p_i \mid \neg r_i \vee \neg p_i \in S \text{ and } S \cup \{r_i\} \text{ is consistent}\}$;

$\quad\quad$ **if** $K_l = \emptyset$ **then** Stop (inconsistent preference statements);

$\quad\quad - \mathcal{P} = \mathcal{P} \setminus \{(r_i|p_i) \mid r_i \wedge p_i \in K_l\}$;

$\quad\quad - l = l + 1$;

$\quad$ **return** $\mathcal{G} = (\mathcal{G}_1, \cdots, \mathcal{G}_{l-1})$, where $\mathcal{G}_j = K_{l-j}$ for $j = 1, \cdots, l-1$

end

$\succeq = (\{\omega_6, \omega_7\}, \{\omega_0, \omega_1, \omega_2, \omega_3, \omega_4\}, \{\omega_5\}) = (\{meat - red - cake, meat - red - ice\_cream\}, \{fish - white - cake, fish - white - ice\_cream, fish - red - cake, fish - red - ice\_cream, meat - white - cake\}, \{meat - white - ice\_cream\}).$

Let us now compute the preference relation associated with $\mathcal{P}$ interpreted following pessimistic semantics (see Algorithm 3.4). The less preferred outcomes are the outcomes which do not satisfy any preference statement in $\mathcal{P}$, i.e., they do not satisfy any of the formulas *fish*, $red \wedge meat$ and $white \wedge cake$. So, $E_1 = \{\omega_5\}$. We remove $(|fish)$ and $(white|cake)$ from $\mathcal{P}$ since they are satisfied. We get $\mathcal{P} = \{(red|meat)\}$. E_2 is the set of outcomes which do not satisfy $meat \wedge red$. We have $E_2 = \{\omega_0, \omega_1, \omega_2, \omega_3, \omega_4\}$. We remove $(red|meat)$. Lastly, $E_3 = \{\omega_6, \omega_7\}$. The preference relation associated with $\mathcal{P}$ is $(\{\omega_6, \omega_7\}, \{\omega_0, \omega_1, \omega_2, \omega_3, \omega_4\}, \{\omega_5\})$. So, $\mathcal{P}$ interpreted following pessimistic semantics and $\mathcal{G}$ induce the same preference relation.

4.3 Positive and Negative Preferences

The logical representations of negative preferences and positive preferences in terms of weighted formulas exhibit very similar behaviors, however, in an opposite (i.e., dual) way. The first type of preference can be represented by a possibilistic logic base while the second type of preference can be represented by a guaranteed possibilistic logic base. Consider a negative preference (ϕ, α) and a positive preference (φ, β). These two formulas induce the following constraints on their associated tolerance distribution and satisfaction distribution, respectively: $\forall \omega \in \Omega$,

$$\Pi(\neg \phi) = \max\{\pi(\omega) \mid \omega \not\models \phi\} \leq 1 - \alpha, \tag{4.1}$$

$$\Delta(\phi) = \min\{\delta(\omega) \mid \omega \models \varphi\} \geq \beta. \tag{4.2}$$

Possible functions satisfying the inequalities (4.1) and (4.2) are shown in Figures 4.1 and 4.2, respectively.

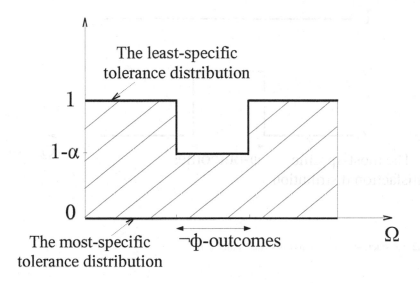

Fig. 4.1 Tolerance distributions associated with (ϕ, α)

We can see that the unique non-trivial tolerance distribution associated with (ϕ, α) is the least-specific tolerance distribution while it is just the opposite, namely, the most-specific satisfaction distribution, regarding (φ, β).

In general, given a possibilistic logic base $\mathbb{T} = \{(\phi_i, \alpha_i) \mid i = 1, \cdots, n\}$ and a guaranteed possibilistic logic base $\mathscr{G} = \{(\varphi_j, \beta_j) \mid j = 1, \cdots, m\}$, the tolerance distribution $\pi_{\mathbb{T}}$ and the satisfaction distribution $\delta_{\mathscr{G}}$, respectively associated with $\mathbb{T}$ and $\mathscr{G}$, are defined as follows: $\forall \omega \in \Omega$,

$$\pi_{\mathbb{T}}(\omega) = \begin{cases} 1 & \text{if } \omega \models \phi_1 \wedge \cdots \wedge \phi_n \\ 1 - \max\{\alpha_i \mid (\phi_i, \alpha_i) \in \mathbb{T}, \omega \not\models \phi_i\} & \text{otherwise} \end{cases},$$

$$\delta_{\mathscr{G}}(\omega) = \begin{cases} 0 & \text{if } \omega \not\models \varphi_1 \vee \cdots \vee \varphi_m \\ \max\{\beta_j \mid (\varphi_j, \beta_j) \in \mathscr{G}, \omega \models \varphi_j\} & \text{otherwise} \end{cases}.$$

Indeed, given $\mathbb{T}$, the higher the priority of a negative preference, the smaller the tolerance degree of any outcome falsifying the preference. On the other hand, given $\mathscr{G}$, the higher the priority of a positive preference, the higher the satisfaction degree of any outcome satisfying the preference. So, the greater the number of negative preferences, the more restricted the set of fully tolerated outcomes. In contrast, the greater

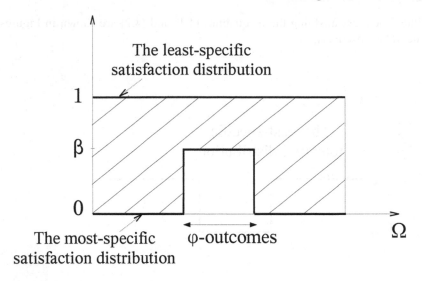

Fig. 4.2 Satisfaction distributions associated with (φ, β)

the number of positive preferences, the larger the set of satisfactory outcomes. In fact, negative preferences act as constraints and positive preferences act as wishes. The former are conjunctively combined while the latter are disjunctively combined.

Any complete preorder can be represented in a compact way by means of a set of negative preferences or a set of positive preferences [7, 2]. Consequently, a set of negative preferences can be translated into a set of positive preferences, and conversely. The translation procedures have been given in [3]. We will not recall these procedures in this chapter. Instead, we are interested in the above comparison between the two representations. More specifically, we have shown in the previous subsection that a set of comparative preference statements obeying the optimistic semantics can be translated into a possibilistic logic base (i.e., a set of negative preferences). Also, a set of comparative preference statements obeying the pessimistic semantics can be translated into a guaranteed possibilistic logic base (i.e., a set of positive preferences). In this subsection we address the following questions:

- Do Algorithms 4.1 and 4.3 have a dual behavior?
- How do comparative preference statements obeying optimistic semantics relate to comparative preference statements obeying pessimistic semantics?

The answer to the first question is positive. Algorithms 4.1 and 4.3 are structurally similar. They differ on the set S, which is equal to $\{\neg r_i \vee p_i\}$ in Algorithm 4.1 and to $\{\neg r_i \vee \neg p_i\}$ in Algorithm 4.3. This difference exhibits a dual behavior of the two algorithms. In fact, $\{\neg r_i \vee p_i\}$ is the syntactic counterpart of the best outcomes given a set of preference statements $\{(r_i|p_i)\}$ obeying optimistic semantics. They are outcomes which do not falsify any preference statement, so they satisfy the set $\{\neg r_i \vee p_i\}$. On the other hand, when dealing with a set of preference statements obeying pessimistic semantics, we compute the worst outcomes given a set of preference statements $\{(r_i|p_i)\}$. They are outcomes which do not satisfy any preference statement $(r_i|p_i)$, so they satisfy the set $\{\neg r_i \vee \neg p_i\}$. Consequently, if $(r_i|p_i)$ is interpreted following optimistic semantics, then $(r_i|\neg p_i)$ is its corresponding preference statement interpreted following pessimistic semantics. Note, however, that their associated preference relations are dual. More precisely, the preference relation associated with $(r_i|p_i)$ following optimistic semantics is (E_1, E_2), where E_1 is the set of $(\neg r_i \vee p_i)$-outcomes and E_2 is the set of $(r_i \wedge \neg p_i)$-outcomes. The preference relation associated with $(r_i|\neg p_i)$ following pessimistic semantics is $\succeq' = (E_2, E_1)$. In general, we have the following translation [2]:

Proposition 4.1. *Let $\mathscr{P} = \{(r_i|p_i) \mid i = 1, \cdots, n\}$ and $\mathscr{P}' = \{(r_i|\neg p_i) \mid i = 1, \cdots, n\}$ be two consistent sets of comparative preference statements. Let $\succeq$ and $\succeq'$ be the preference relations associated with $\mathscr{P}$ and $\mathscr{P}'$ following optimistic and pessimistic semantics, respectively. Then $\succeq = (E_1, \cdots, E_m)$ and $\succeq' = (E_m, \cdots, E_1)$.*

Example 4.5. (Example 4.1 continued)
We have $\mathscr{P} = \{(|fish), (red|meat), (white|cake)\}$. The preference relation associated with $\mathscr{P}$ following optimistic semantics is $\succeq = (\{\omega_0\}, \{\omega_1, \omega_4, \omega_5, \omega_6, \omega_7\}, \{\omega_2, \omega_3\})$. Let $\mathscr{P}' = \{(|\neg fish), (red|\neg meat), (white|\neg cake)\}$, which is equivalent to $\{(|meat), (red|fish), (white|ice\_cream)\}$. The preference relation associated with $\mathscr{P}'$ following pessimistic semantics is $\succeq' = (\{\omega_2, \omega_3\}, \{\omega_1, \omega_4, \omega_5, \omega_6, \omega_7\}, \{\omega_0\})$.

4.4 Conditional Preference Networks and Weighted Preferences

As in conditional logics, priorities are not explicitly present in the CP-nets-based representation language. In this section we aim at understanding which hidden priorities govern the expression of preferences in CP-nets. We consider again Example 3.30 given in Subsection 3.5.2.

Example 4.6.
Consider four binary variables $V(vest)$, $P(pants)$, $S(shirt)$ and $C(shoes)$ with $Dom(V) = \{V_b, V_w\}$, $Dom(P) = \{P_b, P_w\}$, $Dom(S) = \{S_r, S_w\}$ and $Dom(C) = \{C_r, C_w\}$. The subscripts b, w and r stand for *black, white* and *red*, respectively. We have

$$\begin{aligned}
\Omega = \{&V_bP_bS_rC_r, V_bP_bS_wC_r, V_bP_wS_rC_r, V_bP_wS_wC_r, \\
&V_wP_bS_rC_r, V_wP_bS_wC_r, V_wP_wS_rC_r, V_wP_wS_wC_r, \\
&V_bP_bS_rC_w, V_bP_bS_wC_w, V_bP_wS_rC_w, V_bP_wS_wC_w, \\
&V_wP_bS_rC_w, V_wP_bS_wC_w, V_wP_wS_rC_w, V_wP_wS_wC_w\}.
\end{aligned}$$

Suppose that Peter expresses preferences represented by the CP-net N depicted in Figure 4.3. This CP-net means that other thing being equal, Peter prefers

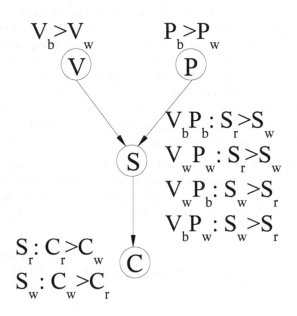

Fig. 4.3 A CP-net, N

(P_1): a black vest to a white vest,
(P_2): black pants to white pants,
(P_3): when vest and pants have the same color, a red shirt to a white shirt; otherwise, a white shirt, and
(P_4): when the shirt is red, red shoes; otherwise, white shoes.

The preference relation $\succ_N$ associated with N is depicted in Figure 4.4.

The above preferences are comparative preference statements of the form "in context r, p is preferred to $\neg p$", where r may be a tautology. Such a preference can be represented by a weighted formula $(\neg r \vee p, 1 - \alpha)$, which stands for "when r is true, it is somewhat imperative to have p true". Interpreted as a possibilistic logic formula, each outcome which falsifies $\neg r \vee p$ gets a tolerance degree equal to α. It gets a tolerance degree equal to 1 if it satisfies the formula.

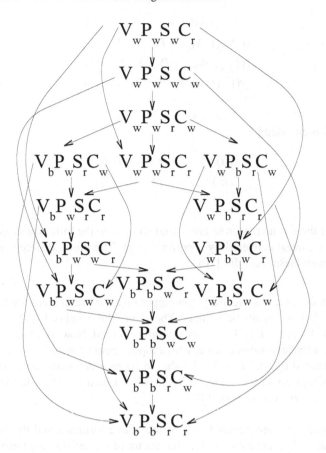

Fig. 4.4 The partial order $\succ_N$ associated to the CP-net N

Example 4.7. (Example 4.6 continued)
(P_1) and (P_2) are encoded by means of

$$(i) : \{(V_b, 1 - \alpha)\}$$

and

$$(ii) : \{(P_b, 1 - \beta)\},$$

respectively. (P_3) is encoded by

$$(iii) : \{(\neg V_b \vee \neg P_b \vee S_r, 1 - \gamma)\},$$
$$(iv) : \{(\neg V_w \vee \neg P_w \vee S_r, 1 - \eta)\},$$
$$(v) : \{(\neg V_w \vee \neg P_b \vee S_w, 1 - \delta)\},$$
$$(vi) : \{(\neg V_b \vee \neg P_w \vee S_w, 1 - \varepsilon)\}.$$

Lastly, (P_4) is encoded by

$$(vii) : \{(\neg S_r \vee C_r, 1 - \theta)\},$$
$$(viii) : \{(\neg S_w \vee C_w, 1 - \rho)\}.$$

Note that there is no reason to give equal weights to the formulas associated with the different contexts covered by a preference P_i. Therefore, different weights are associated with these formulas [10].

Since one does not know precisely how imperative the preferences are, the weights will be handled in a symbolic manner. Therefore, the weights $1 - \alpha$, $1 - \beta$, $1 - \gamma$, $1 - \eta$, $1 - \delta$, $1 - \varepsilon$, $1 - \theta$ and $1 - \rho$ are not rank-ordered. However, they are assumed to belong to a linearly ordered scale, with a top element (denoted by 1) and a bottom element (denoted by 0). Thus, $1 - (.)$ should be regarded here just as denoting an order-reversing map on this scale, with $1 - (0) = 1$, and $1 - (1) = 0$. On this scale, one has $1 > 1 - \alpha$ as soon as $\alpha \neq 0$.

Table 4.2 gives the satisfaction levels of the above formulas and the sixteen possible outcomes. The last column gives the vector of the satisfaction levels.

Although the values of the weights are unknown, a partial order over the 16 outcomes can be naturally induced. For example, $V_b P_b S_r C_r$ is preferred to all remaining outcomes since it is the only outcome that satisfies all Peter's preferences. Also, $V_w P_b S_w C_w$ is preferred to $V_w P_w S_r C_r$ since the former falsifies $(V_b, 1 - \alpha)$ while the latter falsifies both $(V_b, 1 - \alpha)$ and $(P_b, 1 - \beta)$. This partial order (called basic partial order) is depicted in Figure 4.5.

Indeed, an outcome ω is naturally preferred to an outcome ω' when the set of formulas falsified by ω is included in the set of formulas falsified by ω'. Thus, ω is preferred to ω' only when the components of its associated satisfaction vector are equal to 1 for those components that are different in the two satisfaction vectors associated with ω and ω'.

However, the basic partial order does not give indication about the priority between the formulas. This priority should be induced by comparabilities in $\succ_N$ between outcomes which are incomparable w.r.t. the basic partial order. For example, $V_w P_b S_r C_w$ is preferred to $V_w P_w S_r C_w$ w.r.t. the CP-net while the two outcomes are incomparable w.r.t. the basic partial order since $V_w P_b S_r C_w$ falsifies $(V_b, 1 - \alpha)$,

Table 4.2 Satisfaction levels

	(i)	(ii)	(iii)	(iv)	(v)	(vi)	(vii)	(viii)	Satisfaction levels
$V_b\ P_b\ S_r\ C_r$	1	1	1	1	1	1	1	1	$(1,1,1,1,1,1,1,1)$
$V_b\ P_b\ S_w\ C_r$	1	1	γ	1	1	1	1	ρ	$(1,1,\gamma,1,1,1,1,\rho)$
$V_b\ P_w\ S_r\ C_r$	1	β	1	1	1	ε	1	1	$(1,\beta,1,1,1,\varepsilon,1,1)$
$V_b\ P_w\ S_w\ C_r$	1	β	1	1	1	1	1	ρ	$(1,\beta,1,1,1,1,1,\rho)$
$V_w\ P_b\ S_r\ C_r$	α	1	1	1	δ	1	1	1	$(\alpha,1,1,1,\delta,1,1,1)$
$V_w\ P_b\ S_w\ C_r$	α	1	1	1	1	1	1	ρ	$(\alpha,1,1,1,1,1,1,\rho)$
$V_w\ P_w\ S_r\ C_r$	α	β	1	1	1	1	1	1	$(\alpha,\beta,1,1,1,1,1,1)$
$V_w\ P_w\ S_w\ C_r$	α	β	1	η	1	1	1	ρ	$(\alpha,\beta,1,\eta,1,1,1,\rho)$
$V_b\ P_b\ S_r\ C_w$	1	1	1	1	1	1	θ	1	$(1,1,1,1,1,1,\theta,1)$
$V_b\ P_b\ S_w\ C_w$	1	1	γ	1	1	1	1	1	$(1,1,\gamma,1,1,1,1,1)$
$V_b\ P_w\ S_r\ C_w$	1	β	1	1	1	ε	θ	1	$(1,\beta,1,1,1,\varepsilon,\theta,1)$
$V_b\ P_w\ S_w\ C_w$	1	β	1	1	1	1	1	1	$(1,\beta,1,1,1,1,1,1)$
$V_w\ P_b\ S_r\ C_w$	α	1	1	1	δ	1	θ	1	$(\alpha,1,1,1,\delta,1,\theta,1)$
$V_w\ P_b\ S_w\ C_w$	α	1	1	1	1	1	1	1	$(\alpha,1,1,1,1,1,1,1)$
$V_w\ P_w\ S_r\ C_w$	α	β	1	1	1	1	θ	1	$(\alpha,\beta,1,1,1,1,\theta,1)$
$V_w\ P_w\ S_w\ C_w$	α	β	1	η	1	1	1	1	$(\alpha,\beta,1,\eta,1,1,1,1)$

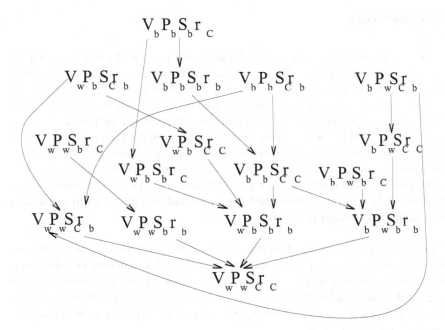

Fig. 4.5 Basic partial order

$(\neg V_w \vee \neg P_b \vee S_w, 1 - \delta)$ and $(\neg S_r \vee C_r, 1 - \theta)$ while $V_w P_w S_r C_w$ falsifies $(V_b, 1 - \alpha)$, $(P_b, 1 - \beta)$ and $(\neg S_r \vee C_r, 1 - \theta)$.

These additional strict preferences are due to the fact that preferences in CP-nets depend on the structure of the graph, i.e., they are parent-dependent. More precisely, since preferences over the values of a variable depend on the values of its parents, the application of the ceteris paribus semantics implicitly gives priority to father nodes. For example, we have $V_w P_b S_r C_w \succ_N V_w P_w S_r C_w$ due to $P_b > P_w$. Indeed, $V_w P_w S_r C_w$ is less preferred than $V_w P_b S_r C_w$ since the former falsifies $(P_b, 1 - \beta)$ while the latter falsifies $(\neg V_w \vee \neg P_b \vee S_w, 1 - \delta)$ (they both falsify $(V_b, 1 - \alpha)$ and $(\neg S_r \vee C_r, 1 - \theta)$). More specifically, when two outcomes ω and ω' differ in the value of one variable only, ω is preferred to ω' w.r.t. a CP-net if and only if

- the set of formulas falsified by ω is a strict subset of the set of formulas falsified by ω', or
- ω' falsifies a parent node preference while ω falsifies a child node preference.

Therefore, $1 - \alpha$ and $1 - \beta$ are incomparable. They are strictly greater than $1 - \gamma$, $1 - \eta$, $1 - \delta$ and $1 - \varepsilon$. The latter are incomparable but strictly greater than $1 - \theta$ and $1 - \rho$. Lastly, $1 - \theta$ and $1 - \rho$ are incomparable [10].

4.5 Conclusion

When a user's preferences cannot be fulfilled, she is generally ready to give up or weaken some preferences. The preferences to be sacrificed are generally those which considered as not too important for her. However, users do not always have the cognitive capability to determine which preferences are less important. The presence of priorities greatly facilitates this task. This concern motivated this chapter. More specifically, compact preference representation languages can be divided into two categories: weighted languages and unweighted languages. We provided procedures for the translation of conditional logics and conditional preference networks into weighted propositional logic formulas. These procedures make hidden priorities explicit in these unweighted languages and thus permit us to understand the underpinning priority in the latter.

Interestingly, these results show that optimistic and pessimistic semantics in conditional logics exhibit similar behavior w.r.t. defeasibility, although in a dual way. More specific preferences are given priority over less specific preferences. On the other hand, conditional preference networks do not obey the defeasibility principle. Instead, preferences associated with parent nodes are given priority over preferences associated with child nodes.

References

1. Benferhat, S., Dubois, D., Prade, H.: Representing default rules in possibilistic logic. In: Nebel, B., Rich, C., Swartout, W.R. (eds.), 3rd International Conference of Principles of Knowledge Representation and Reasoning, pp. 673-684. Morgan Kaufmann, (1992)

2. Benferhat, S., Dubois, D., Kaci, S., Prade, H.: Bridging logical, comparative and graphical possibilistic representation frameworks. In: Benferhat, S., Besnard, P. (eds.), 6th European Conference on Symbolic and Quantitative Approaches to Reasoning and Uncertainty, pp. 422-431. Springer, (2001)
3. Benferhat, S., Dubois, D., Kaci, S., Prade, H.: Possibilistic logic representation of preferences: relating prioritized goals and satisfaction levels expressions. In: van Harmelen, F. (eds.), 15th European Conference on Artificial Intelligence, pp. 685-689. IOS Press, (2002)
4. Benferhat, S., Kaci, S.: A possibilistic logic handling of strong preferences. In: Smith, M.H., Gruver, W.A. (eds.), International Fuzzy Systems Association, pp. 962-967. (2001)
5. Brafman, R.I., Domshlak, C.: Introducing variable importance tradeoffs into CP-nets. In: Darwiche, A., Friedman, N. (eds.), 18th International Conference on Uncertainty in Artificial Intelligence, pp. 69-76. Morgan Kaufmann, (2002)
6. Brewka, G., Niemelä, I., Truszczynski, M.: Answer set optimization. In: Gottlob, G., Walsh, T. (eds.), 18th Joint Conference on Artificial Intelligence, pp. 867-872. Morgan Kaufmann, (2003)
7. Coste-Marquis, S., Lang, J., Liberatore, P., Marquis, P.: Expressive power and succinctness of propositional languages for preference representation. In: Dubois, D., Welty, C.A., Williams, M.A. (eds.), 9th International Conference on Principles of Knowledge Representation and Reasoning, pp. 203-212. AAAI Press, (2004)
8. Domshlak, C., Rossi, F., Venable, K.B., Walsh, T.: Reasoning about soft constraints and conditional preferences: complexity results and approximation techniques. In: Gottlob, G., Walsh, T. (eds.), 18th Joint Conference on Artificial Intelligence, pp. 215-220. Morgan Kaufmann, (2003)
9. Goldsmith, J., Lang, J., Truszczynski, M., Wilson, N.: The computational complexity of dominance and consistency in CP-nets. In: Kaelbling, L.P., Saffiotti, A. (eds.), 19th Joint Conference on Artificial Intelligence, pp. 144-149. Professional Book Center, (2005)
10. Kaci, S., Prade, H.: Mastering the processing of preferences by using symbolic priorities. In: Ghallab, M. Spyropoulos, C.D., Fakotakis, N., Avouris, N.M. (eds.), 18th European Conference on Artificial Intelligence, pp. 376-380. IOS Press, (2008)

Chapter 5
What Psychology Has to Say About Preferences

5.1 Introduction

In the previous chapters we addressed various problems related to the representation of and reasoning with preferences. These problems are mainly grounded in mathematical and philosophical approaches representing how the users are expected to behave [25, 26]. Therefore, a preference relation is usually supposed to be transitive, different completion principles are used when preferences are incomplete, and so on. Nevertheless, preferences should benefit from special attention to the hypotheses we intend to consider. This is because preferences fundamentally differ from beliefs and knowledge; they are purely subjective information. Accordingly, it is worth trying to turn to experimental sciences in order to support (or not) the hypotheses, methods, etc. In this chapter we are interested in psychology of preferences.

Psychology is an academic and experimental science which consists of studying human behaviors. The purpose of a psychological analysis is not to refute theoretical methods. Instead, it only gives a prescriptive analysis showing how people are likely to behave, which method is more plausible w.r.t. human behavior, etc. The need of such analysis has been recently stressed in the artificial intelligence community. For example, it has been shown that human inference is consistent with System P [30] (see [15, 2]) and that System P constitutes a psychologically sound base of rationality postulates for the evaluation of non-monotonic reasoning systems. Qualitative decision making has also been studied by psychologists [6].

Although preferences have been mainly and extensively studied by philosophers, economists and mathematicians, they have also attracted (for a relatively short time) the attention of psychologists. This chapter is not intended to give a detailed exposition of their works. Instead, we shed light on a selection of works and explore the opinion of psychologists in the light of some insights when dealing with preferences.

5.2 Origins of Preferences

One of the main functions of preferences is orienting decision making in order to guide behavior and to reach adaptive goals. The psychological study of human preferences has revealed a variety of origins of our preferences. Some are or seem biologically inherited; others are constructed during human motor or perceptual development, or at later stages of human development. Most of our preferences are context- and social environment-dependent.

Many studies have advocated the idea that some of our preferences are innate and that biological evolution can explain the emergence of forms of social preferences such as food preferences, mate preferences, and preferences for some kinds of objects.

Studies of food preferences have emphasized the idea that despite substantial variation across societies there are broad categories of nutritional needs that apply to all humans, such as carbohydrates, protein, lipids, and vitamins and minerals [34]. It has been shown, for example, that humans and also other species like horses and bears have a preference for sweet foods and drinks [18, 36, 39]. The taste of sweet is often associated with a high concentration of sugar and, therefore, of calories. It is the case, for example, in ripe fruits which provide, in addition, vitamins and minerals. Many pieces of data suggest that early exposure to the taste of sweet is not necessary for a preference for it. For example, one- to three-day-old human infants prefer sweet to non-sweet fluids [17]. Newborn infants, the first time that they taste something sweet, without any prior breast or bottle feeding, smile slightly, licking the upper lip, and sucking. This acceptance response is found also in rats [24], and suggests an innate predisposition to choose and ingest sweet foods or drinks. In contrast, the preference for salty food does not seem innate despite salt being necessary for the body to function properly. Indeed, humans cannot taste salt well until approximately four months in age, at which point they demonstrate a preference for salty over non salty foods. However, this delay in the emergence of a preference for salty foods can be adaptive as well and genetically programed, giving the evolution of food needs during a newborn's development.

Evolutionary explanations have been addressed in plenty of studies to predict the mate selection preferences of both sexes. People seem to prefer universally some standards of beauty such as symmetric faces [22, 41], large eyes, and baby-face features [4, 13], and place relatively equal value on love, kindness, intelligence and good health [8]; but men and women differently rate characteristics such as attractiveness and financial prospects [7, 9]. Whatever the culture, men place a higher value on physical attractiveness and women on financial prospects. Explanations of such differences are grounded in the process of natural selection. According to Buss [8], women produce a relatively small number of gametes compared to men, who produce 12 million sperm per hour; women are fertile for a limited period in a month (men have "plenty of time"), and are pregnant for nine months. So, women are relatively "precious" compared to men for the survival of our species and our evolution and are naturally prone to exercising a greater degree of discrimination when choosing a mate. In addition, the survival and the harmonious development of a child needs resources that a female often cannot provide alone at a sufficient level given the physical and psychological demands of maternity. A mother must ensure the future of her baby, and she must choose a father able to ensure sufficient resources for that, and to protect his family from bad fortune. Similarly, differences have been found between women and men in their preferences for body types. According to Montoya [38] women prefer body types indicative of strength and overall fitness, and men prefer body types indicative of fertility. Both men and women prefer body types indicative of overall health.

Strong evidence in favor of the existence of innate preferences has been provided by Alexander and Hines [1]. They gave two stereotypically masculine toys (a ball and a police car), two stereotypically feminine toys (a soft doll and a cooking pot), and two neutral toys (a picture book and a stuffed dog) to 44 male and 44 female vervet monkeys. They measured how much time monkeys spent with each toy and found that male monkeys showed significantly greater interest in the masculine toys, and the female monkeys greater interest in the feminine toys. No difference was found for the neutral toys. A replication of this study [27] with other toys has shown a similar result, but with non-statistically significant differences. Although no convincing explanation of this preference has been provided, this reinforces the hypothesis of existing innate preferences.

Most of our preferences are not biologically acquired, of course, even preferences about food and relationships. For example, after having the experience of eating something and becoming ill, we do not want to eat that thing again. We learn that some foods can cause illness. To be able to avoid new kinds of food is as necessary as to be able to recognize advantageous ones. Another example is preference for high-fat foods. For example, Birch and Deysher [5] have shown that preschool subjects learn to eat smaller meals with a taste previously associated with a high-calorie snack, and larger meals with a taste previously associated with a low-calorie snack.

More intuitively, it is hardly defendable that preferences for some cosmetic perfume, some sauce or some TV program could be genetically programed, whatever the dependencies between these preferences and some other innate ones.

5.3 The Role of Affect in Human Preferences

Affect has not been always recognized as a fundamental component of judgment and decision-making processes. As pointed out by Slovic et al. [46], the main focus of descriptive decision research has been cognitive rather than affective. Despite this cognitive emphasis, affect is today at the core of several psychological models of decision making, and evidence has been found that affect plays a key role in the preferences selection or elicitation process.

The fundamental nature and importance of affect has been shown by Robert Zajonc and his colleagues (see, e.g., [55]). The central finding is that, when objects are presented to an individual repeatedly, the "mere exposure" is capable of creating a positive attitude or preference for these objects. In the typical study, stimuli such as nonsense phrases, or faces, or Chinese ideographs are presented to an individual with varied frequencies. In a later session, the individual judges these stimuli on liking, or familiarity, or both. The more frequent the prior exposure to a stimulus, the more positive the response. There is much experimental evidence in favor of the role of affect in decision making. For example, it has been found by Hsee and Kunreuther [28] that affect influences decisions about whether or not to purchase insurance. In one study, they found that people were willing to pay twice as much to insure a beloved antique clock (that no longer works and cannot be repaired) against loss in shipment to a new city than to insure a similar clock for which "one does not have any special feeling". In the event of loss, the insurance paid $100 in both cases.

The role of affect in decision making has been explored and explained by Antonio Damasio [14]. Damasio's theory is derived from observations of patients with brain damage that has left their basic intelligence, memory, and capacity for logical thought intact but has impaired their ability to "feel", that is, to have access to the affective value of the consequences of their choices. Without that ability, people make less optimal decisions than non-impaired people do. The key idea of Damasio [14] is that each time we experience something in our daily lives, we construct a somatic marker in memory which is an association between the activated stimuli and our physiological affective state. These somatic markers are very good guides for further evaluations of the consequences of similar facts. As such, they act as preferences, positive for pleasant experiences, and negative for negative ones. Damasio proposes that somatic markers guide attention towards more advantageous options, simplifying the decision process.

Another important and related concept is the one of affect heuristic. Slovic et al. [46] define the affect heuristic as the reliance on feelings of goodness or badness. The affect heuristic had its origin in the early study of risk perception reported by Fischhoff et al. [19]. One of the findings in this study and numerous subsequent studies was that perceptions of risk and society's responses to risk were strongly linked to the degree to which a hazard evoked feelings of dread (see also [44]). Thus, activities associated with cancer are seen as riskier and more in need of regulation than activities associated with less dreaded forms of illness, injury, and death (e.g., accidents). A second finding in the study by Fischhoff et al. has been even more instrumental in the study of the affect heuristic. This is the finding that judgments of risk and benefit are negatively correlated. For many hazards, the greater the perceived benefit, the lower the perceived risk, and vice versa. Smoking, alcoholic beverages, and food additives, for example, tend to be seen as very high in risk and relatively low in benefit, whereas vaccines, antibiotics, and X-rays tend to be seen as high in benefit and relatively low in risk. This negative relationship is noteworthy because it occurs even when the nature of the benefits from an activity is distinct, and qualitatively different from the nature of the risks. That inverse relationship is generated in people's minds and suggested by the fact that risk and benefits generally tend to be positively (if at all) correlated in the world. Activities that bring great benefits may be high or low in risk but activities that are low in benefit are unlikely to be high in risk (if they were, they would be proscribed).

Subsection 3.6 presented a new type of preference called bipolar preference. These preferences make a clear distinction between positive preferences (what the user would really like) and negative preferences (what the user would reject). It has been shown that at the theoretical level there is in general no symmetry between positive preferences and negative preferences in the sense that positive preferences do not just mirror what is not rejected [3]. Relatively recent studies in cognitive psychology have shown that the distinction between positive and negative preferences makes sense. In fact, the two types of preferences are processed separately in the brain, and are felt as different dimensions by people [12, 11]. Moreover, referring to [16], the human mind seems to be expert in the processing of bipolar information, and it is very likely that a large part of this expertise is not acquired, but is the result of the cognitive evolution of the species. At a finer-grained level, the distinction between positive preferences and negative preferences and their separate processing would result from the architectures of the mind and affect systems [11, 31, 42, 10, 16]. The affect system refers to the components of the nervous system involved in positive and negative information processing [11]. Moreover, the affect is not a unitary faculty but rather is composed of a number of distinct processes.

5.4 The Constructive Nature of Preferences

We do, of course, carry a myriad of preferences in our memory. We were born with some of them, such as a fondness for sweets, a dislike of pain, and, perhaps, a fear of snakes. Moreover, we spend our life, particularly in childhood and adolescence, building preferences from our experiences and our wants, needs, and desires. Some of these learned preferences are broad, such as preferring more money to less; others are quite specific, such as liking a particular flavor of ice cream. These well-established preferences are readily available for use. The need for preference construction arises when our known preferences are not sufficient for solving the decision problem that we face. It seems that these more difficult situations have one or more of the following three characteristics. First, some of the decision elements may be totally unfamiliar, such as when choosing what to eat from a menu in a foreign language. Second, the choices available to us may present a conflict among our known preferences, so that tradeoffs must be made. For example, suppose you are choosing between two apartments to rent. One has big windows with a great view but has a cramped kitchen. The other has no view but a well-arranged, spacious kitchen. You know you prefer nice views and large kitchens, but to make this decision you must make a tradeoff between one thing (view) and the other (kitchen). Often, we know our preferences for individual things but do not know the tradeoffs between them. Third, we find it difficult to translate our positive and negative feelings into a numerical response, even when our preferences are clear. For example, suppose you find an apartment with a great view and a big kitchen. Now, the question is, How much rent are you willing to pay for this apartment? That question may be hard to answer. The variability in the ways we construct and reconstruct our preferences yields preferences that are labile, inconsistent, subject to factors we are unaware of, and not always in our own best interest. Indeed, so pervasive is this lability that the very notion of a "true" preference must, in many situations, be rejected. Preferences are the result of a constructive and context-dependent process [54]. An important phenomenon resulting from this constructive nature and well studied in psychological literature is known as preference reversal.

Preference reversal occurs when the preference order between alternatives is reversed if different elicitation methods are employed [32]. Psychologists [20, 29, 50] explain this phenomenon by the fact that preferences are highly sensitive to the way the elicitation process is described and to the mode of response used to express the preference. The academic example to illustrate preference reversals is a gamble, with a probability of winning or losing. It has been observed that users may rank-order differently the alternatives depending on how they process information. Consider the following example [32], consisting of one bet with a high probability of winning a modest amount (the P bet) and one bet with a lower probability of winning a larger payoff (the $ bet):

P bet: $\frac{11}{12}$ chance to win 12 chips;
$\frac{1}{12}$ chance to lose 24 chips;

$ bet: $\frac{2}{12}$ chance to win 79 chips;
$\frac{10}{12}$ chance to lose 5 chips,

where each chip is worth 25 cents. Each participant is asked to first make a choice and then to indicate a minimum selling price for each bet. The experiments reported that the two bets were chosen about equally often across participants. However, the $ bet received a higher selling price.

These findings led to a number of empirical investigations, some of which attempted to eliminate preference reversals but instead replicated and extended them [21]. In particular, the acceptability of an option can depend on whether a negative outcome is evaluated as a cost or as an uncompensated loss [53], and it has been shown also that preferences depend on attractiveness ratings, risk ratings, and the strengths of preferences judgments (see [37]).

The phenomenon of preference reversal has, however, bad consequences on rational theories (e.g., economics) as it invalidates their invariance principle [51, 52]. The latter states that the preference relation over alternatives should be independent of the description of the alternatives or the elicitation process of the preferences. However, Slovic [45] has shown that a preference reversal can imply either the transitivity of the preference relation or the failure of the independence assumption of the preference elicitation process, or both. Consequently, this problem has attracted much attention of economists [23, 40], who attempted to invalidate preference reversals. However they recognized later on the real existence of this phenomenon.

Another consequence resulting from the constructive nature of preferences and its context-dependent sensitivity is the lack of preference transitivity. Although transitivity is generally regarded as a rational assumption, people sometimes express "consistent" intransitive preferences. To illustrate this, consider the following two examples borrowed from [49].

Example 5.1. Let ω_1, ω_2 and ω_3 be three alternatives over two variables X_1 and X_2. We give in Table 5.1 the values of ω_1, ω_2 and ω_3 w.r.t. X_1 and X_2. Suppose that the

Table 5.1

	X_1	X_2
ω_1	2	6
ω_2	3	4
ω_3	4	2

three alternatives are rank-ordered w.r.t. the following decision rule: if the difference between the two alternatives w.r.t. X_1 is strictly greater than 1, prefer the alternative that has the higher value on X_1. If the difference between the alternatives w.r.t. X_1 is less than or equal to 1, prefer the alternative that has the higher value on X_2. Therefore, we have ω_1 preferred to ω_2 and ω_2 preferred to ω_3. However ω_3 is preferred to ω_1.

Example 5.2. Consider a user who would like to buy a car. His initial impulse is to buy the simplest model for \$2,089. Nevertheless, when the salesman presents the optional accessories, he first decides to add power steering, which brings the price to \$2,167, feeling that the price difference is relatively negligible. Then, following the same reasoning, he is willing to add \$47 for a good car radio, and then an additional \$64 for power brakes. By repeating this process several times, our user ends up with a \$2,593 car, equipped with all the available accessories. At this point, however, he may prefer the simplest car over the fancy one, realizing that he is not willing to spend \$504 for all the added features, although each one of them alone seemed worth purchasing.

The intransitivity of preferences has also been observed in a database framework [48].

Example 5.3. I prefer the color of car ω_1 to the color of car ω_2 and the model of car ω_2 to the model of car ω_3, but I have no reason to prefer car ω_1 to car ω_3.

Note that in Examples 5.1 and 5.2, the preference between the first alternative and the last one is reversed while the two alternatives are incomparable in Example 5.3.

The above examples also illustrate the idea that intransitivity does not represent contradictory behavior of the users.

Now that psychologists claim that intransitivity is not a damning fact, the main question is "how to deal with intransitivity?" Following Tversky [49], it seems that the majority of participants who expressed intransitive preferences said that preferences are and should be transitive. This result confirms a previous result [35] where the author indicates that when faced with their own intransitivities, participants tend to modify their choice according to the transitivity property. Tversky [49] intuitively explains this behavior by the fact that given that an alternative ω_2 is preferred to an alternative ω_1, ω_1 can be considered as eliminated and ω_3 should be selected given that ω_3 is preferred to ω_2. Therefore, no intransitivity can occur since ω_1 and ω_3 are not compared.

5.5 Conclusion

This chapter offers an interesting overview of some problems related to preference handling from a psychological point of view. Surprisingly, we encounter many problems from the artificial intelligence framework. In particular, cognitive psychology confirms that preference elicitation constitutes a real bottleneck, pointing out the difficulty of choice when multiple outcomes are present. Moreover, positive and negative preferences have a strong foundation in this framework.

We believe that this chapter is only a first step to increasing researchers' awareness of this valuable topic. Artificial intelligence researchers have claimed responsibility for many notions from the theoretical point of view. For example, several semantics are used in conditional logics and CP-nets, namely, strong, optimistic, pessimistic and ceteris paribus. They correspond to different users' behaviors. It would be worth trying to study the plausibility of these semantics from a psychological point of view.

References

1. Alexander, G.M., Hines, M.: Sex differences in responses to children's toys in a non-human primate (*Cercopithecus aethiops sabaeus*). Evolution and Human Behavior **23**, 467–479 (2002)
2. Benferhat, S., Bonnefon, J.F., da Silva Neves, R.: An experimental analysis of possibilistic default reasoning. In: Dubois, D., Welty, C.A., Williams, M.A. (eds.), 9th International Conference on Principles of Knowledge Representation and Reasoning, pp. 130-140. AAAI Press, (2004)
3. Benferhat, S., Dubois, D., Kaci, S., Prade, H.: Bipolar representation and fusion of preferences in the possibilistic logic framework. In: Fensel, D., Giunchiglia, F., McGuinness, D.L., Williams, M.A. (eds.), 8th International Conference on Principle of Knowledge Representation and Reasoning, pp. 421-432. Morgan Kaufmann, (2002)

4. Berscheid, E., Reis, H.T.: Attraction and close relationships. In: Gilbert, D.T., Fiske, S.T., Lindzey, G. (eds.), The Handbook of Social Psychology, pp. 193-281. McGraw-Hill, New York (1998)
5. Birch, L.L., Deysher, M.: Caloric compensation and sensory specific satiety: Evidence for self regulation of food intake by young children. Appetite **7**, 323-331 (1986)
6. Bonnefon, J.F., Fargier, H.: Comparing sets of positive and negative arguments: Empirical assessment of seven qualitative rules. In: Brewka, G., Coradeschi, S., Perini, A., Traverso, P. (eds.), 17 European Conference on Artificial Intelligence, pp. 130-140. IOS Press, (2006)
7. Buss, D.M.: Sex differences in human mate preferences: Evolutionary hypotheses tested in 37 cultures. Behavioral and Brain Sciences **12**, 1–49 (1989)
8. Buss, D.M.: The Evolution of Desire: Strategies of Human Mating (rev. ed.). New York: Basic Books (2003)
9. Buss, D.M., Shackelford, T.K., Kirkpatrick, L.A., Larsen, R.J.: A half century of American mate preferences: The cultural evolution of values. Journal of Marriage and the Family **63**, 491–503 (2001)
10. Borod, J.C.: The Neuropsychology of Emotion. Oxford University Press (2000)
11. Cacioppo, J.T., Bernston, G.G.: The affect system: Architecture and operating characteristics. Current Directions in Psychological Science **8(5)**, 133–137 (1999)
12. Cacioppo, J.T., Gardner, W.L., Bernston, G.G.: Beyond bipolar conceptualizations and measures: The case of attitudes and evaluative space. Personality and Social Psychology Review **1(1)**, 3–25 (1997)
13. Cunningham, M.R., Roberts, A.R., Barbee, A.P., Druen, P.B., Wu, C.H.: Their ideas of beauty are, on the whole, the same as ours: Consistency and variability in the cross-cultural perception of female physical attractiveness. Journal of Personality and Social Psychology **68**, 261–279 (1995)
14. Damasio, A.: Descartes' Error: Emotion, Reason, and the Human Brain. Putnam (1994)
15. da Silva Neves, R., Bonnefon, J.F., Raufaste, E.: An Empirical Test of Patterns for Nonmonotonic Inference. Annals of Mathematics and Artificial Intelligence **34(1-3)**, 107–130 (2002)
16. da Silva Neves, R., Raufaste, E.: A psychological study of bipolarity in the possibilistic framework. In: Bouchon-Meunier, B., Coletti , G., Yager, G.G. (eds.), 10th International Conference on Information Processing and Management of Uncertainty in Knowledge-Based Systems, pp. 975-981, (2004)
17. Desor, J.A., Maller, O., Turner, R.E.: Taste in acceptance of sugars by human infants. Journal of Comparative and Physiological Psychology **84**, 496–501 (1973)
18. Einstein, M.A., Hornstein, I.: Food preferences of college students and nutritional implications. Journal of Food Science **35**, 429–436 (1970)
19. Fischhoff, B., Slovic, P., Lichtenstein, S., Read, S., Combs, B.: How safe is safe enough? A psychometric study of attitudes towards technological risks and benefits. Policy Sciences **8**, 127–152 (1978)
20. Fischhoff, B., P. Slovic, P., Lichtenstein, S.: Knowing what you want: Measuring labile values. Cognitive processes in choice and decision behavior. T.S. Wallsten (1980)
21. Goldstein, W., Einhorn, H.: Expression theory and the preference reversal phenomena. Psychological Review **94**, 236–254 (1987)
22. Grammer, K., Thornhill, R.: Human (*Homo sapiens*) facial attractiveness and sexual selection: The role of symmetry and averageness. Journal of Comparative Psychology **108**, 233-242 (1994)
23. Grether, D.M., Plott, C.: Economic theory of choice and the preference reversal phenomena. American Economic Review **69**, 623–638 (1979)
24. Grill, H.J., Norgren, R.: Chronically decerebrate rats demonstrate satiation but not bait shyness. Science **201**, 267–269 (1978)
25. Hansson, S.O.: What is ceteris paribus preference? Journal of Philosophical Logic **25**, 307–332 (1996)
26. Hansson, S.O.: The structure of values and norms. Cambridge University Press (2001)
27. Hassett, J.M., Siebert, E.R., Wallen, K.: Sex differences in rhesus monkey toy preferences parallel those of children. Hormones and Behavior **54**, 359-364 (2008)

28. Hsee, C.K., Kunreuther, H.C.: The affection effect in insurance decisions. Journal of Risk and Uncertainty **20**, 141–159 (2000)
29. Kahneman, D., Tversky, A.: Prospect theory: An analysis of decision under risk. Econometrica **37**, 263–291 (1979)
30. Kraus, S., D. Lehmann, D., Magidor, M.: Nonmonotonic reasoning, preferential models and cumulative logics. Artificial Intelligence **44(1-2)**, 167–207 (1990)
31. Larsen, J.T., McGraw, P., Cacioppo, J.T.: Can people feel happy and sad at the same time? Journal of Personality and Social Psychology **81**, 684–696 (2001)
32. Lichtenstein, S., Slovic, P.: Reversals of preference between bids and choices in gambling decisions. Journal of Experimental Psychology **89(1)**, 46–55 (1971)
33. Lichtenstein, S., Slovic, P.: The Construction of Preference, Cambridge University Press (2006)
34. Logue, A.W.: The Psychology of Eating and Drinking. Brunner Routledge, Taylor and Francis Book (2004)
35. MacCrimmon, K.R.: An experimental study of the decision making behavior of business executives. Ph.D. dissertation, University of California (1965)
36. Meiselman, H.L.: The role of sweetness in the food preference of young adults. In: Weiffenbach, J.M. (eds.), Taste and Development, pp. 269-281, Bethesda (1977)
37. Mellers, A.B., Chang, S., Birnbaum, H.M.: Preferences, prices, and ratings in risky decision making. Journal of Experimental Psychology: Human Perception and Performance **18(2)**, 347–361 (1992)
38. Montoya, R.M.: Gender similarities and differences in preferences for specific boy part. Current Research in Social Psychology **13**, pages 133-144 (2007)
39. Peryam, D.R., Polemis, B.W., Kamen, J.M., Eindhoven, J., Pilgrim, F.J.: Food preferences of men in the U.S. armed forces. Chicago: Quartermaster Food and Container Institute for the Armed Forces (1960)
40. Pommerehne, W., Schneider, F., Zweifel, P.: Economic theory of choice and the preference reversal phenomena: A reexamination. American Economic Review **72**, 569–574 (1982)
41. Rhodes, G., Pro.tt, F., Grady, J.M., Sumich, A.: Facial symmetry and the perception of beauty. Psychonomic Bulletin and Review **5**, 659-669 (1998)
42. Rolls, E.T.: Precis of "Brain and Emotion". Behavioral and Brain Sciences **23(2)**, 177–234 (2000)
43. Shuler, G.A., McCord, D.M.: Determinants of Male Attractiveness: "Hotness" Ratings as a Function of Perceived Resources. American Journal of Psychological Research, 10–23 (2000)
44. Slovic, P.: Perception of Risk. Science **236**, 280–285 (1987)
45. Slovic, P.: The Construction of Preference. American Psychologist **50(5)**, 364–371 (1995)
46. Slovic, P., Finucane, M., Peters, E., MacGregor, D.G.: Gilovich, T., Griffin, D., Kahneman, D. (eds.), The affect heuristic. Intuitive Judgment: Heuristics and Biases. pp. 397-420. Cambridge University Press (2002)
47. Slovic, P., Lichtentstein, S.: The relative importance of probabilities and payoffs in risk taking. Journal of Experimental Psychology Monographs **78**, 1–18 (1968)
48. Torlone, R., Ciaccia, P.: Finding the best when it's a matter of preference. In: De Antonellis, V., Castano, S., Catania, B., Guerrini, G. (eds.), 10th Symposium on Advanced Database Systems, pp. 347-360. Edizioni Seneca, (2002)
49. Tversky, A.: Intransitivity of preference. Psychological Review **76**, 31–48 (1969)
50. Tversky, A., Kahneman, D.: The framing of decisions and the psychology of choice. Science **211(4481)**, 453–458 (1981)
51. Tversky, A., Kahneman, D.: Rational choice and the framing of decisions. Journal of Business **59**, 251–278 (1986)
52. Tversky, A., Sattath, S., Slovic, P.: Contingent weighting in judgment and choice. Psychological Review **95**, 371–384 (1988)
53. Tversky, A., Slovic, P., Kahneman, D.: The causes of preference reversal. American Economic Review **80**, 204–217 (1990)
54. Tversky, A., Thaler, R.H.: Anomalies: Preference reversals. Journal of Economic Perspectives **4**, 201–211 (1990)

55. Zajonc, R.B.: Attitudinal effects of mere exposure. Journal of Personality and Social Psychology **9**, Monongraph supplement (1968)

Zajonc, R.B.: Attitudinal effects of mere exposure. Journal of Personality and Social Psychology 9,2 (supplement part 2) (1968)

Part II
Reasoning with Preferences

Chapter 6
Preferences in Argumentation Theory

6.1 Introduction

Argumentation theory is a reasoning process based on constructing arguments, determining conflicts between arguments and determining acceptable arguments. Dung's argumentation framework is an abstract framework based on a set of arguments and a binary defeat relation defined over the set [12]. The output of an argumentation framework is a multi-set of acceptable arguments called acceptable extensions. An extension is a set of arguments which can be used together in order to support a decision, a viewpoint, etc. Thus, it should satisfy two basic requirements: (1) an extension is conflict-free, i.e., no defeat relation holds between arguments in the extension and (2) an extension defends its arguments from any external attack.

The abstract nature of Dung's argumentation framework accounts for the broad range of its applications. Specifically, this framework has been shown to be suitable for reasoning about inconsistent knowledge [1, 2, 5], decision [6], in multi-agent systems [23, 4], etc.

Preferences play an important role in solving conflicts in argumentation theory. Preference-based argumentation frameworks accommodate preferences in argumentation theory. They are an instantiation of Dung's framework where the defeat relation is derived from an attack relation and a preference relation over the set of arguments. More precisely, an argument A defeats an argument B if and only if A attacks B and B is not preferred to A. We say that the preference-based argumentation framework represents the induced Dung's argumentation framework. The extensions of the preference-based argumentation framework are extensions of the Dung's argumentation framework it represents. Different ways are there to compute the preference relation, depending on the strength and nature of knowledge from which the arguments are built. More precisely, an argument is preferred when it is built from more important or prioritized information, which may be pervaded with implicit priorities (e.g., defeasible knowledge) or explicit priorities (e.g., weighted formulas). The preference relation may also be induced by the values promoted by the arguments. An argument is preferred when the value it promotes is more important or preferred. A value may be a goal, a decision, a criterion, a viewpoint, etc.

Unfortunately, preference-based argumentation frameworks run into serious trouble when an argument is attacked by a less preferred argument and not vice versa. More precisely, let us consider two arguments A and B such that A attacks B but B is preferred to A. Following preference-based argumentation frameworks, the attack fails and no defeat relation holds between A and B. Consequently, the two arguments belong together to the acceptable extensions. However, this result is unacceptable since A and B together do not represent a coherent statement. In the first part of this chapter, we focus on this problem. Different proposals have been made to remedy this problem. Nevertheless, a deep analysis of the problematic cases reveals that the flaw is not due to the use of preferences but to a more fundamental problem. More precisely, we show that the preferences and the attack relation have not been properly used together. This is because researchers define on the one hand preference-based argumentation frameworks as an extension of Dung's argumentation framework. Consequently, they replace the not necessarily symmetric defeat relation with a not necessarily symmetric attack relation and a preference relation. On the other hand, they define the acceptable extensions of a preference-based argumentation framework as acceptable extensions of the Dung's argumentation framework it represents. A preference-based argumentation framework with a symmetric conflict relation allows us to prevent the undesirable result [14].

In the second part of the chapter, we provide an overview of existing preference-based argumentation frameworks that correspond to different ways of incorporating preferences in argumentation theory.

In the last part of the chapter, we address the role of preferences in the output of preference-based argumentation frameworks. In fact, the use of preferences (even in the most elaborate way) in preference-based argumentation frameworks has been done in a limited way in the sense that preferences are only used to compute the defeat relation given an attack relation. Then, the output of preference-based argumentation frameworks is a set of acceptable extensions which are equally preferred. The authors of [11] have advocated this problem and defined new extensions that only return the most preferred acceptable extensions. We believe that returning the most preferred acceptable extensions and excluding the other ones is not suitable. This is because all acceptable extensions satisfy minimal requirements of Dung's framework, namely, defense and conflict-freeness; thus, no reason is valid for excluding some of them. Instead, we keep all acceptable extensions but propose different more or less strong ways to rank-order them [14].

6.2 Dung's Argumentation Framework

Dung [12] models argumentation theory by means of a set of arguments and a binary defeat relation over the arguments (called an attack relation by Dung). In Dung's framework, an argument is an abstract entity whose origin and structure are not known. Its role is only determined by its relation with other arguments given the defeat relation. The defeat relation between two arguments means that the user cannot forward the two arguments together without contradicting herself.

Definition 6.1 (Dung's argumentation framework).
Dung's argumentation framework is a tuple $AF = \langle \mathscr{A}, Def \rangle$ where $\mathscr{A}$ is a finite set of arguments and Def is a binary defeat relation defined over $\mathscr{A} \times \mathscr{A}$.

We suppose that Def is an irreflexive binary relation, i.e., there are no self-defeating arguments.

Example 6.1. Let $AF_1 = \langle \mathscr{A}_1, Def_1 \rangle$ be an argumentation framework with $\mathscr{A}_1 = \{A,B,C,D,E,F,G,H\}$ and Def_1 defined by $A\ Def_1\ G$, $D\ Def_1\ C$, $D\ Def_1\ E$, $C\ Def_1\ F$, $F\ Def_1\ C$, $E\ Def_1\ F$ and $F\ Def_1\ E$. Let $AF_2 = \langle \mathscr{A}_2, Def_2 \rangle$ be another argumentation framework, with $\mathscr{A}_2 = \{A,B,C,D\}$ and $A\ Def_2\ B$, $B\ Def_2\ A$, $A\ Def_2\ C$, $B\ Def_2\ C$ and $C\ Def_2\ D$. AF_1 and AF_2 are depicted in Figures 6.1 and 6.2, respectively. An arrow from an argument to another argument represents that the former defeats the latter.

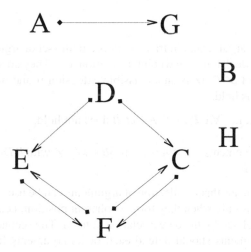

Fig. 6.1 An argumentation framework, AF_1

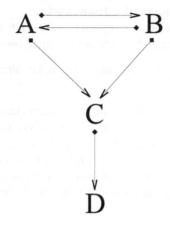

Fig. 6.2 An argumentation framework, AF_2

The output of an argumentation framework is a multi-set of arguments which can be used to defend a decision, a viewpoint, a position, etc. They are called admissible extensions. A subset $\mathscr{S} \subseteq \mathscr{A}$ is an admissible extension if and only if both of the following conditions hold:

- it is *conflict-free*, i.e., $\forall A, B \in \mathscr{S}$, A *Def* B does not hold,

- it *defends* all its elements, i.e., $\forall A \in \mathscr{S}$, if $\exists B \in \mathscr{A} \setminus \mathscr{S}$ with B *Def* A then $\exists C \in \mathscr{S}$ such that C *Def* B.

The first property means that a collection of arguments can be used together in an argumentation process only when they form a coherent position, i.e., no arguments in the collection are related by the defeat relation at hand. The second property means that the set of arguments should defend each of its arguments from any external attack.

Example 6.2. (Example 6.1 continued)
Let us consider the argumentation framework AF_1 given in the previous example. The sets $\{A\}$, $\{D\}$, $\{F\}$, $\{A, B, D, F, H\}$ are some admissible extensions of AF_1.

Consider now AF_2. The sets $\{A\}$, $\{B\}$, $\{A,D\}$ and $\{B,D\}$ are admissible extensions of AF_2.

Acceptable extensions are admissible extensions which satisfy some additional properties. We summarize the most well-known acceptable extensions in the next definition:

Definition 6.2 (Acceptable extensions). [12]
Let $\langle \mathscr{A}, Def \rangle$ be an argumentation framework.

- A subset $\mathscr{S} \subseteq \mathscr{A}$ is a *preferred extension* if and only if it is a maximal (for set inclusion) admissible extension.
- A subset $\mathscr{S} \subseteq \mathscr{A}$ is a *stable extension* if and only if it is a preferred extension that defeats any argument in $\mathscr{A} \setminus \mathscr{S}$.
- A subset $\mathscr{S} \subseteq \mathscr{A}$ is a *complete extension* if and only if it is conflict-free and $\mathscr{S} = \{A \mid A \in \mathscr{A}, \mathscr{S} \text{ defends } A\}$.
- A subset $\mathscr{S} \subseteq \mathscr{A}$ is the *grounded extension* if and only if it is the smallest (for set inclusion) complete extension of $\langle \mathscr{A}, Def \rangle$.

Example 6.3. (Example 6.1 continued)
The set $\{A,B,D,F,H\}$ is the grounded extension and the unique preferred or stable extension of AF_1. The grounded extension of AF_2 is empty. The sets $\{A,D\}$ and $\{B,D\}$ are the preferred or stable extensions of AF_2.

6.3 Preference-Based Argumentation Framework

The abstract nature of Dung's argumentation framework accounts for its large range of applications involving conflicts. Specifically, preference-based argumentation frameworks have been developed in order to take into account preferences over arguments [24, 25, 9, 3, 2, 26, 17, 21].

Recently, researchers [20, 7] motivated this framework by arguing that Dung's framework does not allow to consider preferences over arguments. Therefore, if an argument A defeats an argument B but it turns out that B is preferred to A, then the defeat fails, i.e., a defeat against a more preferred argument does not succeed. The following recent example illustrates this idea.

Example 6.4. (Borrowed from [7])
An agent wants to buy a violin. An expert says that the violin is produced by Stradivari; that is why it is expensive. Based on this information, the agent has a first argument A which claims that the violin is expensive. The agent has a three-year old son who says that the violin was not produced by Stradivari. Thus, the agent has a second argument B which claims that the violin was not produced by Stradivari. Notice that B contradicts the information "the violin is produced by Stradivari" used in A in order to conclude that the violin is expensive.

The authors of [7] model Example 6.4 by a Dung's argumentation framework $\langle \mathscr{A}, Def \rangle$, defined by $\mathscr{A} = \{A, B\}$ and $B\ Def\ A$. Thus, B is the only acceptable argument. Afterward, they criticize this result, arguing that an argument given by an expert is stronger than an argument given by a three-year old child. So, A should be accepted instead of B. Even worse, consider a third argument C which claims that the violin is produced by Stradivari according to the expert. Then, following the above modeling we have $B\ Def\ A$, $B\ Def\ C$ and $C\ Def\ B$. So, the grounded extension is empty while it should be equal to $\{A, C\}$.

The problem raised by Example 6.4 regarding the importance of arguments seems intuitively correct. In fact, an argument provided by an expert should be stronger than an argument provided by a child. However, we think that the flaw is not due to Dung's framework but rather to a misunderstanding of that framework. In fact, the conflict relation between the two arguments A and B is modeled by a defeat relation $B\ Def\ A$ in [7]. We believe that this modeling is the source of the undesirable results. In fact, we should not omit the fact that Dung's argumentation framework is an "abstract" framework which is defined by a set of abstract arguments and a binary relation representing defeat relations between arguments. Indeed, Dung proposed a general and abstract framework and left it to us to define the set of arguments and, more importantly, to fix the defeat relation. Consequently, if we believe that the source of an argument should play a role in the definition of the defeat relation, then we accordingly define this relation. This turns out to have $A\ Def\ B$ instead of $B\ Def\ A$, which faithfully models the problem and returns the intended result, namely A.

By the above observation, we say that Dung's framework does not fail to take into account preferences but should be suitably instantiated for this purpose. This is all the more true if a preference-based argumentation framework is defined as being a representation of Dung's argumentation framework in the sense that its acceptable extensions are acceptable extensions of the Dung's argumentation framework it represents (see Definition 6.4).

Definition 6.3 (Preference-based argumentation framework).
A preference-based argumentation framework is a three-tuple $PAF = \langle \mathscr{A}, Att, \succeq \rangle$ where $\mathscr{A}$ is a finite set of arguments, Att is an irreflexive binary relation (called attack relation) defined over $\mathscr{A} \times \mathscr{A}$ and $\succeq$ is a preorder over $\mathscr{A} \times \mathscr{A}$.

A preference-based argumentation framework can represent an argumentation framework.

Definition 6.4. A preference-based argumentation framework $\langle \mathscr{A}, Att, \succeq \rangle$ represents $\langle \mathscr{A}, Def \rangle$ if and only if $\forall A, B \in \mathscr{A}$, we have

$$A\ Def\ B \text{ iff } (A\ Att\ B \text{ and } not(B \succ A)).$$

We suppose that Att is irreflexive in $\langle \mathscr{A}, Att, \succeq \rangle$ in order to prevent self-defeating arguments in the associated Dung's argumentation framework. In fact, $not(A \succ A)$

is true, so having *A Att A* leads to *A Def A*.

There are always preference-based argumentation frameworks representing Dung's argumentation frameworks and vice versa. More precisely, each preference-based argumentation framework represents one and only one Dung's argumentation framework and each Dung's argumentation framework is represented by at least one but usually several preference-based argumentation frameworks [17].

The acceptable extensions of a preference-based argumentation framework are the acceptable extensions of the unique argumentation framework it represents.

However, it appears that preference-based argumentation frameworks may lead to undesirable results. Let us consider $\langle \mathscr{A}, Att, \succeq \rangle$ with $\mathscr{A} = \{A, B\}$, *B Att A* and $A \succ B$. Dung's argumentation framework represented by $\langle \mathscr{A}, Att, \succeq \rangle$ is $\langle \mathscr{A}, Def \rangle$ with $Def = \emptyset$ since *B Att A* but $A \succ B$. This preference-based argumentation framework models the problem described in Example 6.4 where *A* is "the violin is produced by Stradivari so it is expensive" and *B* is "the violin is not produced by Stradivari". Being expressed by an expert, *A* is strictly preferred to *B*. Since $Def = \emptyset$, both *A* and *B* are accepted. They form together all acceptable extensions. Although the set $\{A, B\}$ is conflict-free in the sense of Dung's framework since *A* and *B* are not related by the defeat relation *Def*, it is not correct to consider that the set is conflict-free. In fact, since *B Att A*, the two arguments are conflicting and one cannot use them without contradicting herself. In Example 6.4, this means that "An expert says that the violin is produced by Stradivari, that is why it is expensive" (argument *A*) and "the violin was not produced by Stradivari" (argument *B*). This fact has been first noticed by Modgil [21] and investigated later by Amgoud and Vesic [7]. While Modgil considers that such a result is not necessarily undesirable, Amgoud and Vesic work on new preference-based argumentation frameworks to deal with the above problem. In our opinion, this is an undesirable result but it is due to a fundamental reason related to the attack relation *Att*. In fact, in the above example, both *A* and *B* are accepted because the attack *B Att A* fails due to the fact that *A* is strictly preferred to *B*. It is worth noticing that in Dung's argumentation framework extensions are conflict-free and any arguments related by *Def* cannot appear in the same extension. This means that the existence of an argument in an extension implies the exclusion of any argument with which it is related by a defeat relation. This crucial principle is not faithfully reported in the above preference-based argumentation framework. In fact, *A* and *B* are conflicting, which means that they cannot appear in the same extension. However, since the attack relation is "asymmetric" (we only have *B Att A*), having $A \succ B$ means that *A* and *B* are not related by *Def*. Indeed, they both belong to the acceptable extensions.

In Example 6.4, and preference-based argumentation frameworks in general, a faithful modeling of the idea that two conflicting arguments *A* and *B* should not appear in the same extension (thus ensuring the conflict-freeness of the extensions) is to exclude one of them from an extension as soon as they are related by the attack relation, whatever the sense in which it is, i.e., *A Att B* or *B Att A* or both. The preference relation is then used to determine the sense of the defeat relation between the two arguments, i.e., *A Def B* or *B Def A* or both. Therefore, we ensure that both arguments will not belong together to the same acceptable extension since they are related by the defeat relation. This idea can be recovered by a "symmetric" attack relation in preference-based argumentation frameworks. Since an attack is intuitively not necessarily symmetric, we will speak about a conflict relation. Therefore, we define a preference-based argumentation framework with a symmetric conflict relation.

Definition 6.5 (Preference-based argumentation framework with a symmetric conflict relation).
A preference-based argumentation framework with a symmetric conflict relation is a three-tuple $PAF = \langle \mathscr{A}, \mathscr{C}, \succeq \rangle$ where $\mathscr{A}$ is a finite set of arguments, $\mathscr{C}$ is an irreflexive and symmetric conflict relation over $\mathscr{A} \times \mathscr{A}$ and $\succeq$ is a preorder over $\mathscr{A} \times \mathscr{A}$.

We equivalently write $A \mathrel{\mathscr{C}} B$ and $(A,B) \in \mathscr{C}$. For the sake of simplicity we refer to both $\langle \mathscr{A}, Att, \succeq \rangle$ and $\langle \mathscr{A}, \mathscr{C}, \succeq \rangle$ as preference-based argumentation frameworks.

Dung's argumentation framework represented by $\langle \mathscr{A}, \mathscr{C}, \succeq \rangle$ is defined in the standard way, i.e.,

$$A \; Def \; B \text{ if and only if } A \mathrel{\mathscr{C}} B, B \mathrel{\mathscr{C}} A \text{ and } not(B \succ A).$$

Example 6.5. (Example 6.4 continued)
The problem is modeled by $\langle \mathscr{A}, \mathscr{C}, \succeq \rangle$ with $\mathscr{A} = \{A,B\}$, $\mathscr{C} = \{(A,B),(B,A)\}$ and $A \succ B$. Then, Dung's argumentation framework represented by $\langle \mathscr{A}, \mathscr{C}, \succeq \rangle$ is $\langle \mathscr{A}, Def \rangle$ with $A \; Def \; B$. The only acceptable extension is $\{A\}$, which is the intended result.

Unfortunately, this is not the end of the story! While a symmetric conflict relation is suitable to prevent two conflicting arguments from belonging to the same extension, it is not unlikely to encounter an asymmetric attack relation. In order to deal with this situation, we should be able to move from an attack relation (possibly asymmetric) to a symmetric conflict relation. How do we construct a conflict relation from an attack relation in a coherent way? In particular, we want to construct $\langle \mathscr{A}, \mathscr{C}, \succeq' \rangle$ from $\langle \mathscr{A}, Att, \succeq \rangle$ such that the acceptable extensions of $\langle \mathscr{A}, Att, \succeq \rangle$ and the acceptable extensions of $\langle \mathscr{A}, \mathscr{C}, \succeq' \rangle$ coincide. Let $\langle \mathscr{A}, Def_1 \rangle$ (or $\langle \mathscr{A}, Def_2 \rangle$) be Dung's argumentation framework represented by $\langle \mathscr{A}, Att, \succeq \rangle$ (or $\langle \mathscr{A}, \mathscr{C}, \succeq' \rangle$). In order to have that $\langle \mathscr{A}, Att, \succeq \rangle$ and $\langle \mathscr{A}, \mathscr{C}, \succeq' \rangle$ return the same acceptable extensions, we will show that

$$\forall A, B \in \mathscr{A}, A \; Def_1 \; B \text{ iff } A \; Def_2 \; B.$$

That is, $\langle \mathscr{A}, Att, \succeq \rangle$ and $\langle \mathscr{A}, \mathscr{C}, \succeq' \rangle$ return the same set of defeat relations.

It is worth noticing here that Def_1 is composed of two types of defeat relations. On the one hand, we have standard defeat relations computed from Att and $\succeq$ following Definition 6.4. On the other hand, we have defeat relations which are not captured by that definition but should be considered in order to repair existing preference-based argumentation frameworks. More precisely, given $\langle \mathscr{A}, Att, \succeq \rangle$ we have $A\ Def_1\ B$ if and only if

- $A\ Att\ B$ and $not(B \succ A)$, or

- $B\ Att\ A$ and $A \succ B$.

  We define $\mathscr{C}$ and $\succeq'$ from Att and $\succeq$ in the following way:

- $\forall A, B \in \mathscr{A}$, $A\ Att\ B$ if and only if $A\ \mathscr{C}\ B$ and $B\ \mathscr{C}\ A$,

- $\succeq = \succeq'$.

  Let us now check whether $\forall A, B \in \mathscr{A}$, $A\ Def_1\ B$ iff $A\ Def_2\ B$. Let A and B be two arguments in $\mathscr{A}$. We distinguish between three cases:

- $A\ Att\ B$ and $A \succ B$.
  This is the simplest case. We have $A\ Def_1\ B$. We also have $A\ \mathscr{C}\ B$, $B\ \mathscr{C}\ A$ and $A \succ' B$. So, we have $A\ Def_2\ B$.

- $B\ Att\ A$ and $A \succ B$.
  This is the troubling case since the attack of B on A does not succeed because A is strictly preferred to B. As previously explained, existing preference-based argumentation frameworks should be repaired in order to accept A and reject B. Therefore, we should have $A\ Def_1\ B$. This is intuitively meaningful since A is attacked by B. Now, given the fact that A or B should be discarded, A becomes a defeater of B since it is preferred. The symmetric conflict relation $A\ \mathscr{C}\ B$ and $B\ \mathscr{C}\ A$ together with $A \succ' B$ leads to $A\ Def_2\ B$.

- $A\ Att\ B$ and $(A \approx B$ or $A \sim B)$.
  This is a case where simply replacing the attack relation by a symmetric conflict relation does not return the intended result. In fact, $A\ Att\ B$ and $(A \approx B$ or $A \sim B)$ induce $A\ Def_1\ B$. Now, a symmetric conflict relation between A and B, i.e., $A\ \mathscr{C}\ B$ and $B\ \mathscr{C} A$, together with $A \approx' B$ (or $A \sim' B$), returns both $A\ Def_2\ B$ and $B\ Def_2\ A$.

In order to overcome the problem raised by the third case, let us analyze the behavior of preference-based argumentation frameworks $\langle \mathscr{A}, Att, \succeq \rangle$. In the first two cases, being strictly preferred, A becomes stronger and "wins" any conflict it is involved in, whatever the attacker or the attacked argument. In the third case, $A\ Att\ B$ and $(A \approx B$ or $A \sim B)$ results in $A\ Def_1\ B$, which means that A is at least as strong as B in this conflict. Indeed, what matters when working with a symmetric conflict relation is which argument is "stronger". Let $A \overline{\succ}_s B$ (or $A \overline{\succeq}_s B$) denote "A is stronger than B" (or "A is at least as stronger as B"). Given a preference-based argumentation framework $\langle \mathscr{A}, Att, \succeq \rangle$, we define $\mathscr{C}$ and $\overline{\succeq}_s$ as follows:

- $((A\ Att\ B$ or $B\ Att\ A)$ and $A \succ B)$ iff $(A\ \mathscr{C}\ B$, $B\ \mathscr{C}\ A$ and $A \overline{\succ}_s B)$,
- $(A\ Att\ B$ and $(A \approx B$ or $A \sim B))$ iff $(A\ \mathscr{C}\ B$, $B\ \mathscr{C}\ A$ and $A \overline{\succeq}_s B)$.

Therefore, we define an argumentation framework with a symmetric conflict relation and a strongness relation.

Definition 6.6 (Strongness-based argumentation framework).
A strongness-based argumentation framework is a three-tuple $SAF = \langle \mathscr{A}, \mathscr{C}, \overline{\succeq}_s \rangle$, where $\mathscr{A}$ is a finite set of arguments, $\mathscr{C}$ is an irreflexive and symmetric conflict relation over $\mathscr{A} \times \mathscr{A}$ and $\overline{\succeq}_s$ is an ordering relation over $\mathscr{A} \times \mathscr{A}$.

The strongness relation $\overline{\succeq}_s$ is an ordering relation (and not a preorder) because it is not necessarily reflexive or transitive. In fact, from the construction of $\mathscr{C}$ and $\overline{\succeq}_s$, $\overline{\succeq}_s$ is reflexive, i.e., $A \overline{\succeq}_s A$ means that A *Att* A holds. However, *Att* is irreflexive. The following is a counterexample against the transitivity of $\overline{\succeq}_s$.

Example 6.6. Consider $\langle \mathscr{A}, Att, \succeq \rangle$ with $\mathscr{A} = \{A, B, C\}$, A *Att* B, B *Att* C, C *Att* A and $A \approx B \approx C$. Following the construction of $\mathscr{C}$ and $\overline{\succeq}_s$ we have

- $A \mathscr{C} B$, $B \mathscr{C} A$ and $A \overline{\succeq}_s B$ (given A *Att* B and $A \approx B$),
- $B \mathscr{C} C$, $C \mathscr{C} B$ and $B \overline{\succeq}_s C$ (given B *Att* C and $B \approx C$),
- $C \mathscr{C} A$, $A \mathscr{C} C$ and $C \overline{\succeq}_s A$ (given C *Att* A and $C \approx A$).

So, we have $A \overline{\succeq}_s B$ and $B \overline{\succeq}_s C$ but $A \overline{\succeq}_s C$ does not hold.

However, $\overline{\succeq}_s$ being non-transitive is not a damning criticism since although $\succeq$ is supposedly a preorder in Definition 6.3, the properties of a preorder (reflexivity and transitivity) are not used. What matters is only the ordering between pairwise arguments involved in an attack relation (see Definition 6.4).

Given a strongness-based argumentation framework $\langle \mathscr{A}, \mathscr{C}, \overline{\succeq}_s \rangle$, we define Dung's argumentation framework in the standard way:

$$A \; Def \; B \text{ if and only if } A \mathscr{C} B, B \mathscr{C} A \text{ and } not(B \overline{\succ}_s A).$$

Then, we show the following result:

Proposition 6.1. *Let $\langle \mathscr{A}, Att, \succeq \rangle$ be a preference-based argumentation framework. Let $\langle \mathscr{A}, \mathscr{C}, \overline{\succeq}_s \rangle$ be a strongness-based argumentation framework such that $\mathscr{C}$ and $\overline{\succeq}_s$ are constructed from Att and $\succeq$ as previously given. Let $\langle \mathscr{A}, Def_2 \rangle$ be Dung's argumentation framework represented by $\langle \mathscr{A}, \mathscr{C}, \overline{\succeq}_s \rangle$.*

1. If $(A \; Att \; B$ and $not(B \succ A))$ then $A \; Def_2 \; B$.
2. If $(A \; Att \; B$ and $B \succ A)$ then $B \; Def_2 \; A$.

Proof

1. Suppose $(A \; Att \; B$ and $not(B \succ A))$ and prove $A \; Def_2 \; B$.
   $not(B \succ A)$ means that $A \succ B$ or $A \approx B$ or $A \sim B$. We distinguish between two cases:

   - $A \; Att \; B$ and $A \succ B$
     From the construction of $\overline{\succeq}_s$ we have $A \mathscr{C} B$, $B \mathscr{C} A$ and $A \overline{\succ}_s B$. Indeed, we have $A \; Def_2 \; B$.

- $A\ Att\ B$ and $(A \approx B$ or $A \sim B)$
  From the construction of $\overline{\succeq}_s$ we have $A\ \mathscr{C}\ B$, $B\ \mathscr{C}\ A$ and $A\overline{\succeq}_sB$. $A\overline{\succeq}_sB$ means that $not(B\overline{\succ}_sA)$ is true. So, we have $A\ \mathscr{C}\ B$, $B\ \mathscr{C}\ A$ and $not(B\overline{\succ}_sA)$. Indeed, we get $A\ Def_2\ B$.

2. Suppose that $A\ Att\ B$ and $B \succ A$ and prove $B\ Def_2\ A$.
   By construction we have $A\ \mathscr{C}\ B$, $B\ \mathscr{C}\ A$ and $B\overline{\succ}_sA$. Therefore, $B\ Def_2\ A$. ∎

Item 1 states that any defeat relation a la Dung induced by $\langle \mathscr{A}, Att, \succeq \rangle$ is recovered by $\langle \mathscr{A}, \mathscr{C}, \overline{\succeq}_s \rangle$ in $\langle \mathscr{A}, Def_2 \rangle$. Item 2 states that defeat relations which should be considered but not captured by Definition 6.4 are also recovered by $\langle \mathscr{A}, \mathscr{C}, \overline{\succeq}_s \rangle$ in $\langle \mathscr{A}, Def_2 \rangle$. Therefore Proposition 6.1 shows that $\langle \mathscr{A}, \mathscr{C}, \overline{\succeq}_s \rangle$ is complete.

However, the proposition does not tell us whether any defeat relation induced by $\langle \mathscr{A}, \mathscr{C}, \overline{\succeq}_s \rangle$, i.e., Def_2, corresponds to a defeat relation induced by $\langle \mathscr{A}, Att, \succeq \rangle$. The latter property ensures that $\langle \mathscr{A}, Att, \succeq \rangle$ and $\langle \mathscr{A}, \mathscr{C}, \overline{\succeq}_s \rangle$ induce the same defeat relations. The following proposition states that the answer is positive. Therefore $\langle \mathscr{A}, \mathscr{C}, \overline{\succeq}_s \rangle$ is sound.

Proposition 6.2. *Let $\langle \mathscr{A}, Att, \succeq \rangle$ be a preference-based argumentation framework. Let $\langle \mathscr{A}, \mathscr{C}, \overline{\succeq}_s \rangle$ be a strongness-based argumentation framework such that $\mathscr{C}$ and $\overline{\succeq}_s$ are constructed from Att and $\succeq$ as previously given. Let $\langle \mathscr{A}, Def_2 \rangle$ be Dung's argumentation framework represented by $\langle \mathscr{A}, \mathscr{C}, \overline{\succeq}_s \rangle$. $\forall A, B \in \mathscr{A}$, if $A\ Def_2\ B$ then one of the following two statements holds:*

- *$A\ Att\ B$ and $not(B \succ A)$,*
- *$B\ Att\ A$ and $A \succ B$.*

Proof
Suppose that $A\ Def_2\ B$, i.e., $A\ \mathscr{C}\ B$, $B\ \mathscr{C}\ A$ and $not(B\overline{\succ}_sA)$. From the construction of $\mathscr{C}$ and $\overline{\succeq}_s$ we have that any two conflicting arguments are totally ordered w.r.t. $\overline{\succeq}_s$. Therefore we distinguish between two cases. A first case where $A\ \mathscr{C}\ B$, $B\ \mathscr{C}\ A$ and $A\overline{\succ}_sB$ which means that $(A\ Att\ B$ or $B\ Att\ A)$ and $A \succ B$. Note that $A \succ B$ means that $not(B \succ A)$ is true. So we have either $A\ Att\ B$ and $not(B \succ A)$ or $B\ Att\ A$ and $A \succ B$. In the second case, we have $A\ \mathscr{C}\ B$, $B\ \mathscr{C}\ A$ and $A\overline{\succeq}_sB$ which is equivalent to $A\ Att\ B$ and $(A \approx B$ or $A \sim B)$. So $A\ Att\ B$ and $not(B \succ A)$ holds. ∎

Propositions 6.1 and 6.2 show that given the construction of $\mathscr{C}$ and $\overline{\succeq}_s$ from Att and $\succeq$, we correctly move from $\langle \mathscr{A}, Att, \succeq \rangle$ to $\langle \mathscr{A}, \mathscr{C}, \overline{\succeq}_s \rangle$ in the sense that the two frameworks induce the same defeat relations. Therefore, their acceptable extensions coincide.

In light of the above results, it is more suitable to speak about a symmetric conflict relation and an ordering relation $\overline{\succeq}_s$ reflecting the relative "strongness" between arguments. The latter may be a given preference relation or derived from an attack relation and a preference relation as previously shown. In the following we abstract this level of detail on how the conflict relation and the preference or strongness relation are obtained.

In order to avoid any confusion and without loss of what has been previously presented, we suppose that we deal with a standard preference-based argumentation framework with a symmetric conflict relation and a preference relation. This simplification only aims at keeping the usual terminology used in existing preference-based argumentation frameworks. To summarize, we have the following:

- A preference-based argumentation framework is a three-tuple $PAF = \langle \mathscr{A}, \mathscr{C}, \succeq \rangle$ where $\mathscr{A}$ is a set of arguments, $\mathscr{C}$ is an irreflexive and symmetric conflict relation defined over $\mathscr{A} \times \mathscr{A}$ and $\succeq$ is a preorder over $\mathscr{A} \times \mathscr{A}$.

- A preference-based argumentation framework $\langle \mathscr{A}, \mathscr{C}, \succeq \rangle$ represents Dung's argumentation framework if and only if $\forall A, B \in \mathscr{A}$, we have

$$A \; Def \; B \; \text{iff} \; (A \; \mathscr{C} \; B, B \; \mathscr{C} \; A \; \text{and} \; not(B \succ A)).$$

Example 6.7. (Borrowed from [17])
Let $\langle \mathscr{A}, \mathscr{C}, \succeq \rangle$ be a preference-based argumentation framework with $\mathscr{A} = \{A,B,C,D,E,F,G,H\}$, $\mathscr{C} = \{(A,G),(G,A),(C,D),(D,C),(C,F),(F,C),$ $(D,E),(E,D),(E,F),(F,E)\}$ and $\succeq: A \approx D \succ B \approx C \approx E \approx F \succ G \approx H$. Dung's argumentation framework represented by $\langle \mathscr{A}, \mathscr{C}, \succeq \rangle$ is $\langle \mathscr{A}, Def \rangle$ with $A \; Def \; G$, because $A \; \mathscr{C} \; G$, $G \; \mathscr{C} \; A$ and $G \succ A$ does not hold. Similarly, we have $D \; Def \; C$, $C \; Def \; F$, $F \; Def \; C$, $D \; Def \; E$, $E \; Def \; F$ and $F \; Def \; E$. No other defeat relations hold. This argumentation framework is AF_1, given in Example 6.1. For example, the grounded extension is $\{A,B,D,F,H\}$.

6.4 Where Does the Preference Relation Come from?

The preference relation over arguments can be computed in different ways, depending on the structure of the arguments. In the following subsections, we review some of them.

6.4.1 Implicit Priorities

The introduction of preferences in argumentation theory was first proposed by Simari and Loui [24]. In their framework, an argument is a tuple $\langle H, h \rangle$, where H is a set of formulas and h is a formula. H is called the support of the argument and h is its conclusion. By abuse of language we say that $\langle H, h \rangle$ is an argument for h. Inspired by non-monotonic reasoning, the authors build their arguments from a set of defeasible knowledge, denoted by $\mathbb{D}$. They also consider a consistent set of knowledge denoted by K. Generally, $K \cup \mathbb{D}$ is inconsistent. The tuple $\langle H, h \rangle$ is an argument if and only if it satisfies the following properties:

- $K \cup H \vdash h$,

- $K \cup H$ is consistent,
- $\nexists H' \subset H$ such that $K \cup H' \vdash h$,

where $H \subseteq \mathbb{D}$.

When we deal with non-defeasible knowledge, the set K is not necessary. See the following subsections.

Example 6.8 (Inspired by [24]).
Let $\mathbb{D} = \{\phi \Rightarrow \psi, \xi \wedge \psi \Rightarrow \varphi, \Theta \Rightarrow \Upsilon\}$ be a set of defeasible rules. Let $K = \{\phi, \xi\}$. The two arguments $A = \langle \{\phi \Rightarrow \psi, \xi \wedge \psi \Rightarrow \varphi\}, \varphi \rangle$ and $B = \langle \{\phi \Rightarrow \psi\}, \psi \rangle$ are constructed from $\mathbb{D}$.

We say that an argument can be activated if the premise of each rule in its support is true. In the above example, A can be activated as soon as ϕ and ξ are true while B can be activated as soon as ϕ is true. This notion defines the specificity between two arguments. We say that an argument is more specific than another argument if and only if each time the former can be activated the latter can also be activated, but the reverse is not true. In the above example, A is more specific than B because when ϕ and ξ are true, both A and B can be activated. On the other hand, if only ϕ is true then B can be activated but not A. The specificity relation defines the preference relation. Being more specific makes an argument preferred.

The structure of arguments in terms of support and conclusion defines two types of conflict between arguments. Let $A = \langle H, h \rangle$ and $B = \langle H', h' \rangle$ be two arguments.

- A and B disagree when their conclusions are contradictory, i.e., $K \cup \{h, h'\}$ is inconsistent. We say that A and B rebut each other.
- A provides a counterargument against B when its conclusion contradicts a formula used in support of B. Formally, there exists an argument $\langle H_2, h_2 \rangle$ such that $H_2 \subseteq H'$ and $K \cup \{h, h_2\}$ is inconsistent.

In both cases we have $A \, \mathscr{C} \, B$ and $B \, \mathscr{C} \, A$.

6.4.2 Explicit Priorities

In the previous subsection, rules are pervaded with implicit priorities due to their defeasible nature. In some applications, information is provided with explicit priorities representing its certainty or priority. Information may be totally or partially rank-ordered. Different proposals have been made to compare sets of prioritized information (cf. Chapter 3). We refer the reader to [10] for further comparisons. In this section we recall possibilistic logic-based comparison [9].

Definition 6.7 (The level of an argument).
Let $\Sigma = \{(\phi_i, \alpha_i) \mid i = 1, \cdots, n\}$ be a set of weighted propositional logic formulas

with $\alpha_i \in (0,1]$. Let $\Sigma^* = \{\phi_i \mid (\phi_i, \alpha_i) \in \Sigma\}$ and $A = \langle H, h \rangle$ be an argument such that $H \subseteq \Sigma^*$. The level of A w.r.t. Σ, denoted by $level_\Sigma(A)$, is defined by

$$level_\Sigma(A) = \min\{\alpha_i \mid (\phi_i, \alpha_i) \in \Sigma, \phi_i \in H\}.$$

Example 6.9. Let $\Sigma = \{(a, .9), (a \vee b, .85), (\neg a, .8), (\neg a \vee \neg b, .8), (d, .4), (\neg d, .3)\}$. Let $\langle \mathscr{A}, \mathscr{C}, \succeq' \rangle$ be a preference-based argumentation framework where the arguments in $\mathscr{A}$ are built from $\Sigma^* = \{a, a \vee b, \neg a, \neg a \vee \neg b, d, \neg d\}$. We have $\mathscr{A} = \{A, B, C, D, E, F, G, H\}$ with $A = \langle \{d\}, d \rangle$, $B = \langle \{a \vee b\}, a \vee b \rangle$, $C = \langle \{\neg a\}, \neg a \rangle$, $D = \langle \{a\}, a \rangle$, $E = \langle \{\neg a, a \vee b\}, b \rangle$, $F = \langle \{a, \neg a \vee \neg b\}, \neg b \rangle$, $G = \langle \{\neg d\}, \neg d \rangle$ and $H = \langle \{\neg a \vee \neg b\}, \neg a \vee \neg b \rangle$. Therefore $\mathscr{C} = \{(A, G), (G, A), (C, D), (D, C), (D, E), (E, D), (C, F), (F, C), (F, E), (E, F)\}$. We also have $level_\Sigma(A) = .4$, $level_\Sigma(B) = .85$, $level_\Sigma(C) = .8$, $level_\Sigma(D) = .9$, $level_\Sigma(E) = .8$, $level_\Sigma(F) = .8$, $level_\Sigma(G) = .3$ and $level_\Sigma(H) = .8$.

An argument is preferred in possibilistic logic-based comparison when the least certain or prioritized formulas it contains are more certain or prioritized. Formally, we write the following definition.

Definition 6.8. Let $\Sigma = \{(\phi_i, \alpha_i) \mid i = 1, \cdots, n\}$ be a set of weighted propositional logic formulas with $\alpha_i \in (0, 1]$. Let $\Sigma^* = \{\phi_i \mid (\phi_i, \alpha_i) \in \Sigma\}$. Let $A = \langle H, h \rangle$ and $B = \langle H', h' \rangle$ be two arguments such that $H \subseteq \Sigma^*$ and $H' \subseteq \Sigma^*$. Then, A is *at least as preferred as* B, denoted by $A \succeq B$, iff

$$level_\Sigma(A) \geq level_\Sigma(B).$$

A is strictly preferred to B, denoted by $A \succ B$, iff $A \succeq B$ holds but $B \succeq A$ does not.

Example 6.10. (Example 6.9 continued)
We have $D \succ' B \succ' E \approx' H \approx' F \approx' C \succ' A \succ' G$. Dung's argumentation framework represented by $\langle \mathscr{A}, \mathscr{C}, \succeq' \rangle$ is $\langle \mathscr{A}, Def \rangle$ with A Def G, D Def C, C Def F, F Def C, D Def E, E Def F and F Def E. The set $\{A, B, D, F, H\}$ is the grounded extension and also the unique preferred or stable extension. Note that $\langle \mathscr{A}, \mathscr{C}, \succeq' \rangle$ and the preference-based argumentation framework $\langle \mathscr{A}, \mathscr{C}, \succeq \rangle$ given in Example 6.7 represent the same Dung's argumentation framework although $\succeq$ and $\succeq'$ are different.

6.4.3 Value-Based Argumentation Framework

In some applications, the arguments need to be compared not on the basis of their internal structure but with respect to the viewpoints or decisions they promote. This may be due to the fact that the internal structure of the arguments is not available or because the values must be considered. This is particularly true in persuasion dialogues when the preference over values induces the preference over arguments promoting the values [8]. Thus, if two arguments are conflicting then the argument promoting a preferred value is accepted. For example, suppose that two parents discuss whether their son can watch the soccer game on the TV or whether he should prepare for his exam. Watching the game allows their son to discuss it with his friends, which promotes his sociability. On the other hand, preparing for his exam promotes his education. If the parents consider that sociability is not more important than education, then the child should prepare for his exam.

Bench-Capon [8] developed an argumentation framework which models the above considerations. Like Dung's framework, he considers abstract arguments. Moreover, he considers (i) a set of values promoted by the arguments and (ii) a set of audiences, following Perelman [22], where each audience corresponds to a preference relation over values.

Definition 6.9 (Value-based argumentation framework). [8]
A value-based argumentation framework is a five-tuple, $VAF = \langle \mathscr{A}, \mathscr{C}, V, val, \mathscr{D} \rangle$, where $\mathscr{A}$ is a finite set of arguments, $\mathscr{C}$ is an irreflexive and symmetric conflict relation over $\mathscr{A} \times \mathscr{A}$, V is a nonempty set of values, val is a function which maps from elements of $\mathscr{A}$ to elements of V and $\mathscr{D}$ is the set of possible audiences. An audience specific argumentation framework is a five-tuple, $VAF_a = \langle \mathscr{A}, \mathscr{C}, V, val, >_a \rangle$, where $a \in \mathscr{D}$ is an audience and $>_a$ is a partial order over $V \times V$.

It is worth noticing that $\mathscr{C}$ is independent of val, in the sense that two arguments promoting the same value may conflict.

In order to be as close as possible to the preference-based argumentation frameworks presented in this chapter, we focus on audience-specific value-based argumentation frameworks.

Definition 6.10 (Audience-specific value-based argumentation framework).
$\langle \mathscr{A}, \mathscr{C}, V, val, >_a \rangle$ represents $\langle \mathscr{A}, \mathscr{C}, \succeq \rangle$ if and only if $\forall A, B \in \mathscr{A}$, we have

$$A \succeq B \text{ if and only if } (val(A) >_a val(B) \text{ or } val(A) = val(B)).$$

Concerning the existence of audience-specific value-based argumentation frameworks representing a preference-based argumentation framework, the situation is the same as between preference-based argumentation frameworks and argumentation frameworks. Each audience-specific value-based argumentation framework represents precisely one preference-based argumentation framework, and each preference-based argumentation framework is represented by an equivalence class of alphabetic variants of audience-specific value-based argumentation frameworks [17]. The acceptable extensions of an audience-specific value-based argumentation framework are again simply the acceptable extensions of the unique preference-based argumentation framework it represents.

Example 6.11. (Example 6.7 continued)
Let $\langle \mathscr{A}, \mathscr{C}, V, val, >_a \rangle$ be a value-based argumentation framework with $\mathscr{A}$ and $\mathscr{C}$ as given in Example 6.7, and $V = \{v_1, v_2, v_3\}$, $val(A) = val(D) = v_1$, $val(B) = val(C) = val(E) = val(F) = v_2$ and $val(G) = val(H) = v_3$, and $v_1 >_a v_2 >_a v_3$. We can check that this value-based argumentation framework is represented by

the preference-based argumentation framework $\langle \mathscr{A}, \mathscr{C}, \succeq \rangle$ in Example 6.7. For example, the grounded extension of $\langle \mathscr{A}, \mathscr{C}, V, val, >_a \rangle$ is the grounded extension of $\langle \mathscr{A}, \mathscr{C}, \succeq \rangle$ and therefore, as shown in Example 6.7, is $\{A, B, D, F, H\}$.

6.4.4 Extended Value-Based Argumentation Framework

In Bench-Capon's framework an argument promotes at most one value. However, in practice it is possible to have arguments which promote multiple values. Moreover, in Bench-Capon's framework, a value v_1 being more important than (or preferred to) a value v_2 is interpreted as any argument promoting v_1 being preferred to any argument promoting v_2. One can also imagine other ways to compare the arguments promoting v_1 and v_2. Kaci and van der Torre [17] extend Bench-Capon's framework in order to take into account the above considerations. More specifically, they consider (i) arguments promoting multiple values and (ii) various kinds of preferences over values.

In order to model the fact that an argument may promote multiple values, the function *val* in Definition 6.9 has been replaced by a function *arg* from V to $2^{\mathscr{A}}$ such that $arg(v)$ is the set of arguments promoting the value v. This extension has the consequence that it can no longer be said that an argument is preferred to another argument if the value promoted by the former is preferred to the value promoted by the latter. This is because each argument may promote multiple values. The question is, how do we rank-order the arguments in $\mathscr{A}$ given preferences over the set of values? This calls for the second extension. Actually Bench-Capon's interpretation of "v_1 is preferred to v_2" is that any argument promoting v_1 is preferred to any argument promoting v_2. Making the connection with preference representation, we see that this is strong semantics (see Subsection 3.4.1).

Given that arguments can now promote multiple values, strong semantics is likely to induce a cyclic preference relation over arguments. Moreover, Kaci and van der Torre observed that optimistic and pessimistic semantics can be used as well in this argumentation framework. Formally, we have the following definition [17].

Definition 6.11 (Preference semantics).
Let $\mathscr{A}$ be a set of arguments and $\succeq$ be a preference relation over $\mathscr{A} \times \mathscr{A}$. Let V be a set of values, $v_1, v_2 \in V$ and *arg* be a function from V to $2^{\mathscr{A}}$.

- $\succeq$ satisfies $v_1 \gg_{st} v_2$, v_1 is *strongly* preferred to v_2 if and only if $\forall A \in \min(arg(v_1)\backslash arg(v_2), \succeq), \forall B \in \max(arg(v_2)\backslash arg(v_1), \succeq)$ we have $A \succ B$.

- $\succeq$ satisfies $v_1 \gg_{opt} v_2$, v_1 is *optimistically* preferred to v_2 if and only if $\forall A \in \max(arg(v_1)\backslash arg(v_2), \succeq), \forall B \in \max(arg(v_2)\backslash arg(v_1), \succeq)$ we have $A \succ B$.

- $\succeq$ satisfies $v_1 \gg_{pes} v_2$, v_1 is *pessimistically* preferred to v_2 if and only if $\forall A \in \min(arg(v_1)\backslash arg(v_2), \succeq), \forall B \in \min(arg(v_2)\backslash arg(v_1), \succeq)$ we have $A \succ B$.

Note that the above definition translates preference semantics from propositional logic to argumentation framework. Indeed, outcomes correspond to arguments while preferences over propositional formulas correspond to preferences over values. Ceteris paribus semantics does not make sense in argumentation frameworks. Note also that strong semantics can be written in terms of optimistic or pessimistic semantics [17]. For the sake of simplicity we only focus on optimistic and pessimistic semantics.

Instead of a partial order over the values, Kaci and van der Torre use a preference specification which is a set of preference statements of the form $\mathcal{P} = \{v_i \gg_\rhd v_j\}$, where $v_i, v_j \in V$ and $\rhd \in \{opt, pes\}$. $\gg_\rhd$ is not necessarily transitive or irreflexive. As in preference representation, a preference relation $\succeq$ is a model of $\mathcal{P}$ if and only if $\succeq$ satisfies each $v_i \gg_\rhd v_j$ in $\mathcal{P}$. A set of preference statements $\mathcal{P}$ is consistent if and only if it has a model. As in Bench-Capon's framework where the preference relation over arguments is induced by a partial order over values, in this framework, the preference relation over arguments is induced by $\mathcal{P}$. The new framework is called the value-specification argumentation framework.

Definition 6.12 (Value-specification argumentation framework). [17]
A value-specification argumentation framework is a five-tuple $\langle \mathcal{A}, \mathcal{C}, V, arg, \gg_\rhd \rangle$ where $\mathcal{A}$ is a finite set of arguments, $\mathcal{C}$ is an irreflexive and symmetric conflict relation over $\mathcal{A} \times \mathcal{A}$, V is a set of values, arg is a function from V to $2^{\mathcal{A}}$, and $\gg_\rhd \subseteq V \times V$ is a set of preference statements over V with $\rhd \in \{opt, pes\}$.

Inspired by conditional logics for preference representation explored in Section 3.4, Kaci and van der Torre associate a unique complete preorder with $\mathcal{P}$ depending on whether $\rhd = opt$ or $\rhd = pes$.

Definition 6.13. $\langle \mathcal{A}, \mathcal{C}, \succeq \rangle$ represents $\langle \mathcal{A}, \mathcal{C}, V, arg, \gg_\rhd \rangle$ if and only if $\succeq$ satisfies each $v_1 \gg_\rhd v_2$ in $\gg_\rhd$. $\langle \mathcal{A}, \mathcal{C}, V, arg, \gg_\rhd \rangle$ represents $\langle \mathcal{A}, \mathcal{C}, \succeq \rangle$ if and only if $\rhd = opt$ (or $\rhd = pes$) and $\succeq$ is the least- (or most-) specific relation among the $\succeq'$ such that $\langle \mathcal{A}, \mathcal{C}, \succeq' \rangle$ represents $\langle \mathcal{A}, \mathcal{C}, V, arg, \gg_\rhd \rangle$.

Concerning the existence of value-specification argumentation frameworks representing preference-based argumentation frameworks, the situation is different from before. For each value-specification argumentation framework there is at most one preference-based argumentation framework it represents, and for each preference-based argumentation framework there is at least one value-specification argumentation framework that represents it [17].

The acceptable extensions of a value-specification argumentation framework are the acceptable extensions of the unique preference-based argumentation framework it represents, if such a framework exists.

Example 6.12. (Borrowed from [17])
Let $\langle \mathcal{A}, \mathcal{C}, V, arg, \gg_\rhd \rangle$ be a value-specification argumentation framework defined by $\mathcal{A} = \{A, B, C, D, E, F, G, H\}$ with

A: "the soccer game is going to be very interesting, many people will watch the game because it is Barcelona against Arsenal",

B: "one should not always do the same as her friends, but also develop an idea herself of what is good to do",

C: "I have to watch the game, because Barcelona has not been in the final for six years",

D: "you better not watch the game, you have an exam tomorrow and you have to prepare for it",

E: "I have to watch the game, because I want to discuss it tomorrow with my friends",

F: "you are not going to watch television tonight, because you have been watching television for three evenings in a row, and television is unhealthy, dumb and uninspiring",

G: "the soccer game is going to be boring, because the first half was already won by 6-0",

H: "a child must go to school; education is important because it gives more options later on".

$\mathscr{C}$ is the conflict relation given in Example 6.7, $V = \{v_1, v_2, v_3, v_4, v_5, v_6\} = \{health, short term pleasure, education, enjoy, social, alone\}$ with $arg(v_1) = \{F\}$, $arg(v_2) = \{G, H\}$, $arg(v_3) = \{D, H\}$, $arg(v_4) = \{C, E\}$, $arg(v_5) = \{A, E\}$, $arg(v_6) = \{B, F\}$, and $\mathscr{P} = \{v_1 \gg_{opt} v_2, v_3 \gg_{opt} v_4, v_5 \gg_{opt} v_6\}$. Let $\succeq$ be a preference relation over $\mathscr{A} \times \mathscr{A}$ defined by $A \approx D \succ B \approx C \approx E \approx F \succ G \approx H$. We can check that $\succeq$ satisfies each preference in $\mathscr{P}$. Then, $\langle \mathscr{A}, \mathscr{C}, \succeq \rangle$ represents $\langle \mathscr{A}, \mathscr{C}, V, arg, \gg_{opt} \rangle$. We can also check that $\succeq$ is the least-specific preorder among the $\succeq'$ such that $\langle \mathscr{A}, \mathscr{C}, \succeq' \rangle$ represents $\langle \mathscr{A}, \mathscr{C}, V, arg, \gg_{opt} \rangle$, so $\langle \mathscr{A}, \mathscr{C}, V, arg, \gg_{opt} \rangle$ represents $\langle \mathscr{A}, \mathscr{C}, \succeq \rangle$.

We can check that $\langle \mathscr{A}, \mathscr{C}, \succeq \rangle$ is the preference-based argumentation framework given in Example 6.7. Therefore for example the grounded extension of $\langle \mathscr{A}, \mathscr{C}, V, arg, \gg_{opt} \rangle$ is $\{A, B, D, F, H\}$.

6.4.5 Arguing About Preferences

Modgil [21] developed a preference-based argumentation framework in which the arguments are abstract entities and the preference relation over the set of arguments is not defined by external information (e.g., ordered values or information pervaded with implicit or explicit priorities). Instead, preferences over arguments are supported by arguments. More precisely, in the instantiation of a defeat relation a la Dung in a preference-based argumentation framework, i.e., (*A Def B*) iff (*A $\mathscr{C}$ B*, *B $\mathscr{C}$ A* and *not*(*B $\succ$ A*)), the condition *not*(*B $\succ$ A*) is supported by an argument. In other words, when two arguments *A* and *B* are conflicting, *A* defeats *B* only if there is no argument claiming that *B* is preferred to *A*. Modgil calls his framework "extended argumentation framework".

Definition 6.14 (Extended argumentation framework). [21]

An extended argumentation framework is a three-tuple $\langle \mathscr{A}, \mathscr{C}, \mathscr{H} \rangle$ such that $\mathscr{A}$ is a finite set of arguments and

- $\mathscr{C} \subseteq \mathscr{A} \times \mathscr{A}$ is an irreflexive and symmetric conflict relation,

- $\mathscr{H} \subseteq \mathscr{A} \times \mathscr{C}$: $(A, (B, D))$ stands for "A claims that D is preferred to B",

- if $(A, (B, D)), (A', (D, B)) \in \mathscr{H}$ then $(A, A'), (A', A) \in \mathscr{C}$.

Example 6.13. (Borrowed from [21])

Let $\langle \mathscr{A}, \mathscr{C}, \mathscr{H} \rangle$ be an extended argumentation framework with

- $\mathscr{A} = \{A, B, D, D', E\}$,
- $\mathscr{C} = \{(A, B), (B, A), (D, D'), (D', D)\}$ and
- $\mathscr{H} = \{(D, (B, A)), (D', (A, B)), (E, (D, D'))\}$.

Given that the argument E claims that $D' \succ D$ and E is not defeated we have that D' *Def* D. Consequently, $B \succ A$, so B *Def* A. The set of acceptable arguments is $\{E, D', B\}$.

6.4.6 Preference-Based Argumentation Framework with Fuzzy Preference Relation

Existing preference-based argumentation frameworks rely on a crisp preference relation over the set of arguments. However, one may need to quantify the truth of the preferences. So, instead of specifying that an argument A is preferred to another argument B, we specify how much the statement "A is preferred to B" is true. This degree may also be considered as an intensity of preference. Kaci and Labreuche [15, 16] developed a valued preference-based argumentation framework which is based on a fuzzy preference relation in addition to the conflict relation. A fuzzy preference relation over $\mathscr{A} \times \mathscr{A}$ is a function $P : \mathscr{A} \times \mathscr{A} \rightarrow [0, 1]$. $P(A, B)$ is the degree of credibility of the statement "A is strictly preferred to B". $P(A, B) = 1$ means that the previous statement is certainly validated, $P(A, B) = 0$ means that the previous statement is certainly non-validated, and $P(A, B) = .5$ means that it is unknown whether the previous statement is validated or not.

We suppose that we directly work on P, and not on a fuzzy preference relation R which evaluates the degree of credibility of the statement "A is at least as preferred as B". In fact P is induced by R in order to evaluate "strict" preferences. Actually, P is a fuzzy strict preference relation. We simply speak about a fuzzy preference relation. See Section 2.3.

Definition 6.15 (Valued preference-based argumentation framework). [15, 16]

A valued preference-based argumentation framework is a three-tuple $VPAF =$

$\langle \mathscr{A}, \mathscr{C}, P \rangle$ where $\mathscr{A}$ is a finite set of arguments, $\mathscr{C}$ is an irreflexive and symmetric conflict relation defined over $\mathscr{A} \times \mathscr{A}$ and P is a function defined from $\mathscr{A} \times \mathscr{A}$ to $[0, 1]$.

Given a conflict relation, the fuzzy preference relation allows us to quantify the defeat relation. Intuitively, the more the statement "A is strictly preferred to B" is true, the less is the strength of the defeat of B on A. Argumentation frameworks with varied-strength defeat relations have been recently developed.

Definition 6.16 (Argumentation framework with varied-strength defeats). [13] An argumentation framework with varied-strength defeats (AFV) is a three-tuple $\langle \mathscr{A}, Def, VDef \rangle$ where $\langle \mathscr{A}, Def \rangle$ is a Dung's argumentation framework and $VDef$ is a function defined from Def to $[0, 1]$.

Any bipolar linearly ordered scale with top, bottom and neutral elements can be used, as can also the unit interval $[0, 1]$. The parts of the scale above and below the neutral element are symmetric.

$VDef(A, B)$ is the degree of credibility of the statement "A defeats B". Values 0, .5 and 1 for $VDef(A, B)$ mean that the validity of the previous statement is certainly false, unknown and certainly true respectively.

We say that A *defeats* B w.r.t. $\langle \mathscr{A}, Def, VDef \rangle$ iff (A *Def* B and $VDef(A, B) > 0$). Therefore, the two situations where, for $A, B \in \mathscr{A}$, $not(A$ *Def* $B)$ and (A *Def* B but $VDef(A, B) = 0$) will be considered as equivalent.

Martínez et al. [20] offer a qualitative representation of a valued defeat relation where $VDef$ is represented by a (pre)order.

The representation theorem which holds between a standard preference-based argumentation framework and Dung's argumentation framework can also be translated in this framework.

Definition 6.17. [15, 16]
A valued preference-based argumentation framework $\langle \mathscr{A}, \mathscr{C}, P \rangle$ represents an argumentation framework with varied-strength defeats $\langle \mathscr{A}, Def, VDef \rangle$ iff $VDef = \mathscr{C}$ and

$$VDef(A, B) = 1 - P(B, A),$$

with $A \mathscr{C} B$, $B \mathscr{C} A$. Other $VDef(., .)$ are equal to 0.

Note that the Boolean condition $not(B \succ A)$ in Definition 6.4 is extended into the credibility value $1 - P(B, A)$.

A valued preference-based argumentation framework represents precisely one argumentation framework with varied-strength defeats and an argumentation framework with varied-strength defeats is represented by at least one valued preference-based argumentation framework [15, 16].

The extension of standard preference-based argumentation frameworks to deal with a fuzzy preference relation raises an important question regarding the computation of acceptable extensions in the new framework. The extensions of a valued preference-based argumentation framework are the acceptable extensions of the argumentation framework with the varied-strength defeats it represents.

Recall that the basic notions in Dung's framework to compute acceptable extensions are "defense" and "conflict-freeness". These two notions have been extended to deal with a valued defeat relation.

Definition 6.18 (Defense in AFV). [20]
Let $\langle \mathscr{A}, Def, VDef \rangle$ be an argumentation framework with varied-strength defeats. The set $\mathscr{S} \subseteq \mathscr{A}$ defends $A \in \mathscr{A}$ w.r.t. $\langle \mathscr{A}, Def, VDef \rangle$ iff for all $B \in \mathscr{A}$ such that B Def A and $VDef(B,A) > 0$, there exists $C \in \mathscr{S}$ with

$$C \text{ } Def \text{ } B \text{ and } VDef(C,B) \geq VDef(B,A).$$

That is, the defense provided by $\mathscr{S}$ in favor of A is successful if the defeat of C on B is stronger than or equal to the defeat of B on A.

We can see from the above definition that if a set of arguments $\mathscr{S}$ defends an argument A w.r.t. $\langle \mathscr{A}, Def, VDef \rangle$, then $\mathscr{S}$ also defends A w.r.t. $\langle \mathscr{A}, Def \rangle$. This implies that there are less situations where a defense holds with $\langle \mathscr{A}, Def, VDef \rangle$ than with $\langle \mathscr{A}, Def \rangle$.

Regarding the notion of conflict-freeness, the authors of [20] do not consider the strength of defeats and simply use conflict-freeness defined in Dung's framework. On the other hand, the strength of defeats has been considered in [13] where a set of arguments is α-conflict-free if the strength of defeat relations between arguments of the set sum up to no more than α. Therefore, α represents an inconsistency tolerance degree.

Definition 6.19 (α-conflict-free). [13]
Let $\langle \mathscr{A}, Def, VDef \rangle$ be an argumentation framework with varied-strength defeats. $\mathscr{S} \subseteq \mathscr{A}$ is α-conflict-free w.r.t. $\langle \mathscr{A}, Def, VDef \rangle$ iff

$$\sum_{A,B \in \mathscr{S}} VDef(A,B) \leq \alpha.$$

When $\alpha = 0$, Definition 6.19 reduces to the conflict-freeness of Dung's framework.

From the concepts of defense and conflict-free defined above, acceptable extensions can be defined in a similar way as that for the Boolean case.

Example 6.14. (Borrowed from [16])
Let $\langle \mathscr{A}, \mathscr{C}, P \rangle$ be a preference-based argumentation framework with a fuzzy preference relation with $\mathscr{A} = \{A,B,C,D\}$, $\mathscr{C} = \{(A,B),(B,A),(C,B),(B,C),(A,D),(D,A),(C,D),(D,C)\}$, $P(B,A) = 1, P(A,B) = 0, P(D,C) = 1, P(C,D) = 0$ and all other values of $P(.,.)$ are .5. We have $VDef(D,C) = 1$, $VDef(C,B) = .5$, $VDef(B,C) = .5$,

$VDef(B,A) = 1$, $VDef(A,D) = .5$ and $VDef(D,A) = .5$. The other values of $VDef$ vanish. The defeat relations and their strengths are depicted in Figure 6.3.

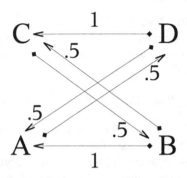

Fig. 6.3 An argumentation framework with varied-strength defeats

We fix $\alpha = 0$. There are two maximal (for set inclusion) conflict-free sets of arguments, $\mathscr{S}_1 = \{A,C\}$ and $\mathscr{S}_2 = \{B,D\}$. However, $\{A,C\}$ is not admissible since the defeat of B on A ($VDef(B,A) = 1$) is stronger than the defense that $\mathscr{S}_1$ can provide. In fact, we have $VDef(C,B) = .5$.

Besides the interest in using a fuzzy preference relation in argumentation frameworks, this relation also allows us to refine standard preference-based argumentation frameworks. More precisely, recall that in preference-based argumentation frameworks we have

$$(A \ Def \ B) \text{ iff } (A \ \mathscr{C} \ B, B \ \mathscr{C} \ A \text{ and } not(B \succ A)).$$

Then, $A \ Def \ B$ holds when $A \succ B$, $A \sim B$ or $A \approx B$. One may consider that the defeat of A on B is stronger if it holds with $A \succ B$ rather than with $A \sim B$ or $A \approx B$. The following example illustrates this idea.

Example 6.15.
Consider the original version of Example 6.14 given in [11]. Let $\langle \mathscr{A}, \mathscr{C}, \succeq \rangle$ be a preference-based argumentation framework with $\mathscr{A} = \{A, B, C, D\}$ and $\mathscr{C} = \{(A,B), (B,A), (C,B), (B,C), (A,D), (D,A), (C,D), (D,C)\}$ and $B \succ A$, $D \succ C$. Dung's argumentation framework represented by $\langle \mathscr{A}, \mathscr{C}, \succeq \rangle$ is depicted in Figure 6.4.

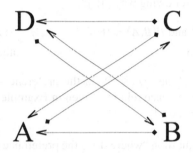

Fig. 6.4 Dung's argumentation framework represented by $\langle \mathscr{A}, \mathscr{C}, \succeq \rangle$

There are two stable extensions, $\mathscr{S}_1 = \{A, C\}$ and $\mathscr{S}_2 = \{B, D\}$. The authors of [11] have noticed that $\mathscr{S}_1$ should not be considered as a stable extension as each argument in $\mathscr{S}_1$ is less preferred to at least one argument in $\mathscr{S}_2$. In fact, we have $B \succ A$ and $D \succ C$. Therefore, $\mathscr{S}_2$ should be considered the only stable extension as it is preferred to $\mathscr{S}_1$.

Kaci and Labreuche [16] noticed that the problem of discarding $\mathscr{S}_1$ from the set of stable extensions is deeper than the preference relation over arguments considered individually. In fact, the preference relation over arguments together with the conflict relation lead to varied levels in the way $\mathscr{S}_1$ and $\mathscr{S}_2$ defend their arguments. More precisely, C in $\mathscr{S}_1$ defends A against the defeat from B. Similarly, D in $\mathscr{S}_2$

defends B against the defeat from C. However, these two situations are not similar. In the first situation, one may consider that the defense is not so strong since the defeating argument B is strictly preferred to A while there is no evidence of relative strength between C and B. On the other hand, in the second situation, one may consider that the defense is stronger since the defender D is strictly preferred to C and there is no evidence of relative strength between C and B. From this analysis, it is concluded that $\mathscr{S}_1$ does not sufficiently defend its elements.

Therefore, Example 6.15 suggests that the defeat relation $A \; Def \; B$ defined by $(A \; \mathscr{C} \; B, B \; \mathscr{C} \; A$ and $A \succ B)$ is stronger than the defeat relation $A' \; Def \; B'$ defined by $(A' \; \mathscr{C} B', B' \; \mathscr{C} \; A'$ and $(A' \approx B'$ or $A' \sim B'))$. In order to get this result, a preference-based argumentation framework with a fuzzy preference relation $\langle \mathscr{A}, \mathscr{C}, P \rangle$ is associated with a preference-based argumentation framework $\langle \mathscr{A}, \mathscr{C}, \succeq \rangle$ such that P is constructed from $\succeq$ in the following way [15]:

$$P(A,B) = 1 \text{ and } P(B,A) = 0 \qquad\qquad \text{if } A \succ B, \qquad (6.1)$$
$$P(A,B) = .5 \qquad\qquad\qquad\qquad\qquad \text{otherwise.}$$

We can check that the resulting $\langle \mathscr{A}, \mathscr{C}, P \rangle$ is the preference-based argumentation framework with a fuzzy preference relation given in Example 6.14. The unique acceptable extension is $\mathscr{S}_2 = \{B, D\}$.

In this framework, the question "where does the preference relation come from?" is also raised. As in standard preference-based argumentation frameworks, we can imagine different ways to compute a fuzzy preference relation over $\mathscr{A} \times \mathscr{A}$. The preference relation presented in Subsection 6.4.2 and computed from weighted propositional logic formulas can be extended to the fuzzy case as follows [15]:

$$P(A,B) = \begin{cases} 0 & \text{if } level_\Sigma(A) < level_\Sigma(B) \\ level_\Sigma(A) - level_\Sigma(B) & \text{if } level_\Sigma(A) \geq level_\Sigma(B) \end{cases}.$$

This fuzzy preference relation induces the following valued defeat relation:

$$VDef(A,B) = \begin{cases} 1 & \text{if } level_\Sigma(A) > level_\Sigma(B) \\ 1 + level_\Sigma(A) - level_\Sigma(B) & \text{if } level_\Sigma(A) \leq level_\Sigma(B) \end{cases}.$$

Intuitively, $VDef$ means that the defeat $Def(A,B)$ is certainly true when the level of A is strictly greater than the level of B. On the other hand, if A defeats a stronger argument B then the more B is stronger than A, the less is the defeat $VDef(A,B)$.

6.5 Higher Use of Preferences in Preference-Based Argumentation Frameworks

The role of preferences in existing preference-based argumentation frameworks is limited to determining which argument is stronger in a conflict relation. However, preferences may have a greater role and refine the output of a preference-based argumentation framework. This problem was first advocated in [11], where the authors use Example 6.15 to claim that some extensions should be removed given the preference relation at hand. For this purpose, they focus on stable extensions and define super-stable extensions which are the preferred stable extensions. In the previous subsection we have shown that preference-based argumentation frameworks with a fuzzy preference relation are able to solve the problem raised by Example 6.15. Another way to tackle this problem is to keep all acceptable extensions and rank-order them w.r.t. the preference relation $\succeq$.

The question now is how to use the preference relation over the set of arguments in order to rank-order the acceptable extensions. This question raises two questions:

(1) Should we use the preference relation as initially provided?
(2) How do we compare sets of arguments?

The following example illustrates which kind of preference relation is suitable.

Example 6.16. [14]
Let $\langle \mathscr{A}, \mathscr{C}, \succeq \rangle$ with $\mathscr{A} = \{A, B, C, D, E, F\}$, $\mathscr{C} = \{(A,D), (D,A), (B,C), (C,B), (B,F), (F,B), (D,E), (E,D), (A,F), (F,A), (C,E), (E,C), (A,E), (E,A), (C,F), (F,C), (C,D), (D,C), (D,F), (F,D), (B,E), (E,B)\}$. $\succeq$ is defined by $E \succ B \succ A$ and $F \succ D$. We have three stable extensions, $S_1 = \{A, C\}$, $S_2 = \{B, D\}$ and $S_3 = \{E, F\}$. Figure 6.5 depicts the stable extensions and the partial preorder $\succeq$. An arrow from an argument to another argument represents that the former is strictly preferred to the latter.

Let us first compare S_1, S_2 and S_3 w.r.t. the partial preorder $\succeq$. Consider a preference semantics between sets which states that "S_i is preferred to S_j if and only if any argument in S_j is strictly less preferred w.r.t. $\succeq$ to at least one argument in S_i". Let $>_1$ be the preference relation over $2^{\mathscr{A}} \times 2^{\mathscr{A}}$ w.r.t. this semantics. We have that $S_3 >_1 S_2$ since $E \succ B$ and $F \succ D$. On the other hand, S_1 is incomparable to both S_2 and S_3. However, one may consider that S_3 is preferred to S_1 as $E \succ A$ while C is incomparable to both E and F. Similarly, S_2 is preferred to S_1 since $B \succ A$ while C is incomparable to both B and D. Therefore, we have $S_3 >_1 S_2 >_1 S_1$. The transitivity of $>_1$ is intuitively meaningful since there is only one "step" from E to B while there are two steps from E to A in the partial preorder $\succeq$.

Counting the length of the preferences path and ignoring incomparability in a partial preorder is known in preference representation as "linearization" of the partial preorder, which means that a complete preorder consistent with the partial preorder is computed. Based on this idea, we use insights from preference representation. In particular, we compute a unique complete preorder consistent with $\succeq$ following the

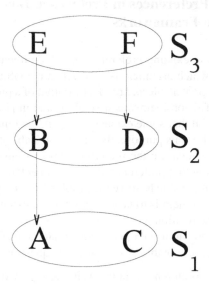

Fig. 6.5 The partial preorder $\succeq$ and the stable extensions of $\langle \mathscr{A}, \mathscr{C}, \succeq \rangle$

minimal and maximal specificity principles. We informally explain the computation of the unique complete preorder w.r.t. these principles. We refer the reader to Section 3.4 for a formal description. Let $\succeq$ be a partial preorder and $\succeq_* = (E_1, \cdots, E_n)$ be its unique associated complete preorder. Recall that the lower k is, the more preferred are arguments in E_k. Let $\succ$ be the strict preference relation associated with $\succeq$.

1. Following the minimal specificity principle, each argument is considered as *preferred* as possible in the preorder, i.e., in the lowest possible rank k. This method is based on the principle that an argument is satisfactory unless the contrary is stated. The resulting preorder is denoted by $\succeq_h = (E_1, \cdots, E_n)$. We put in E_1 the arguments which are not dominated w.r.t. $\succ$. E_2 is the set of the arguments which are only dominated by the arguments in E_1, and so on.

2. Following the maximal specificity principle, each argument is put as *low* as possible in the preorder, i.e., in the greatest possible rank k. This method is based on the principle that an argument is not satisfactory unless the contrary is stated. The resulting preorder is denoted by $\succeq_l = (E'_1, \cdots, E'_m)$. We put in E'_m the arguments

which do not dominate any other argument w.r.t. $\succ$. E'_{m-1} is the set of arguments which only dominate the arguments in E'_m, and so on.

Example 6.17. (Example 6.16 continued)
We have $\succeq$: $E \succ B, B \succ A, F \succ D$.

We first compute $\succeq_l$. We have $E_1 = \{C, E, F\}$. The arguments which are dominated by arguments in E_1 only are B and D. So $E_2 = \{B, D\}$. We remove $E \succ B$ and $F \succ D$ since they are satisfied. So we now have $B \succ A$. Only A is dominated by arguments in E_2, so $E_3 = \{A\}$. Therefore $\succeq_l = (\{C, E, F\}, \{B, D\}, \{A\})$.

Let us now compute $\succeq_h$. We have $E'_3 = \{A, C, D\}$. The arguments which only dominate the arguments in E'_3 are B and F. So $E'_2 = \{B, F\}$. We remove $B \succ A$ and $F \succ D$ since they are satisfied. So we have $E \succ B$. E is the only argument which dominates arguments in E'_2. So $E'_1 = \{E\}$. Therefore $\succeq_h = (\{E\}, \{B, F\}, \{A, C, D\})$.

Recall that the aim is to rank-order the acceptable extensions. This is a three-step process:

1. compute the acceptable extensions of a preference-based argumentation framework $\langle \mathscr{A}, \mathscr{C}, \succeq \rangle$; let $\mathscr{E}$ be this set,

2. compute a complete preorder $\succeq_*$ ($\succeq_h$ or $\succeq_l$) consistent with $\succeq$,

3. rank-order the sets in $\mathscr{E}$ given $\succeq_*$.

As in preference representation, comparing two sets of arguments Σ_1 and Σ_2 turns to compare $\Sigma_1 \setminus \Sigma_2$ and $\Sigma_2 \setminus \Sigma_1$; otherwise we may obtain undesirable results.

Example 6.18. (Borrowed from [14])
Consider a preference-based argumentation framework $\langle \mathscr{A}, \mathscr{C}, \succeq \rangle$ with $\mathscr{A} = \{A, B, C, D\}$, $\mathscr{C} = \{(B, D), (D, B)\}$ and $A \succ D$, $B \succ C$. Dung's argumentation framework $\langle \mathscr{A}, Def \rangle$ represented by $\langle \mathscr{A}, \mathscr{C}, \succeq \rangle$ is defined by $B\ Def\ D$ and $D\ Def\ B$. We have two preferred extensions, $P_1 = \{A, B, C\}$ and $P_2 = \{A, C, D\}$. We have that $\succeq_h = \succeq_l = (\{A, B\}, \{C, D\})$. Suppose that $\Sigma_1 \subseteq \mathscr{A}$ is preferred to $\Sigma_2 \subseteq \mathscr{A}$ if and only if any argument in Σ_1 is strictly preferred to any argument in Σ_2 w.r.t. $\succeq_h$ (or $\succeq_l$). Following this semantics, P_1 and P_2 are incomparable since no argument in P_1 is strictly preferred to any argument in P_2 and vice versa. However, this is rather an undesirable result since the incomparability here is due to the fact that P_1 and P_2 share some arguments. If we only focus on non-common arguments, i.e., $P_1 \setminus P_2$ and $P_2 \setminus P_1$, then we have that P_1 is preferred to P_2 since $P_1 \setminus P_2 = \{B\}$, $P_2 \setminus P_1 = \{D\}$ and $B \succ_h D$ (also $B \succ_l D$).

One may imagine different ways to compare sets of arguments. In [14] we have translated preference semantics from propositional logic to argumentation theory, as already done in extended value-based argumentation frameworks (see Subsection 6.4.4). We present here a more complete definition.

Definition 6.20 (Comparison semantics).
Let Σ_1 and Σ_2 be two subsets of $\mathscr{A}$. Let $\succeq$ be a complete preorder over $\mathscr{A} \times \mathscr{A}$.

- Σ_1 is at least as strongly preferred as Σ_2, denoted by $\Sigma_1 \geq_{st} \Sigma_2$, iff $\Sigma_2 \subseteq \Sigma_1$, or

$$\forall A \in \Sigma_1 \setminus \Sigma_2, \forall B \in \Sigma_2 \setminus \Sigma_1, A \succeq B.$$

- Σ_1 is at least as optimistically preferred as Σ_2, denoted by $\Sigma_1 \geq_{opt} \Sigma_2$, iff $\Sigma_2 \subseteq \Sigma_1$, or

$$\forall A \in \max(\Sigma_1 \setminus \Sigma_2, \succeq), \forall B \in \max(\Sigma_2 \setminus \Sigma_1, \succeq), A \succeq B.$$

- Σ_1 is at least as pessimistically preferred as Σ_2, denoted by $\Sigma_1 \geq_{pes} \Sigma_2$, iff $\Sigma_2 \subseteq \Sigma_1$, or

$$\forall A \in \min(\Sigma_1 \setminus \Sigma_2, \succeq), \forall B \in \min(\Sigma_2 \setminus \Sigma_1, \succeq), A \succeq B.$$

Σ_1 and Σ_2 are equally preferred w.r.t. some semantics $\triangleright$ ($\triangleright \in \{st, opt, pes\}$) if and only if $\Sigma_1 \succeq_\triangleright \Sigma_2$ and $\Sigma_2 \succeq_\triangleright \Sigma_1$. Σ_1 is strictly preferred to Σ_2 w.r.t. $\triangleright$ ($\triangleright \in \{st, opt, pes\}$) if and only if $\Sigma_1 \succeq_\triangleright \Sigma_2$ holds but $\Sigma_2 \succeq_\triangleright \Sigma_1$ does not.

Example 6.19. (Borrowed from [14])
We first consider $\succeq_h$. We have

- $S_3 >_{st} S_2$ and $S_3 >_{st} S_1$ while S_1 and S_2 are incomparable w.r.t. $\geq_{st}$,
- $S_3 >_{opt} S_2$, $S_1 >_{opt} S_2$ and $S_1 =_{opt} S_3$,
- $S_3 >_{pes} S_2 >_{pes} S_1$. We can also check that $S_3 >_{pes} S_1$ holds.

Let us now consider $\succeq_l$. Then,

- $S_3 >_{st} S_2 >_{st} S_1$,
- $S_3 >_{opt} S_2 >_{opt} S_1$. We can also check that $S_3 >_{opt} S_1$ holds,
- $S_3 >_{pes} S_2$, $S_3 >_{pes} S_1$ and $S_1 =_{pes} S_2$.

6.6 Conclusion

Preferences play an important role in solving conflicts between arguments. Preferences can be present in preference-based argumentation frameworks in different ways. This had led to several preference-based argumentation frameworks based on prioritized information, values, fuzzy preference relations, etc.

So far, preference-based argumentation frameworks with symmetric conflict relation have been considered as a special case of preference-based argumentation frameworks [18, 19]. Recently, it has been argued that existing preference-based argumentation frameworks suffer from flaws as they may violate the conflict-freeness of acceptable extensions. We have shown that a symmetric conflict relation should not be considered as a special case of an attack relation in preference-based argumentation frameworks but as the right way to model incompatibility between arguments in order to faithfully represent Dung's argumentation framework. It allows us to satisfy conflict-freeness of acceptable extensions.

If we are provided with an asymmetric attack relation and a preference relation, a preference-based argumentation framework with a symmetric conflict relation can be defined which properly uses together these two notions.

Besides, a symmetric conflict relation is more suitable for modeling incompatibility between arguments, in particular when the latter cannot be described in terms of an attack relation, e.g., natural language processing.

Inspired by conditional logics for preference representation (see Subsection 3.4), in which sets of outcomes are compared following different semantics, we argued for greater use of preferences in the output of preference-based argumentation frameworks. We proposed different ways to rank-order the acceptable extensions.

References

1. Amgoud, L., Cayrol C.: A reasoning model based on the production of acceptable arguments. Annals of Mathematics and Artificial Intelligence **34**, 197–216 (2002)
2. Amgoud, L., Cayrol C.: Inferring from inconsistency in preference-based argumentation frameworks. International Journal of Approximate Reasoning **29(2)**, 125–169 (2002)
3. Amgoud, L., Cayrol, C., LeBerre, D.: Comparing arguments using preference orderings for argument-based reasoning. In: Manaris, B., Marquis, P. (eds.), 8th International Conference on Tools with Artificial Intelligence, pp. 400-403. IEEE, (1996)
4. Amgoud, L., Dimopoulos, Y., Moraitis, P.: A unified and general framework for argumentation-based negotiation. In: Durfee, E.H., Yokoo, M., Huhns, M.N., Sheory, O. (eds.), 6th International Joint Conference on Autonomous Agents and Multiagent Systems, pp. 158. IFAAMAS, (2007)
5. Amgoud, L., Kaci, S.: An argumentation framework for merging conflicting knowledge bases. International Journal of Approximate Reasoning **45(2)**, 321–340 (2007)
6. Amgoud, L., Prade, H.: Using arguments for making and explaining decisions. Artificial Intelligence **173(3-4)**, 413–436 (2009)
7. Amgoud, L., Vesic, S.: Repairing preference-based argumentation frameworks. In: Boutilier, G. (eds.), 21st International Joint Conference on Artificial Intelligence, pp. 665-670. (2009)
8. Bench-Capon, T.J.M..: Persuasion in practical argument using value-based argumentation frameworks. Journal of Logic and Computation **13(3)**, 429–448 (2003)
9. Benferhat, S., Dubois, D., Prade, H.: Argumentative inference in uncertain and inconsistent knowledge bases. In: Heckerman, D., Mamdani, E.H. (eds.), 9th Annual Conference on Uncertainty in Artificial Intelligence, pp. 411-419. Morgan Kaufmann, (1993)
10. Benferhat, S., Dubois, D., Prade, H.: Some syntactic approaches to the handling of inconsistent knowledge bases: A comparative study Part 2: The prioritized case. Logic at work **24**, 473–511 (1998)
11. Dimopoulos, Y., Moraitis, P., Amgoud, L.: Extending argumentation to make good decisions. In: Rossi, F., Tsoukiàs, A. (eds.), 1st International Conference on Algorithmic Decision Theory, pp. 225-236. Springer, (2009)
12. Dung, P.M.: On the acceptability of arguments and its fundamental role in nonmonotonic reasoning, logic programming and n-person games. Artificial Intelligence **77**, 321–357 (1995)
13. Dunne, P.E., Hunter, A., McBurney, P., Parsons, S., Wooldridge, M.: Inconsistency tolerance in weighted argument systems. In: Sierra, C., Castelfranchi, C., Decker, K.S., Sichman, J.S. (eds.), 8th International Joint Conference on Autonomous Agents and Multiagent Systems, pp. 851-858. IFAAMAS, (2009)
14. Kaci, S.: Refined preference-based argumentation frameworks. In: Baroni, P., Giacomin, M., Simari, G. (eds.), 3rd International Conference on Computational Models of Argument, pp. 299-310. IOP Press, (2010)
15. Kaci, S., Labreuche, C.: Argumentation framework with fuzzy preference relations. In: Hüllermeier, E., Kruse, R., Hoffmann, F. (eds.), 13th Conference on Information Processing and Management of Uncertainty in Knowledge-Based Systems Conference, pp. 554-563. Springer, (2010)

16. Kaci, S., Labreuche, C.: Preference-based argumentation framework with varied-preference intensity. In: Coelho, H., Studer, R., Wooldridge, M. (eds.), 19th European Conference on Artificial Intelligence, pp. 1003-1004. IOP Press, (2010)
17. Kaci, S., van der Torre, L.: Preference-based argumentation: Arguments supporting multiple values. International Journal of Approximate Reasoning **48**, 730–751 (2008)
18. Kaci, S., Van der Torre, L., Weydert, E.: On the acceptability of incompatible arguments. In: Mellouli, K. (eds.), 9th European Conferences on Symbolic and Quantitative Approaches to Reasoning with Uncertainty, pp. 247-258. Springer, (2007)
19. Kaci, S., Van der Torre, L., Weydert, E.: Acyclic argumentation: Attack = conflict+ preference. In: Brewka, G., Coradeschi, S., Perini, A., Traverso, P. (eds.), 17th European Conference on Artificial Intelligence, pp. 725-726. IOS Press, (2006)
20. Martínez, D.C., García, A.J., Simari, G.R.: An abstract argumentation framework with varied-strength attacks. In: Brewka, G., Lang, J. (eds.), 11th International Conference on Principles of Knowledge Representation and Reasoning, pp. 135-144. AAAI Press, (2008)
21. Modgil, S.: Reasoning about preferences in argumentation frameworks. Artificial Intelligence **173(9-10)**, 901–934 (2009)
22. Perelman, C.: Justice, Law and Argument. Reidel, Dordrecht (1980)
23. Prakken, H.: Coherence and flexibility in dialogue games for argumentation. Journal of Logic and Computation **15(6)**, 1009–1040 (2005)
24. Simari, G.R., Loui, R.P.: A mathematical treatment of defeasible reasoning and its implementation. Artificial Intelligence **53**, 125–157 (1992)
25. Prakken, H., Sartor, G.: Argument-based extended logic programming with defeasible priorities. Journal of Applied Non-Classical Logics **7**, 25–75 (1997)
26. Stolzenburg, F., García, A.J., Chesñevar, C.I., Simari, G.R.: Computing generalized specificity. Journal of Applied Non-Classical Logics **13(1)**, 87–113 (2003)

Chapter 7
Preferences in Database Queries

7.1 Introduction

Dealing with preferences is an important issue in database querying. Suppose that a user is looking for a hotel in Paris. Due to the large number of hotels in this city, providing more knowledge about the user's preferences in the query will help us eliminate irrelevant hotels and focus only on the relevant ones. Preferences act as filters which return relevant answers rank-ordered according to their satisfaction level.

The database community has perceived in a timely way, the importance of preferences in queries. The integration of preferences in database queries, however, comes with many complex issues regarding the representation of and reasoning about preferences. This work was originated by Lacroix and Lavency [20]. They extend classical database queries with preferences in such a way that the desired tuples are those which first satisfy the classical query and then the preferences at hand. Afterwards, several approaches were proposed in order to express complex preferences. In particular, the skyline operator [3] compares pairs of tuples w.r.t. different dimensions. The best tuples are those which are not dominated by any other tuple in any dimension. This is the Pareto dominance. However, the skyline operator is not expressive enough to support many natural preferences, e.g., conditional preferences. Kiessling [19] formulates preferences in database queries by means of preference constructors and composition operators. The result of a query is then retrieved using the BMO ("Best Matches Only") operator, which returns tuples which are closest to the user's preferences. Chomicki [9, 10] generalized this proposal and represents preferences by a general logical formula. The associated preference over tuples is a partial order. The winnow operator selects the best tuples, which are those tuples that are not dominated w.r.t. this order. In the same line of research, the partial order is represented using a CP-net by Brafman and Domshlak [6] and an incomplete CP-net by Ciaccia [11]. Here also, the best tuples are those which are not dominated by any other tuples w.r.t. the associated order.

151

While the CP-net-based approaches are explicitly based on comparative preference statements obeying ceteris paribus semantics, it turns out that Chomicki's approach can also be encoded by comparative preference statements obeying strong semantics. Based on conditional logics for preference representation, da Silva Neves and Kaci [17] formulate preferences in database queries using comparative preference statements obeying different semantics. The associated preference relation is a total preorder and the best tuples are those which are not dominated by any other tuple. This framework is also a ranking approach. It offers an iterative version of the winnow operator already advocated by Torlone and Ciaccia [21].

The above approaches offer a qualitative representation of preferences. Quantitative preferences have also been used in database queries [1, 13, 14, 16]. For example, PREFER is a system in which quantitative preferences are obtained by weighting the importance of attributes. Attribute domains are also assumed to be numeric. Therefore, a weighted aggregation function is used to compute a score for each tuple. A tuple is preferred if its score is higher. Chang [8] and Motro [18] assume that numerical information about values of the tuples' domains is available (membership function in [8] and "distances" between values in [18]).

In this chapter we give an overview of the above-mentioned approaches with a particular emphasis on qualitative approaches which use compact languages for preference representation.

7.2 Preliminaries

A relational schema is denoted by $\mathscr{R}(A)$, where $\mathscr{R}$ is the name of the relation and $A = A_1, \cdots, A_l$ is a set of l attributes. Each attribute A_i takes its values in a domain denoted by $Dom(A_i)$. A tuple t over a schema $\mathscr{R}(A)$ associates with each attribute A_i in A a value taken from $Dom(A_i)$. The notation $t.A_i$ refers to the value given to the attribute A_i in the tuple t. An instance r over $\mathscr{R}$ is a nonempty finite set of tuples over $\mathscr{R}(A)$. In Table 7.1 we give the correspondences between database terminology and the one used in the previous chapters.

Table 7.1 Database terminology

Database terminology	Usual terminology
attribute	variable
schema	set of variables
tuple	outcome
relation	feasible outcomes

Example 7.1. Let $Meal(dish, wine)$ be a relational schema with $Dom(dish) = \{meat, fish\}$ and $Dom(wine) = \{red, white, rosé\}$. Let $r = Dom(dish) \times$

$Dom(wine) = \{meat - red, meat - white, meat - rosé, fish - red, fish - white, fish - rosé\}$.

7.3 Database Queries with Preferences

Lacroix and Lavency [20] extend classical database queries with preferences. Given the set of tuples returned by the classical query, preferences select those tuples which are desired.

Example 7.2.
Let $\mathscr{R}(dish, wine, dessert)$ be a relational schema modeling meals such that $Dom(dish)$ = $\{fish, meat\}$, $Dom(wine)$ = $\{white, red\}$ and $Dom(dessert) = \{cake, ice\_cream\}$. Let $r = \{t_0, t_1, t_2, t_3, t_4, t_5, t_6, t_7\}$ be an instance of $\mathscr{R}$ with

$$t_0 : fish - white - ice\_cream, t_1 : fish - white - cake,$$
$$t_2 : fish - red - ice\_cream, t_3 : fish - red - cake,$$
$$t_4 : meat - white - ice\_cream, t_5 : meat - white - cake,$$
$$t_6 : meat - red - ice\_cream, t_7 : meat - red - cake.$$

Suppose that a user asks for *meat*-based meals and from among such meals, she prefers those which are composed of *red wine*. The main query selects *meat*-based meals; they are $t_4 : meat - white - ice\_cream$, $t_5 : meat - white - cake$, $t_6 : meat - red - ice\_cream$ and $t_7 : meat - red - cake$. Now, the preferred meals are t_6 and t_7 as they are composed of *red* wine. If there are no meals composed of both *meat* and *red* wine then the answer to the above query will be *meat*-based meals with another kind of wine. For example, if we were provided with $r' = \{t_0, t_1, t_2, t_3, t_4, t_5\}$ then the preferences are void. The answer to the query is $\{t_4, t_5\}$. Now, if $r'' = \{t_0, t_1, t_2, t_3\}$ then the answer to the classical query is empty. Consequently, the preferences are also void.

This approach also allows for nested preferences, i.e., some preferences are more important than others. For example, the user may prefer *meat*-based meals which are composed of *red* wine and *cake*. But if such meals are not possible then *meat*-based meals with *red* wine but not *cake* are preferred to *meat*-based meals with *cake* but not *red* wine.

7.4 Database Queries with the Skyline Operator

The skyline operator [3] compares the tuples w.r.t. all the attributes. A tuple t_1 is preferred to (or dominates) a tuple t_2 if and only if t_1 is at least as preferred as t_2

w.r.t. all attributes and strictly preferred w.r.t. at least one attribute. This is Pareto dominance. The skyline operator returns all the tuples which are not dominated by any other tuple.

Example 7.3. Consider the relation schema $Car(id, model, price)$ given in Table 7.2. Suppose that a user would prefer the cheapest car given a model. The skyline query

Table 7.2 Example of a relational database

id	model	price
01	206	11500
02	306	15900
03	BMW	21400
04	306	13200
05	BMW	23000

is written as SELECT * FROM Car SKYLINE OF model DIFF, price MIN. The result of the query is (01,206,11500), (04,306,13200) and (03,BMW,21400).

Although the skyline approach is mainly based on a numerical scale of the domains, we can conceptually extend it to qualitative preferences over non-numerical domains.

Example 7.4. (Example 7.1 continued)
Let $\succeq_1$ and $\succeq_2$ be two preference relations defined, respectively, as *meat* $\succ_1$ *fish* and *red* $\succ_2$ *white* $\succ_2$ *rosé*. Let $\succeq_P$ be the preference relation representing Pareto dominance. We have

$$meat - red \succ_P meat - white, meat - white \succ_P meat - rosé,$$
$$meat - red \succ_P meat - rosé, meat - rosé \succ_P fish - rosé,$$
$$meat - red \succ_P fish - red, fish - red \succ_P fish - white,$$
$$meat - red \succ_P fish - white, fish - red \succ_P fish - rosé,$$
$$meat - red \succ_P fish - rosé, fish - white \succ_P fish - rosé.$$

The result of the skyline operator is $meat - red$.

Suppose now that the tuple $meat - red$ does not belong to r. Then, the result of the skyline operator is $meat - white$ and $fish - red$. These two tuples are incomparable because $meat - white$ is preferred to $fish - red$ w.r.t. the main dish ($meat \succ_1 fish$) but $fish - red$ is preferred to $meat - white$ w.r.t. the wine ($red \succ_2 white$).

Several algorithms have been developed to compute the result of the skyline operator. We refer the reader to [3, 10, 21] for further details.

It is recognized that Pareto dominance is not expressive enough to represent complex preferences. This is especially true when preferences need to express interactions between attributes. For example, the skyline operator cannot express that *white* wine is preferred when *fish* is served and *red* wine is preferred otherwise. To overcome this shortcoming, the skyline operator has been extended in order to support complex preferences. In the following subsections, we give an overview of the main approaches.

7.5 Database Queries with Preference Constructors

The pioneering work in the quest for expressing complex preferences in database queries was proposed by Kiessling [19]. A user's preferences are expressed by a partial order obtained by an algebraic formalism. Different ways have been proposed for constructing such an order by composing basic preferences. This order can also be obtained by an aggregation of partial orders by means of constructors, e.g., intersection, union, difference, and prioritized composition. These constructors will be further presented in the next subsection.

Given such a preference representation in database queries, the result of a query is the set of tuples which are not dominated w.r.t. the partial order at hand. This resembles the skyline operator. Kiessling calls his operator "Best Matches Only".

Torlone and Ciaccia [21] use an explicit partial order in database queries. Unlike Kiessling's approach, they compute the best tuples in an iterative way. More precisely, they compute the best tuples, which are those tuples that are not dominated by the partial order at hand. Then, they focus on the remaining tuples and compute the best among them w.r.t. the partial order, and so on.

Example 7.5. (Example 7.1 continued)
Let $\succeq$ be a partial order defined by $meat - red \succ meat - white$ and $fish - white \succ fish - red$. The best tuples are $meat - red$, $fish - white$, $meat - rosé$ and $fish - rosé$. The next best tuples are $meat - white$ and $fish - red$.

7.6 Database Queries with Logical Formulas

Chomicki [10] proposed a variant of Kiessling's approach. He represents the partial order in a concise, i.e., compact, way by means of a first-order logical formula denoted by $C(t_1, t_2)$[1] and called *a preference formula*. $C(t_1, t_2)$ defines a preference relation $\succ_C$ over $\mathscr{R}(A)$ in the following way:

$$t_1 \succ_C t_2 \text{ iff } C(t_1, t_2).$$

---

[1] Sometimes we write C for short.

Example 7.6. (Example 7.1 continued)
We have $r = Dom(dish) \times Dom(wine) = \{meat - red, meat - white, meat - rosé,$
$fish - red, fish - white, fish - rosé\}$.

Let $\succ_{C_1}$ be a preference relation over $Meal(dish, wine)$ defined by a preference formula C_1 as follows:

$$t \succ_{C_1} t' \text{ iff } ((t.dish = meat \land t.wine = red \land t'.dish = meat \land t'.wine = white) \lor$$
$$(t.dish = fish \land t.wine = white \land t'.dish = fish \land t'.wine = red)).$$

The preference relation $\succ_{C_1}$ is depicted in Figure 7.1a.

Let $\succ_{C_2}$ be a preference relation over $Meal(dish, wine)$ defined by a preference formula C_2 as follows:

$$t \succ_{C_2} t' \text{ iff } ((t.wine = red \land t'.wine = white) \lor$$
$$(t.dish = fish \ \land \ t.wine = white \ \land \ t'.dish = fish \ \land \ t'.wine = rosé) \lor$$
$$(t.dish = fish \land t.wine = rosé \land t'.dish = fish \land t'.wine = red)).$$

The preference relation $\succ_{C_2}$ is depicted in Figure 7.1b.

The task of computing the set of undominated tuples is accomplished by the winnow operator, denoted by $W_C(r)$, given an instance r and a preference formula C. $W_C(r)$ is defined as follows [10]:

$$W_C(r) = \{t_1 \mid \nexists t_2 \in r, t_2 \succ_C t_1\}.$$

Note that $W_C(r)$ corresponds to $\max(r, \succ_C)$.

Example 7.7. (Example 7.1 continued)
We have $W_{C_1}(r) = \{meat - red, fish - white, meat - rosé, fish - rosé\}$ and $W_{C_2}(r) = \{meat - red, meat - rosé\}$. Note that $W_{C_2}(r)$ is not empty although $\succ_{C_2}$ is cyclic.

Chomicki [10] also proposed two ways to compose preference relations: unidimensional and multidimensional compositions. In the former, preference relations over the same schema are composed producing a new preference relation over the same schema. In the latter preference relations over several schemas are composed producing a new preference relation over the Cartesian product of these schemas. For simplicity we will consider in this chapter unidimensional composition only. Examples of unidimensional composition are booelan (intersection, union and difference) and prioritized composition (called also lexicographical product).

Let $\succ_{C_1}$ and $\succ_{C_2}$ be two preference relations associated with the preference formulas C_1 and C_2, respectively. The intersection (or union, difference) of $\succ_{C_1}$ and $\succ_{C_2}$, denoted by $\succ_C = \succ_{C_1} \cap \succ_{C_2}$ (or $\succ_C = \succ_{C_1} \cup \succ_{C_2}$, $\succ_C = \succ_{C_1} - \succ_{C_2}$) is defined by the formula $C = C_1 \land C_2$ (or $C = C_1 \lor C_2$, $C = C_1 \land \neg C_2$). The prioritized composition $\succ_C$ of $\succ_{C_1}$ and $\succ_{C_2}$ giving priority to $\succ_{C_1}$ has the following reading: prefer according to $\succ_{C_2}$ unless $\succ_{C_1}$ is applicable. It is defined as

$$t_1 \succ_C t_2 \text{ iff } (t_1 \succ_{C_1} t_2) \vee ((t_1 \sim_{C_1} t_2) \wedge (t_1 \succ_{C_2} t_2)).$$

In this chapter we restrict ourselves to preference formulas which are constructed from atomic formulas using logical connectives $\wedge, \vee, \neg$. An atomic formula (or literal) has the form $A = v$ or $A \neq v$, where A is an attribute and v is a constant. This restriction is made without any loss of generality. In fact, preferences of the form "t is preferred to t' when $t.A < t'.A$" can be modeled in our setting by comparing all possible values of the attribute A. This also includes the case of preferences induced by skyline queries which state that a tuple t is preferred to a tuple t' when it is good or better w.r.t. all attributes and strictly better w.r.t. at least one attribute.

In order to compare Chomicki's framework to other frameworks, we need to standardize the notations. In Chomicki's approach, preference queries are based on a preference formula which is a first-order formula C such that t is preferred to t' if and only if $C(t,t')$. We know that any logical formula can be written in the form $C_1 \vee \cdots \vee C_l$, where each C_i is of the form $c_{i,1} \wedge \cdots \wedge c_{i,m}$, with $c_{i,j}$ an atomic formula. More precisely, $c_{i,j}$ has the form $A = v$ or $A \neq v$, where A is an attribute and v is a constant.

Lemma 7.1. *[17]*
Let C be a preference formula such that $C = C_1 \vee \cdots \vee C_l$. Then, $\succ_C = \succ_{C_1} \cup \cdots \cup \succ_{C_l}$.

Following Chapter 3, we denote a comparative preference statement by $p > q$, which expresses a preference for p over q, where p and q are formulas.

Given a formula $C = C_1 \vee \cdots \vee C_l$, we construct a set of comparative preference statements $\mathscr{P}_C = \{s_1 : p_1 > q_1, \cdots, s_l : p_l > q_l\}$ such that s_i is the name of the comparative preference statement and p_i (or q_i) is the part of C_i concerning the tuple t (or t'). More precisely, $s_i : p_i > q_i$ is built from C_i as follows:

- Recall that C_i is a first-order formula concerning two tuples t and t'. Let $S_t \subset \{c_{i,1}, \cdots, c_{i,m}\}$ be the set of atomic formulas in C_i concerning t.
- For each atomic formula $c_{i,j}$ in S_t we define $f(c_{i,j})$ as follows:

$$f(c_{i,j}) = \begin{cases} v_A & \text{if } c_{i,j} \text{ is of the form } A = v \\ \neg v_A & \text{if } c_{i,j} \text{ is of the form } A \neq v \end{cases}$$

When there is no ambiguity we omit A from v_A and $\neg v_A$.
- Then, $p_i = f(c_{i,1}) \wedge \cdots \wedge f(c_{i,m})$.

We define q_i in a similar way for t'.

Example 7.8. Consider again the preference formula C_1 given in Example 7.1. We have $t \succ_{C_1} t'$ iff $((t.dish = meat \wedge t.wine = red \wedge t'.dish = meat \wedge t'.wine = white) \vee (t.dish = fish \wedge t.wine = white \wedge t'.dish = fish \wedge t'.wine = red))$.
Then, $C_1 = C_{11} \vee C_{12}$, where

$C_{11} = (t.dish = meat) \wedge (t.wine = red) \wedge (t'.dish = meat) \wedge (t'.wine = white)$ and
$C_{12} = (t.dish = fish) \wedge (t.wine = white) \wedge (t'.dish = fish) \wedge (t'.wine = red)$.
So, $\mathscr{P}_{C_1} = \{s_1 : meat \wedge red > meat \wedge white, s_2 : fish \wedge white > fish \wedge red\}$.

Lemma 7.2. *[17]*
*Let $C = C_1 \vee \cdots \vee C_l$ be a preference formula and $\{(s_1) : p_1 > q_1, \cdots, (s_l) : p_l > q_l\}$
be the set of comparative preference statements constructed from C. Then, for $i =
1, \cdots, l$ and $\forall t, t'$ two tuples of an instance r of a relational schema $\mathscr{R}(A)$, we have*

$$t \succ_{C_i} t' \text{ iff } t \models p_i \text{ and } t' \models q_i.$$

Example 7.9. (Example 7.8 continued)
We can check that $t \succ_{C_{11}} t'$ iff $t \models meat \wedge red$ and $t' \models meat \wedge white$. Also, $t \succ_{C_{12}} t'$
iff $t \models fish \wedge white$ and $t' \models fish \wedge red$.

7.7 Database Queries with a CP-net

The standard interpretation of preferences of the form "prefer p to q" in the database
community is "*each tuple satisfying p is preferred to each tuple satisfying q*" [10].
This semantics corresponds to strong preferences in Chapter 3. As noticed in [2,
6], such semantics is too strong and may lead to cyclic preferences when several
comparative preference statements are dealt with.

Example 7.10. (Example 7.1 continued)
Let $\succ_{C_3}$ be defined over $Meal(dish, wine)$ by a preference formula C_3 defined as
follows:

$$t \succ_{C_3} t' \text{ iff } ((t.wine = red \wedge t'.wine \neq red) \vee$$
$$(t.dish = fish \wedge t.wine = white \wedge t'.dish = fish \wedge t'.wine \neq white)).$$

We have $\mathscr{P}_{C_3} = \{s_1 : red > \neg red, s_2 : fish \wedge white > fish \wedge \neg white\}$. Then, $\succ_{C_3} = \succ_{s_1}$
$\cup \succ_{s_2}$. Following s_1 we have

$$meat - red \succ_{s_1} meat - white, meat - red \succ_{s_1} meat - rosé,$$
$$meat - red \succ_{s_1} fish - white, meat - red \succ_{s_1} fish - rosé,$$
$$fish - red \succ_{s_1} meat - white, fish - red \succ_{s_1} meat - rosé,$$
$$fish - red \succ_{s_1} fish - white, fish - red \succ_{s_1} fish - rosé.$$

Following s_2 we have

$$fish - white \succ_{s_2} fish - red, fish - white \succ_{s_2} fish - rosé.$$

Since $\succ_{C_3} = \succ_{s_1} \cup \succ_{s_2}$ we have, therefore, both $fish - red \succ_{C_3} fish - white$ and
$fish - white \succ_{C_3} fish - red$.

It is worth noticing that the other preference semantics (i.e., optimistic, pessimistic, ceteris paribus) may also lead to inconsistent preferences. However, strong semantics has the most requirements; thus it and has a better "chance" of leading to inconsistency.

In order to overcome the above problem raised by the union composition, the authors of [6] proposed a weaker preference semantics based on ceteris paribus semantics together with CP-nets.

Example 7.11. (Borrowed from [17])
Let N be a CP-net over two attributes *dish* and *wine* depicted in Figure 7.2a., with $Dom(dish) = \{fish, meat\}$ and $Dom(wine) = \{white, red, rosé\}$. N is based on three preference statements: *fish* > *meat*, *fish* ∧ *white* > *fish* ∧ ¬*white* and *meat* ∧ *red* > *meat* ∧ ¬*red*. The first statement is an unconditional preference since *dish* is a root node. The other two statements are conditional preferences. An ordering over values of the attribute *wine* is given for each value of *dish*. In CP-net notation these preferences are written *fish* : *white* > ¬*white* and *meat* : *red* > ¬*red*, respectively. N induces the partial order depicted in Figure 7.2b.:

- *fish* − *white* ≻ *meat* − *white*, *fish* − *red* ≻ *meat* − *red* and *fish* − *rosé* ≻ *meat* − *rosé* (according to *fish* > *meat*).
- *fish* − *white* ≻ *fish* − *red*, *fish* − *white* ≻ *fish* − *rosé* (according to *fish* ∧ *white* > *fish* ∧ ¬*white*).
- *meat* − *red* ≻ *meat* − *white*, *meat* − *red* ≻ *meat* − *rosé* (according to *meat* ∧ *red* > *meat* ∧ ¬*red*).

Note, however, that the acyclicity of preference relations induced by an acyclic CP-net is due to the hierarchical structure of preferences, i.e., preferences over values of a child node depend on the values of its parent nodes. The use of ceteris paribus semantics without its being together with an acyclic CP-net does not guarantee the acyclicity of the associated preference relation.

Example 7.12. (Example 7.10 continued)
Following ceteris paribus semantics, s_1 leads to

$$fish - red \succ_{s_1} fish - white, fish - red \succ_{s_1} fish - rosé,$$
$$meat - red \succ_{s_1} meat - white, meat - red \succ_{s_1} meat - rosé$$

and s_2 leads to

$$fish - white \succ_{s_2} fish - red, fish - white \succ_{s_2} fish - rosé.$$

Therefore, we have both *fish* − *red* preferred to *fish* − *white* (following s_1) and *fish* − *white* preferred to *fish* − *red* (following s_2).

Although the CP-net approach guarantees acyclic preference relations, the computation of the winnow operator is, however, expensive from a computational point of view. This is because the winnow operator $(W_N(r) = \{t_1 \mid \nexists t_2 \in r, t_2 \succ_N t_1\})$ is based on pairwise comparisons, called dominance queries, between tuples which are NP-hard in CP-nets [5]. In order to overcome this computational limitation of CP-nets, the authors of [6] have weakened dominance queries into ordering queries. The idea consists of replacing the partial order $\succ_N$ associated with N with a complete order $\succ$ such that $\forall t_1, t_2 \in D_1 \times \cdots \times D_l$, if $t_1 \succ_N t_2$ then $t_1 \succ t_2$. Indeed, $\succ$ is one of the complete orders extending (or consistent with) $\succ_N$.

7.8 Database Queries with an Incomplete CP-net

Ciaccia [11] argued that the CP-net approach may lead to counter-intuitive results when the CP-net is incomplete. To illustrate this, we give the following example:

Example 7.13. (Borrowed from [11])
Consider a CP-net over three binary variables R, T and P, which respectively stand for *RestaurantType*, *Table* and *Price*. We have $Dom(R) = \{it, chn\}$ (Italian or Chinese), $Dom(T) = \{in, out\}$ (inside or outside) and $Dom(P) = \{low, high\}$. Let

$$r = \{it - in - low, it - in - high,$$
$$it - out - low, it - out - high,$$
$$chn - in - low, chn - in - high,$$
$$chn - out - low, chn - out - high\}.$$

The CP-net and its associated order are depicted in Figure 7.3. The best outcome w.r.t. this preference relation is $it - in - low$. Suppose now that the CP-net is incomplete and the preference statement $it : in > out$ is dropped. This means that the user has no preference for sitting inside or outside an Italian restaurant. Suppose also that r is composed of $it - in - low$ and $it - out - high$ only. The two tuples are incomparable, so they are both preferred. However, one may prefer $it - in - low$ to $it - out - high$ because in an Italian restaurant, the user prefers to pay a low price. On the other hand, she has no preference for sitting inside or outside.

In order to solve the problem raised by the above example, Ciaccia first replaced ceteris paribus semantics by strong semantics. However, the strong semantics is not satisfactory since it may lead to cyclic preferences even if the CP-net is acyclic. In the above example, interpreting the two statements $it : in > out$ and $it : low > high$ following strong semantics leads to preferring $it - in - high$ to $in - out - low$ following the first statement and preferring $it - out - low$ to $it - in - high$ following the second statement. Consequently, Ciaccia has weakened strong semantics in order to compare incomparable outcomes only. When the CP-net is complete, the two semantics return identical results.

7.9 Database Queries with Comparative Preference Statements

As presented in the previous sections, two main preference semantics have been used in database queries: strong and ceteris paribus semantics. Each framework argues for the use of a unique semantics. However, this restriction has a side effect as it makes database preference queries not expressive enough.

Example 7.14. (Example 7.2 continued)
Suppose that Clara is asked to express her preferences over $\mathcal{R}(dish, wine, dessert)$. She provides three comparative preference statements:

$s_1 : fish > meat,$
$s_2 : red \wedge cake > white \wedge ice\_cream,$ and
$s_3 : fish \wedge white > fish \wedge red.$

Moreover, she provides additional information that she is vegetarian. Consequently, any *fish*-based meal should be preferred to any *meat*-based meal[2]. That is, s_1 should be interpreted following strong semantics, i.e., any meal composed of *fish* is preferred to any meal composed of *meat*.

Let $\succeq$ be the partial order associated with $\{s_1, s_2, s_3\}$. Using strong semantics on s_1, s_2 and s_3 is too strong and leads to cyclic preferences. In fact, we have both $t_0 \succ t_3$ and $t_3 \succ t_0$, for example. Now, using ceteris paribus semantics on s_1, s_2 and s_3 leads to the partial order depicted in Figure 7.4a. However, this semantics makes $t_3 : fish - red - cake$ and $t_5 : meat - white - cake$ (also t_0 and t_7, and t_2 and t_4) incomparable while one would expect that t_3 is preferred to t_5 (also t_0 is preferred to t_7, and t_2 is preferred to t_4) since Clara is vegetarian.

In order to capture Clara's preferences regarding *fish* and *meat*, it is more suitable to use strong semantics with the comparative preference statement s_1. It is intuitively arguable for us to apply ceteris paribus semantics to s_2 and s_3 since no further information is given about these preferences. Figure 7.4b. depicts the partial order associated with s_1, s_2 and s_3, with s_1 obeying strong semantics and s_2 and s_3 obeying ceteris paribus semantics. We have $W_C(r) = \{t_1\} = \{fish - white - cake\}$. We can check that any *fish*-based meal is preferred to any *meat*-based meal w.r.t. this order.

One may deal with the comparative preference statement s_1 and the fact that Clara is vegetarian by simply ignoring the tuples t_4, t_5, t_6 and t_7 as they are meals composed of meat. However, this drastic solution is not the right way to deal with such a preference since it may be the case that the restaurant has no *fish*-based meals and Clara is hungry and would absolutely like to eat something. So, she may accept a *meat*-based meal, then eat dessert and drink wine without eating the *meat*. In such a case, $meat - red - cake$ should be preferred to $meat - white - ice\_cream$ following s_2.

---

[2] We suppose that a vegetarian person eats fish but not meat.

Indeed, a good preference system should not use a unique semantics for all comparative preference statements but allow the user to express her preferences w.r.t. different semantics simultaneously.

In order to handle the simultaneous use of strong and ceteris paribus preferences in database queries, da Silva Neves and Kaci use Algorithm 3.5 presented in Subsection 3.4.9 for strong and ceteris paribus semantics.

The preorder returned by the algorithm is faithful w.r.t. preference queries since it represents an iterated version of the winnow operator [17]. A set of comparative preference statements interpreted following strong (or ceteris paribus) semantics is denoted by $\mathscr{P}_{>_{st}}$ (or $\mathscr{P}_{>_{cp}}$).

Proposition 7.1 states that the best tuples w.r.t. the preorder returned by Algorithm 3.5 are exactly the result of the winnow operator.

Proposition 7.1. *[17]*
Let $\mathscr{P} = \mathscr{P}_{>_{st}} \cup \mathscr{P}_{>_{cp}}$. Let $\succeq = (E_1, \cdots, E_m)$ be the preorder associated with $\mathscr{P}$ following Algorithm 3.5. Let r be an instance of $\mathscr{R}(A)$. Then,

$$W_{\mathscr{P}}(r) = E_1.$$

Example 7.15. (Example 7.2 continued)
We have $\mathscr{P} = \mathscr{P}_{>_{st}} \cup \mathscr{P}_{>_{cp}}$ with $\mathscr{P}_{>_{st}} = \{s_1 : fish >_{st} meat\}$ and $\mathscr{P}_{>_{cp}} = \{s_2 : red \wedge cake >_{cp} white \wedge ice\_cream, s_3 : fish \wedge white >_{cp} fish \wedge red\}$. We refer the reader to Chapter 3 for a formal description of Algorithm 3.5.

$$\begin{aligned}\mathscr{C}(\mathscr{P}) &= \{(L(s_1), R(s_1))\} \cup \{(L(s_2), R(s_2)), (L(s_3), R(s_3))\} \\ &= \{(\{t_0, t_1, t_2, t_3\}, \{t_4, t_5, t_6, t_7\})\} \cup \{(\{t_3, t_7\}, \{t_0, t_4\}), (\{t_0, t_1\}, \{t_2, t_3\})\}.\end{aligned}$$

We have $E_1 = \{t_1\}$. We replace $(L(s_3), R(s_3))$ with $(\{t_0\}, \{t_2\})$ since $t_1 \in L(s_3)$, $t_3 \in R(s_3)$ and t_1 is preferred to t_3 w.r.t. ceteris paribus semantics. We also replace $(L(s_1), R(s_1))$ with $(\{t_0, t_2, t_3\}, \{t_4, t_5, t_6, t_7\})$. We get $\mathscr{L}(\mathscr{P}) = \{(\{t_0, t_2, t_3\}, \{t_4, t_5, t_6, t_7\})\} \cup \{(\{t_3, t_7\}, \{t_0, t_4\}), (\{t_0\}, \{t_2\})\}$. We repeat the same reasoning and get $E_2 = \{t_3\}$, $E_3 = \{t_0\}$, $E_4 = \{t_2\}$, $E_5 = \{t_5, t_6, t_7\}$ and $E_6 = \{t_4\}$. Indeed, $\succeq = (\{t_1\}, \{t_3\}, \{t_0\}, \{t_2\}, \{t_5, t_6, t_7\}, \{t_4\})$. We have $W_{\mathscr{P}}(r) = E_1 = \{t_1\}$.

Recall that the result of the winnow operator is the set of the best tuples w.r.t. a user's preferences. However, one may wish to know which are the next preferred tuples. Algorithm 3.5 has a nice property as at each iteration it computes the best tuples w.r.t. the current set of tuples. Formally, we have the following result, which generalizes Proposition 7.1:

Proposition 7.2. *[17]*
Let $\mathscr{P} = \mathscr{P}_{>_{st}} \cup \mathscr{P}_{>_{cp}}$. Let $\succeq = (E_1, \cdots, E_m)$ be the preorder associated with $\mathscr{P}$ following Algorithm 3.5 Let r be an instance of $\mathscr{R}(A)$. Then,

$$\forall i = 1, \cdots, m, E_i = W_{\mathscr{P}}^i(r),$$

where $W_{\mathscr{P}}^1(r) = W_{\mathscr{P}}(r)$ and $W_{\mathscr{P}}^{n+1}(r) = W_{\mathscr{P}}(r \setminus \bigcup_{i=1, \cdots, n} W_{\mathscr{P}}^i(r))$.

Indeed, $W_{\mathscr{P}}^1(r)$ is the set of the best tuples, $W_{\mathscr{P}}^2(r)$ is the set of next immediate best tuples, etc.

Example 7.16. (Example 7.2 continued)
Let $r' = r \backslash W_{\mathscr{P}}(r) = \{t_0, t_2, t_3, t_4, t_5, t_6, t_7\}$. We can check that $W_{\mathscr{P}}(r') = W_{\mathscr{P}}^2(r) = \{t_3\} = E_2$. Also, $W_{\mathscr{P}}^3(r) = E_3$, $W_{\mathscr{P}}^4(r) = E_4$, $W_{\mathscr{P}}^5(r) = E_5$ and $W_{\mathscr{P}}^6(r) = E_6$.

Note that computing a complete preorder associated with a set of preference statements allows us to associate a score with each tuple. A tuple t which belongs to the stratum E_i in $\succeq$ will get a score i. Therefore, this framework is a ranking approach. It captures queries with $top - k$ scores [7]. For example, the set E_3 in $\succeq$ is composed of tuples that differ from the best tuples (the result of the winnow operator) in two scores. Also, $E_2 \cup E_3$ is the set of tuples that differ from the best ones in at most two scores.

This framework is a generalization of Chomicki's and Brafman and Domshlak's framework. More precisely, it recovers these frameworks when a unique semantics is used [17]. We first consider the case of querying databases with a CP-net. Recall that CP-nets are based on comparative preference statements of the form $r \wedge p > r \wedge q$ (r may be a tautology) which obey ceteris paribus semantics, i.e., $t \succ_N t'$ iff $t \models r \wedge p$ and $t' \models r \wedge q$ and t, t' are the same otherwise. Each preference statement $r \wedge p > r \wedge q$ is written in this framework as $r \wedge p >_{cp} r \wedge q$. So, $\mathscr{P} = \mathscr{P}_{>_{cp}} = \{s_j : r_j \wedge p_j >_{cp} r_j \wedge q_j\}$, where $r_j \wedge p_j > r_j \wedge q_j$ is expressed in the preference tables associated with the CP-net at hand. Indeed, we can still apply Algorithm 3.5 with an input $\mathscr{P}_{>_{cp}}$. Then, we have the following result [17]:

Proposition 7.3. *Let N be a CP-net and $\mathscr{P}_{>_{cp}}$ be the set of comparative preference statements built from N. Let $\succeq = (E_1, \cdots, E_m)$ be the preorder associated with $\mathscr{P}_{>_{cp}}$ following Algorithm 3.5. Let r be an instance of a relational schema $\mathscr{R}(A)$. Then,*

$$\forall i = 1, \cdots, m, W_N^i(r) = E_i.$$

Example 7.17. (Borrowed from [6])
Let N be a CP-net built on three attributes, *dish*, *wine* and *dessert*, taking their values in $\{fish, meat\}$, $\{white, red\}$ and $\{cake, ice\_cream\}$, respectively. The CP-net N and its associated partial order are depicted in Figure 7.5.

We have $\mathscr{P}_{>_{cp}} = \{fish >_{cp} meat, fish \wedge white >_{cp} fish \wedge red, meat \wedge red >_{cp} meat \wedge white, white \wedge cake >_{cp} white \wedge ice\_cream, red \wedge ice\_cream >_{cp} red \wedge cake\}$. Then, $\mathscr{C}(\mathscr{P}_{>_{cp}}) = \{(\{t_0, t_1, t_2, t_3\}, \{t_4, t_5, t_6, t_7\}), (\{t_0, t_1\}, \{t_2, t_3\}), (\{t_6, t_7\}, \{t_4, t_5\}), (\{t_1, t_5\}, \{t_0, t_4\}), (\{t_2, t_6\}, \{t_3, t_7\})\}$. Let us now apply Algorithm 3.5 on $\mathscr{P}_{>_{cp}}$. We get $\succeq = (E_1, E_2, E_3, E_4, E_5, E_6, E_7)$ with $E_1 = \{t_1\}$, $E_2 = \{t_0\}$, $E_3 = \{t_2\}$, $E_4 = \{t_3, t_6\}$, $E_5 = \{t_7\}$, $E_6 = \{t_5\}$ and $E_7 = \{t_4\}$. We can check that $E_i = W_N^i(r)$ for $i = 1, \cdots, 7$.

Let us now show how this framework captures Chomicki's framework. We first present the encoding of a unique preference relation $\succ_C$. As previously observed, comparative preference statements are interpreted in Chomicki's approach following strong semantics. So, given a formula C, a set of strong preferences is constructed, $\mathscr{P}_{>_{st}} = \{p_1 >_{st} q_1, \cdots, p_l >_{st} q_l\}$, as previously described. Algorithm 3.5 is again used with an input $\mathscr{P}_{>_{st}}$.

Proposition 7.4. *[17]*
Let r be an instance of $\mathscr{R}(A)$. Let C be a preference formula and $\mathscr{P}_{>_{st}}$ be the set of strong preferences built from C. Let $\succeq = (E_1, \cdots, E_m)$ be the preorder associated with $\mathscr{P}_{>_{st}}$ following Algorithm 3.5. Then,

$$\forall i = 1, \cdots, m, W_C^i(r) = E_i.$$

Example 7.18. (Example 7.1 continued)
Let us consider $\succ_{C_1}$. We have $\mathscr{P}_1 = \{meat \wedge red >_{st} meat \wedge white, fish \wedge white >_{st} fish \wedge red\}$. Applying Algorithm 3.5 returns (E_1, E_2) with $E_1 = \{meat - red, fish - white, meat - rosé, fish - rosé\}$ and $E_2 = \{meat - white, fish - red\}$. Indeed, $E_1 = W_{C_1}(r)$ and $E_2 = W_{C_1}^2(r)$.

We now consider $\succ_{C_2}$. We have $\mathscr{P}_2 = \{red >_{st} white, fish \wedge white >_{st} fish \wedge rosé, fish \wedge rosé >_{st} fish \wedge red\}$. Following Algorithm 3.5, $\mathscr{P}_2$ is inconsistent and the associated preorder is (E_1, E_2) with $E_1 = \{meat - red, meat - rosé\}$ and $E_2 = \emptyset$. So, we have $W_{C_2}(r) = E_1$ and $W_{C_2}^2(r) = E_2$.

Let us now give the encoding of the composition of preference queries. Let C_1, C_2 be two preference formulas and $\succ_{C_1}$, $\succ_{C_2}$ be two preference relations over the same relational schema. As observed in Section 7.6, we distinguish between two types of composition: boolean and prioritized. Boolean composition is represented by intersection, union and difference, which are defined by $C_1 \wedge C_2$, $C_1 \vee C_2$ and $C_1 \wedge \neg C_2$, respectively. Since any logical formula can be written in a disjunctive form, the above encoding can be used to encode the boolean composition.

Regarding prioritized composition, the same reasoning can be applied. Let $\succ_p$ be the prioritized composition of $\succ_{C_1}$ over $\succ_{C_2}$. Recall that we have

$$t \succ_p t' \text{ iff } ((t \succ_{C_1} t') \vee (t \sim_{C_1} t' \wedge t \succ_{C_2} t')).$$

Given that $t \succ_p t'$ iff $((t \succ_{C_1} t') \vee (t \sim_{C_1} t' \wedge t \succ_{C_2} t'))$ can be written in terms of a new preference formula C [17],

$$C(t,t') \equiv C_1(t,t') \vee (\neg C_1(t,t') \wedge \neg C_1(t',t) \wedge C_2(t,t')),$$

and that this formula can be written a disjunctive form, the above encoding can be applied to encode the prioritized composition.

Example 7.19. (Example 7.1 continued)
Let $\succ_{C_4}$ and $\succ_{C_5}$ be two preference relations defined by

$t \succ_{C_4} t'$ iff $(t.wine = red \wedge t'.wine \neq red)$ and
$t \succ_{C_5} t'$ iff $((t.dish = fish \wedge t.wine = white) \wedge (t'.dish = fish \wedge t'.wine \neq white))$.

Let $\succ_p$ be the prioritized composition of $\succ_{C_5}$ over $\succ_{C_4}$. The preference relations $\succ_{C_4}, \succ_{C_5}$ and $\succ_p$ are depicted in Figure 7.6. After simplification we have that $C(t,t')$ is equivalent to

$(t.dish = meat \wedge t.wine = red \wedge t'.wine \neq red) \vee (t.wine = red \wedge t'.dish = meat \wedge$
$t'.wine \neq red) \vee (t.wine = red \wedge t'.wine = rosé) \vee (t.dish = fish \wedge t.wine = white \wedge$
$t'.dish = fish \wedge t'.wine \neq white).$

The set of comparative preference statements associated with C is $\mathscr{P}_{>_{st}} = \{meat \wedge$ $red >_{st} \neg red, red >_{st} meat \wedge \neg red, red >_{st} rosé, fish \wedge white >_{st} fish \wedge \neg white\}$. Applying Algorithm 3.5 returns $\succeq = (E_1, E_2, E_3, E_4)$ with $E_1 = \{meat - red\}$, $E_2 = \{fish - white\}$, $E_3 = \{fish - red\}$ and $E_4 = \{meat - white, meat - rosé, fish - rosé\}$.

From Figure 7.6c. we can check that $meat - red$ is the most preferred tuple, $fish - white$ is immediately less preferred, $fish - red$ is less preferred and lastly $meat - white$, $meat - rosé$ and $fish - rosé$ are the least preferred tuples.

Chomicki [10] has noticed that a tuple belongs to the result of the winnow operator as soon as it is not dominated by any other tuple even if it does not dominate any other tuple.

Example 7.20. Consider again the preference formula C_1 given in Example 7.1 defined by
$t \succ_{C_1} t'$ iff $((t.dish = meat \wedge t.wine = red \wedge t'.dish = meat \wedge t'.wine = white) \vee$
$\qquad (t.dish = fish \wedge t.wine = white \wedge t'.dish = fish \wedge t'.wine = red))$
and an instance r of $Meal(dish, wine)$ defined by $\{meat - red, meat - white, meat - rosé, fish - red, fish - white, fish - rosé\}$. We have $W_{C_1}(r) = \{meat - red, meat - rosé, fish - white, fish - rosé\}$.

In the above example, the meals with wine which is neither red nor white (i.e., $meat - rosé, fish - rosé$) are not related w.r.t. $\succ_{C_1}$ to any other meal. Thus, they are not dominated and belong to $W_{C_1}(r)$. If this result is undesirable and the user would like to discard such meals, Chomicki's approach needs to rewrite the preference formula C_1 as follows:

$t \succ_{C_1'} t'$ iff $((t.dish = meat \wedge t.wine = red \wedge t'.dish = meat \wedge t'.wine \neq white) \vee$
$(t.dish = fish \wedge t.wine = white \wedge t'.dish = fish \wedge t'.wine \neq red)).$

Therefore, we have $W_{C_1'}(r) = \{meat - red, fish - white\}$.

In da Silva and Kaci's approach, they do not need to rewrite the preference formula. In fact, the set of comparative preference statements associated with C_1 is $\mathscr{P}_{>_{st}} = \{meat \wedge red >_{st} meat \wedge white, fish \wedge white >_{st} fish \wedge red\}$. Its associated preorder $\succeq = (\{meat - red, meat - rosé, fish - white, fish - rosé\}, \{meat - white, fish - red\})$ computed following the Algorithm 3.5 is the least-specific preorder which satisfies $\mathscr{P}_{>_{st}}$. As explained in Subsection 3.4, the least-specific principle puts a tuple in the highest possible rank in the preorder. Indeed, since $meat - rosé$ and $fish - rosé$ are undominated w.r.t. $\succ_{C_1}$, they belong to the first stratum in $\succeq$.

Now, if one wants to discard such meals then this turns to putting in each stratum in $\succeq$ tuples that are not dominated and also dominate other tuples. This reasoning corresponds to the most-specific principle, which behaves in an opposite way to the least-specific principle (see Subsection 3.4).

Example 7.21. (Example 7.20 continued)
We have $\mathcal{P}_{>_{st}} = \{s_1 : meat \wedge red >_{st} meat \wedge white, s_2 : fish \wedge white >_{st} fish \wedge red\}$.
Then, $\mathcal{L}(\mathcal{P}_{>_{st}}) = \{(L(s_1),R(s_1)),(L(s_2),R(s_2))\} = \{(\{meat-red\},$
$\{meat-white\}),(\{fish-white\},\{fish-red\})\}$. We apply Algorithm 3.6 and get
$E_1 = \{meat-white, meat-rosé, fish-red, fish-rosé\}$ and $E_2 = \{meat-red,$
$fish-white\}$. Then, $\succeq= (E_1', E_2')$ with $E_1' = \{meat-red, fish-white\}$ and
$E_2' = \{meat-white, meat-rosé, fish-red, fish-rosé\}$.

7.10 Conclusion

Managing users' preferences is an important problem in database querying. With the aim of highlighting the use of compact preference representation languages, developed in AI, we shed light on these approaches in database querying. They offer a compact way to represent users' preferences. Each approach is based on an operator, which selects the best tuples given a preference query. Different operators have been used: skyline, winnow, Best, etc., but the difference is only a matter of terminology. They are all based on the same principle. Given the preference relation over tuples induced by the preferences, the best tuples are those which are not dominated by any other tuple.

In some situations, the presented approaches (except Kiessling) do not deal with the case of a empty-result answers, i.e., there is no tuple which satisfies all the user's preferences. This problem occurs when the database is incomplete. One possible solution to this problem may be a stratification of the user's preferences [15]. Then, different approaches may be used to rank-order the available tuples. Nevertheless, the predominant way, a research topic to tackle this problem is by the introduction of fuzzy preferences or the weakening of queries (see, e.g., [4, 12]).

References

1. Agrawal, R., Wimmers, E.L.: A framework for expressing and combining preferences. In: Chen, W., Naughton, J.F., Bernstein, P.A. (eds.), International Conference on Management of Data, pp. 297-306. ACM, (2000)
2. Benferhat, S., Kaci, S.: A possibilistic logic handling of strong preferences. In: Smith, M.H., Gruver, W.A. (eds.), International Fuzzy Systems Association, pp. 962-967. (2001)
3. Börzsönyi, S., Kossmann, D., Stocker, K.: The Skyline operator. 17th International Conference on Data Engineering, pp. 421-430. IEEE Computer Society, (2001)
4. Bosc, P., Pivert, O.: Some approaches for relational databases flexible querying. Journal of Intelligent Information Systems 1, 323–354 (1992)

5. Boutilier, C., Brafman, R.I., Domshlak, C., Hoos, H.H., Poole, D.: CP-nets: A tool for representing and reasoning with conditional ceteris paribus preference statements. Journal of Artificial Intelligence Research **21**, 135–191 (2004)
6. Brafman, R.I., Domshlak, C.: Database preference queries revisited. Technical Report TR2004-1934, Cornell University, Computing and Information Science. (2004)
7. Bruno, N., Chaudhuri, S., Gravano, L.: Top-k selection queries over relational databases: Mapping strategies and performance evaluation. ACM Transactions on Database Systems **27(2)**, 153–187 (2002)
8. Chang, C.L.: Deduce – A deductive query language for relational data base. In: Chen, C.G. (eds.), Pattern Recognition and Artificial Intelligence, pp. 108-134. Academic Press, New York (1976)
9. Chomicki, J.: Querying with intrinsic preferences. 18th International Conference on Data Engineering, pp. 34-51. IEEE Computer Society, (2002)
10. Chomicki, J.: Preference formulas in relational queries. ACM Transactions on Database Systems **28**, 1–40 (2003)
11. Ciaccia, P.: Querying databases with incomplete CP-nets. In: Delgrande, J., Kiessling, W. (eds.), 3rd Multidisciplinary Workshop on Advances in Preference Handling. Electronic proceedings, (2007)
12. Dubois, D., Prade, H.: Bipolarity in flexible querying. In: Yager, Y.Y., Andreasen, T. (eds.), 5th International Conference on Flexible Query Answering Systems, pp. 174-182. Springer, (2007)
13. Fagin, R.: Combining fuzzy information from multiple systems. In: Paredaens, J., Van Gucht, D. (eds.), 15th ACM SIGACT-SIGMOD-SIGART Symposium on Principles of Database Systems, pp. 216-226. ACM Press, (1996)
14. Fagin, R., Wimmers, E.L.: Incorporating user preferences in multimedia queries. In: Afrati, F.N., Kolaitis, P.G. (eds.), 6th International Conference on Database Theory, pp. 247-261. Springer, (1997)
15. Hadjali, A., Kaci, S., Prade, H.: Database preferences queries- A possibilistic logic approach with symbolic priorities. Annals of Mathematics and Artificial Intelligence. Accepted.
16. Hristidis, V., Koudas, N., Papakonstantinou, Y.: PREFER: A system for the efficient execution of multi-parametric ranked queries. In: Aref, W.G. (eds.), ACM SIGMOD International Conference on Management of Data, pp. 259-269. ACM Press, (2001)
17. da Silva Neves, R., Kaci, S.: Preference formulas in relational queries. Logic Journal of the Interest Group in Pure and Applied Logic **18**, 464–483 (2010)
18. Motro, A.: Supporting goal queries in relational database. In: Kerschberg, L. (eds.), 1st International Conference on Expert Database Systems, pp. 85-96. (1986)
19. Kiessling, W.: Foundations of preferences in database systems. In: Lochovsky, F.H., Shan, W. (eds.), 28th International Conference on Very Large Data Bases, pp. 311-322. Morgan Kaufmann, (2002)
20. Lacroix, M., Lavency, P.: Preferences: Putting more knowledge into queries. In: Stocker, P.M., Kent, W., Hammersley, P. (eds.), 13th International Conference on Very Large Data Bases, pp. 217-225. Morgan Kaufmann, (1987)
21. Torlone, R., Ciaccia, P.: Finding the best when it's a matter of preference. In: Ciaccia, P., Rabitti, F., Soda, G. (eds.), 10th Symposium on Advanced Database Systems, pp. 347-360. (2002)

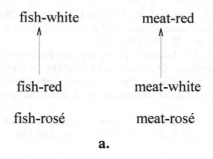

a.

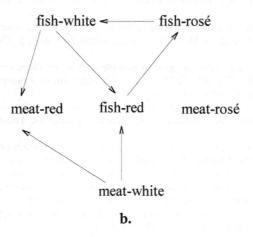

b.

Fig. 7.1 Preference relations $\succ_{C_1}$ and $\succ_{C_2}$

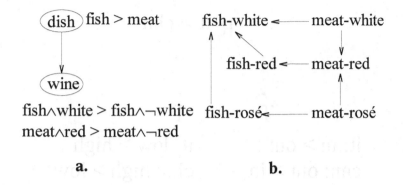

Fig. 7.2 A CP-net and its associated order (Example 7.11)

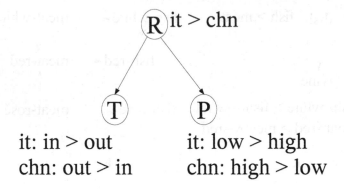

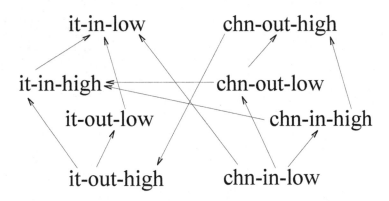

Fig. 7.3 A CP-net and its associated order (Example 7.13)

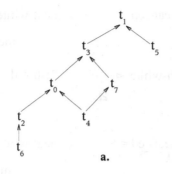

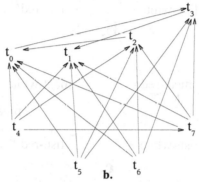

Fig. 7.4 a.: The partial order induced by ceteris paribus semantics (Example 7.14), **b.**: The partial order induced by ceteris paribus and strong semantics (Example 7.14)

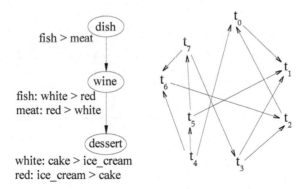

Fig. 7.5 A CP-net N and its associated partial order (Example 7.17)

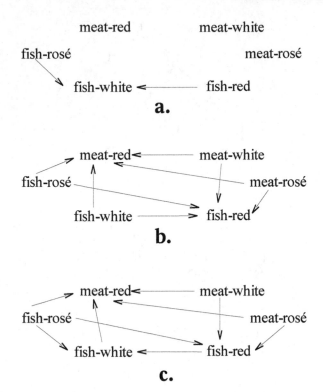

Fig. 7.6 Preference relations **a.**: $\succ_{C_4}$, **b.**: $\succ_{C_5}$, **c.**: $\succ_p$

Chapter 8
Preferences Aggregation

8.1 Introduction

In the previous chapters we focused on problems related to the representation of and reasoning with preferences. In this chapter we highlight the closeness of preference representation and other artificial intelligence fields. In particular, we shed light on conditional logics and relate them to multiple criteria aggregation and temporal reasoning.

Multiple Criteria Aggregation

A classical way of comparing outcomes is using multiple criteria for evaluating them in an absolute manner, using linearly ordered scales. These scales are often numerical, and under the hypothesis that they are commensurable, different aggregation procedures that reflect various combination attitudes can be applied in order to build a complete preorder for rank-ordering the outcomes on the basis of the global evaluations that are obtained. However, in many practical problems (such as multiple criteria analysis and flexible constraints satisfaction problems), a numerical scale, such as [0,1] is too rich to use, and more qualitative scales having a finite number of levels have to be preferred. But the internal operations that can be defined on these latter scales (e.g., [14, 6]) have limited discriminating power since they take values on a finite range.

The problem thus amounts to comparing outcomes represented by evaluation vectors of qualitative criteria evaluations without aggregating them. We assume that preferences are specified through explicit constraints on a complete preorder to be determined over evaluation vectors. These constraints may include preferences between criteria. In addition to the Pareto partial preorder that should constrain any complete preorder between outcomes, one may have some generic preferences that further constrain these complete preorders. For instance, one may state that some criterion is more important than, or as important as, other criteria (maybe in a limited context). One may also have at her disposal some examples of preferences between fully specified outcomes.

Besides, a given compact preference representation language (whatever it is) can be seen as a way of aggregating partial preferences. In particular, the bridges established in Chapter 4 show that a set of comparative preference statements expressed in conditional logics can be seen as a set of weighted logical formulas expressed in possibilistic logic or guaranteed possibilistic logic. Therefore, an outcome can be represented by its evaluation vector of tolerance degrees (in the case of possibilistic logic) or satisfaction degrees (in the case of guaranteed possibilistic logic). The global evaluation of an outcome is then obtained, respectively, by a min-based and a max-based aggregation of its evaluation vector.

The idea of relating the above frameworks comes from the fact that the two frameworks have a set of comparative preference statements as an input. Therefore, the question that naturally arises is, Do the two frameworks return the same result? We investigate this question in the first part of this chapter.

Reasoning about Temporal Information

Representing and reasoning about time and space are important issues in many domains, such as natural language processing, geographic information systems, computer vision, and robot navigation. Qualitative reasoning about temporal and spatial information aims to develop qualitative formalisms to reason about such information using qualitative relations. To this end, several qualitative approaches have been proposed to represent spatial or temporal entities and their relations. For example, Allen [1] represents temporal entities as intervals over a qualitative time scale. Their relations correspond to the different relative positions that may occur between two intervals. For example, "interval I_1 meets interval I_2", "I_1 precedes I_2", etc. This formalism is commonly known as Allen's algebra. In this algebra, an interval is a non-decomposable and abstract entity which is only determined by its start and end points. Given a set of intervals and a set of constraints representing how they should be related, a constraint satisfaction problem consists in finding one or more different solutions which define possible positions of the intervals which satisfy the constraints. However, in some situations, an interval is not a non-decomposable entity. In fact, it is a set of objects which need to be rank-ordered over a qualitative time scale. For example, an interval may be the time allocated to a set of courses which need to be scheduled. So, a relation between two intervals is a constraint between two sets of courses to be scheduled, each in its associated interval. The scheduling of all courses should respect the constraint between the two intervals. Unfortunately, Allen's algebra is not expressive enough for representing intervals whose start and end points are not known and which are composed of objects to be rank-ordered. Nevertheless, it is a powerful algebra for expressing all possible relations between intervals.

While conditional logics and Allen's algebra have been developed for different purposes, they show close, interesting behavior. In particular, the authors of [11] provided an encoding of Allen's algebra in terms of comparative preference statements in conditional logics. Interestingly, this encoding allows us to overcome the shortcomings of Allen's algebra.

8.2 Multiple Criteria Decision

We assume that possible choices are evaluated w.r.t. n criteria. A possible choice is a vector of satisfaction levels $(a_1, \cdots, a_n)$, where a_j is the vector's evaluation w.r.t. a criterion j. We suppose that a_j belongs to a linearly ordered scale $S = \{s_1, \cdots, s_h\}$ with $s_1 < \cdots < s_h$ (commensurateness hypothesis).

Note that a criterion (or vector) corresponds to a variable (or outcome) in the terminology used in the previous chapters. Thus, variables have the same domain. We use the terminology of criteria and vectors since they are more suitable in the framework of multiple criteria decision.

Let $\mathcal{U} = S^n$ be the set of all possible evaluation vectors $v = (a_1, \cdots, a_n)$ (written $v = a_1^i \cdots a_n^i$ for short), called also vectors of attribute values, or vectors for short.

The preference relation $\succeq$ over $\mathcal{U} \times \mathcal{U}$ is expressed in the standard way, as $a_1 \cdots a_n \succeq a_1' \cdots a_n'$, which stands for $v = a_1 \cdots a_n$ is at least as preferred as $v' = a_1' \cdots a_n'$. We also write $a_1 \cdots a_n \succ a_1' \cdots a_n'$ ($v = a_1 \cdots a_n$ is strictly preferred to $v' = a_1' \cdots a_n'$) when $a_1 \cdots a_n \succeq a_1' \cdots a_n'$ holds and $a_1' \cdots a_n' \succeq a_1 \cdots a_n$ does not. Lastly, $a_1 \cdots a_n \approx a_1' \cdots a_n'$ ($v = a_1 \cdots a_n$ and $v' = a_1' \cdots a_n'$ are equally preferred) when both $a_1 \cdots a_n \succeq a_1' \cdots a_n'$ and $a_1' \cdots a_n' \succeq a_1 \cdots a_n$ hold.

The preference relation $\succeq$ is generally specified by means of generic constraints where some or all components may remain unspecified. They are replaced with a variable x_j if the jth component is free to take any value in the scale. This allows us to express various types of preferences, e.g., Pareto ordering, i.e., $\forall x_i \forall x_i'$,

$$x_1 \cdots x_n \succ x_1' \cdots x_n' \text{ if } \forall i, x_i \geq x_i' \text{ and } \exists k, x_k > x_k'.$$

Besides this, other generic constraints of particular interest include those pertaining to the expression of the relative importance of criteria. The greater importance of criterion j w.r.t. criterion k can be expressed in different forms. One way to state it is by exchanging x_j and x_k and writing

$$x_1 \cdots x_j \cdots x_k \cdots x_n \succ x_1 \cdots x_k \cdots x_j \cdots x_n \text{ when } x_j > x_k.$$

Note that this is the counterpart of the relative importance of variables (here criteria) used in TCP-nets, where a variable X being more important than a variable Y is interpreted as "it is more important to see X getting its most preferred assignment than to see Y getting its most preferred assignment".

One may think of other ways of expressing that j is more important than k. For instance, one may restrict the above preferences to extreme values of S for the x_is such that $i \neq j$ and $i \neq k$, since weights of importance in conjunctive aggregation can be obtained in this way for a large family of operators (e.g., [5]). A more drastic way of expressing relative importance would be to use a lexicographic ordering of the vector evaluations based on a linear order of the levels of importance for the criteria. In this case, the problem of ordering the vectors would be immediately solved.

Note that the first view of relative importance above, which is used in the following, is ceteris paribus semantics [10] of subvector (x_j, x_k) w.r.t. (x_k, x_j) for $x_j > x_k$, where the first (or second) component refers to criterion j (or k), all other vector components being equal.

Another way to relate criteria is to express their equal importance. It can be expressed by stating that any two vectors where x_j and x_k are exchanged, and otherwise identical, have the same levels of satisfaction. Formally, we write

$$x_1 \cdots x_j \cdots x_k \cdots x_n \approx x_1 \cdots x_k \cdots x_j \cdots x_n.$$

In addition to generic constraints we may also have particular examples of preferences between some specific vectors.

Given a set of constraints (generic constraints and examples), different approaches have been developed to rank-order evaluation vectors. For example, numerical aggregation procedures return a complete preorder over $\mathcal{U} \times \mathcal{U}$ while qualitative approaches return a partial or complete preorder. Such a preorder should not add any additional constraint. The authors of [7, 12] compared a numerical approach and a qualitative one, namely, Choquet integral and conditional logics. In fact, both approaches consider generic constraints (and possibly examples). Indeed, it would be interesting to compare their outputs.

8.2.1 Multiple Aggregation Decision vs. Conditional Logics

Generic constraints generally induce a strict preference over vectors, i.e.,

$$v \succ v', \text{ with } v, v' \in \mathcal{U}. \tag{8.1}$$

For example, given three criteria X, Y and Z, a relative importance constraint of X over Y is written as

$$xyz_0 \succ yxz_0 \text{ for } x > y, \forall z_0.$$

A set of constraints of the form (8.1) can be written in a compact form as a set of the following constraints [7, 12]:

$$\text{if } v \in \min(\mathscr{U}_1, \succeq) \text{ and } v' \in \max(\mathscr{U}_2, \succeq) \text{ then } v \succ v', \qquad (8.2)$$

where $\mathscr{U}_1$ and $\mathscr{U}_2$ are subsets of $\mathscr{U}$.

This constraint means that any vector in $\min(\mathscr{U}_1, \succeq)$ is preferred to any vector in $\max(\mathscr{U}_2, \succeq)$. Therefore, it corresponds to a preference statement obeying strong semantics in Chapter 3. For the sake of readability, we denote constraints of the form (8.2) as $C(\mathscr{U}_1, \mathscr{U}_2)$.

Generic constraints may also induce equally preferred vectors, i.e.,

$$v \approx v', \text{ with } v, v' \in \mathscr{U}. \qquad (8.3)$$

For example given criteria X, Y, and Z; X and Y having the same importance is written as

$$xyz_0 \approx yxz_0, \forall z_0.$$

Constraints of the form (8.3) can be encoded in conditional logics (see Chapter 3) by means of two non-strict preference statements, $v \succeq v'$ and $v' \succeq v$. Note that these preferences can also be written in a compact way as non-strict preference statements obeying strong semantics of the form [7, 12]:

$$\text{if } v \in \min(\mathscr{U}_1, \succeq) \text{ and } v' \in \max(\mathscr{U}_2, \succeq) \text{ then } v \succeq v', \qquad (8.4)$$

We write such constraints as $CE(\mathscr{U}_1, \mathscr{U}_2)$.

When $\mathscr{U}_1$ and $\mathscr{U}_2$ are composed of a single vector we simply write $v \succ v'$ (or $v \succeq v'$) instead of $C(\{v\}, \{v'\})$ (or $CE(\{v\}, \{v'\})$).

Let $\mathscr{C}$ and $\mathscr{E}\mathscr{Q}$ be the sets of constraints of the form (8.2) and (8.3) respectively, namely, $\mathscr{C} = \{C(\mathscr{U}_i, \mathscr{U}_j)\}$[1] and $\mathscr{E}\mathscr{Q} = \{CE(\mathscr{U}_1, \mathscr{U}_2)\}$.

Following Chapter 3, the set $\mathscr{C} \cup \mathscr{E}\mathscr{Q}$ induces a unique partial preorder over the set of evaluation vectors.

Example 8.1. (Borrowed from [7, 12])
Let us consider two subjects, "mathematics" and "literature", that are evaluated on "a" for good, "b" for medium and "c" for bad with $a > b > c$. Thus, a student having "ac" is good in mathematics and bad in literature. Pareto ordering forces us to have $xy \succ x'y'$ as soon as $(x > x' \text{ and } y \geq y')$ or $(x \geq x' \text{ and } y > y')$ for x, y, x', y' in $\{a, b, c\}$. The Pareto principle induces the following set of constraints:

$\mathscr{C} = \{C(\{aa\}, \{ab, ba, ca\}), C(\{aa, ab\}, \{ac, bb, bc, cb, cc\}), C(\{ac, ba\}, \{bc, cc\}),$
$C(\{bb\}, \{cb, cc, bc\}), C(\{ba\}, \{ca, bb, cb\}), C(\{bc, cb, ca\}, \{cc\}), C(\{ca\}, \{cb\})\}.$

The partial preorder $\succeq_p$ associated with $\mathscr{C}$ is depicted in Figure 8.1a.

Let us extend $\mathscr{C}$ with relative importance constraints. Suppose that mathematics

---

[1] Constraints of the form (8.1) are a special case of constraints of the form (8.2).

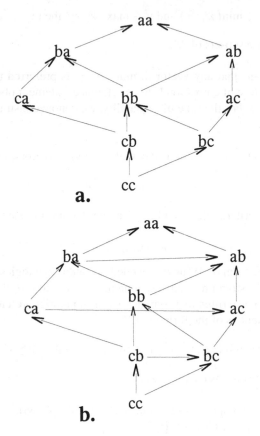

Fig. 8.1 Partial preorders $\succeq_p$ and $\succeq'_p$ associated with $\mathscr{C}$ and $\mathscr{C} \cup \mathscr{C}'$, respectively

is more important than literature. This is modeled by the following relative importance constraint: $xy \succ yx$ for $x > y$. The instantiation of this constraint provides a new set of constraints: $\mathscr{C}' = \{ab \succ ba, ac \succ ca, bc \succ cb\}$.

The partial preorder associated with $\mathscr{C} \cup \mathscr{C}'$ is depicted in Figure 8.1b.

Recall that the aim of this section is to compare a qualitative aggregation approach and a numerical aggregation approach. Since the latter returns a complete preorder over $\mathscr{U} \times \mathscr{U}$, we need to break incomparabilities of the partial preorder returned by the qualitative approach. Therefore, we need to use a completion principle in order to extend the partial preorder associated with $\mathscr{C} \cup \mathscr{E}\mathscr{D}$. Since the set $\mathscr{C} \cup \mathscr{E}\mathscr{D}$ induces a unique partial preorder, the authors of [7, 12] use either the minimal or the maximal specificity principle to compute that complete preorder. This is in agreement with Chapter 3 since strong semantics lies in between optimistic and pessimistic semantics.

Example 8.2. (Example 8.1 continued)
Following the minimal specificity principle, the complete preorder which extends $\succeq'_p$ is $\succeq = (\{aa\}, \{ab\}, \{ba, ac\}, \{ca, bb\}, \{bc\}, \{cb\}, \{cc\})$, while following the maximal specificity principle the complete preorder which extends $\succeq'_p$ is $\succeq' = (\{aa\}, \{ab\}, \{ba\}, \{ac, bb\}, \{bc, ca\}, \{cb\}, \{cc\})$.

Recall that the minimal specificity principle amounts to putting a vector all the higher in the ranking as it is dominated by less vectors according to the constraints. The maximal specificity principle would amount to putting a vector all the lower in the ranking as it is dominated by more vectors according to the constraints.

8.2.2 Numerical Aggregation Approach: Discrete Choquet Integral

The aggregation of vectors of attribute values in the presence of interaction between criteria is essential in many decision-making problems. For this purpose, several multicriteria aggregation approaches have been proposed in literature [8, 9, 5]. In particular, the Choquet integral [8, 9] is a very popular aggregation operator as it allows us to model interactions between criteria. It can represent preferences that cannot be captured by a simple weighted arithmetic mean. Using a particular measure, it aggregates valued attributes describing vectors into a unique value. A Choquet integral is based on a fuzzy measure defined as follows.

Definition 8.1 (Fuzzy measure).
Let $\mathbb{A}$ be the set of attributes and $I(\mathbb{A})$ be the set of all possible subsets of $\mathbb{A}$. A fuzzy measure is a function μ from $I(\mathbb{A})$ to $[0, 1]$ such that:

(i) $\forall I_1, I_2 \in I(\mathbb{A})$ if $I_1 \subseteq I_2$ then $\mu(I_1) \leq \mu(I_2)$,
(ii) $\mu(\emptyset) = 0$ and
(iii) $\mu(\mathbb{A}) = 1$.

A discrete Choquet integral w.r.t. a fuzzy measure μ is defined as follows.

Definition 8.2 (Discrete Choquet integral).
Let μ be a fuzzy measure on $\mathbb{A} = \{a_1, \cdots, a_n\}$. The discrete Choquet integral w.r.t. μ is defined by

$$Ch_\mu(a_1 \cdots a_n) = \sum_{i=1,\cdots,n} (a_{(i)} - a_{(i-1)}) \cdot \mu_{\mathbb{A}_{(i)}},$$

where $a_{(i)}$ indicates that the indices have been permuted so that $0 \leq a_{(1)} \leq \cdots \leq a_{(n)}$, and $\mathbb{A}_{(i)} = \{a_{(i)}, \cdots, a_{(n)}\}$ with $a_{(0)} = 0$.

Example 8.3. (Borrowed from [8, 9, 13])
Let A, B and C be three students evaluated w.r.t. three subjects: mathematics (M), physics (P) and literature (L). Students' grades are summarized in Table 8.1. Using a Choquet integral with a fuzzy measure μ, the global grade for each student is computed as follows:

Table 8.1 Students' grades

student	M	P	L
A	18	16	10
B	10	12	18
C	14	15	15

- student A: $Ch_\mu(A) = Ch_\mu(18, 16, 10)$
  $$= 10 \cdot \mu_{MPL} + (16 - 10) \cdot \mu_{PM} + (18 - 16) \cdot \mu_M,$$
- student B: $Ch_\mu(B) = Ch_\mu(10, 12, 18)$
  $$= 10 \cdot \mu_{MPL} + (12 - 10) \cdot \mu_{PL} + (18 - 12) \cdot \mu_L,$$
- student C: $Ch_\mu(C) = Ch_\mu(14, 15, 15) = 14 \cdot \mu_{MPL} + (15 - 14) \cdot \mu_{PL},$

where μ_X, μ_{XY} and μ_{XYZ} with $X, Y, Z \in \{M, P, L\}$ denote the values of the fuzzy measure μ for the corresponding set of subjects.

The school gives the same importance to mathematics and physics and is more sci-entifically than literarily oriented. Moreover, the school wants to favor well equi-librated students without weak grades, so we should have C preferred to A and A preferred to B, i.e., $C \succ A \succ B$[2]. As indicated before, the fuzzy measure μ models interaction between subjects. Since mathematics and physics have the same im-portance and are more important than literature, we have $\mu_M = \mu_P$, $\mu_M > \mu_L$ and $\mu_P > \mu_L$. Moreover, both mathematics and physics are scientific subjects, and thus considered close, while literature is not. Therefore, the interaction between mathe-matics (or physics) and literature is higher than the interaction between mathematics and physics. Then, $\mu_{ML} = \mu_{PL} > \mu_{PM}$. To summarize, we have the following set of constraints on μ:

$$\mathcal{M} = \begin{cases} \mu_M = \mu_P \\ \mu_M > \mu_L \\ \mu_P > \mu_L \\ \mu_{ML} = \mu_{PL} \\ \mu_{ML} > \mu_{PM} \\ \mu_{PL} > \mu_{PM} \end{cases}.$$

In addition to this set, we consider the constraints $Ch_\mu(C) > Ch_\mu(A)$ and $Ch_\mu(A) > Ch_\mu(B)$, corresponding to the order between the students A, B and C. Table 8.2 gives an example of μ given in [13].

Using the discrete Choquet integral w.r.t. μ given in Table 8.2, we get $Ch_\mu(A) = 13.9$, $Ch_\mu(B) = 13.6$ and $Ch_\mu(C) = 14.9$. Thus, C is preferred to A and A is preferred to B.

---

[2] It has been shown in [13] that there is no weighted arithmetic mean that gives this order over A, B and C.

Table 8.2 Fuzzy measure μ

μ_M	μ_P	μ_L	μ_{PM}	μ_{ML}	μ_{PL}	μ_{MPL}
0.45	0.45	0.3	0.5	0.9	0.9	1

8.2.3 Conditional Logics vs. Choquet Integral

Both conditional logics and the Choquet integral consider constraints (or preference statements) of the form "criterion i is more important than criterion j" and "i and j have the same importance". These constraints may also be expressed in a limited context. Given that conditional logics are a qualitative approach while the Choquet integral is a qualitative one, one may wonder whether the two approaches are equivalent, i.e., they return the same ordering over vectors. This question has been addressed in [7, 12]. The authors compare the two approaches on the basis of Example 8.3. More precisely, they provide an encoding of this example in conditional logics. For this purpose, a qualitative scale $S = \{a,b,c,d,e,f\}$ (with $a > b > c > d > e > f$) is used to encode the students' grades, 18, 16, 15, 14, 12 and 10, respectively given in Table 8.1. Let x, y, and z be the students' grades in mathematics, physics and literature, respectively, so $x,y,z \in \{a,b,c,d,e,f\}$. The second step consists in encoding the constraints over μ, namely, $\mu_M > \mu_L$, $\mu_P > \mu_L$, $\mu_{ML} > \mu_{PM}$, $\mu_{PL} > \mu_{PM}$ and $\mu_P = \mu_M$, by means of generic constraints.

i) M is more important than L: At first sight, this constraint is naturally encoded as

$$xyz \succ zyx \text{ for } x > z, \forall y. \tag{8.5}$$

However, it appears that this encoding is incorrect since it does not recover the ranking over $\mathscr{U}$ induced by the Choquet integral [7, 12]. Let us consider the vectors dfe, efd, ead and dae. Following equation (8.5) we have $dfe \succ efd$ and $dae \succ ead$. However, following Choquet integral we have $Ch_\mu(dfe) = 12.7$, $Ch_\mu(efd) = 12.4$, $Ch_\mu(dae) = 14.8$ and $Ch_\mu(ead) = 15.6$. So, we have dfe preferred to efd but dae not preferred to ead. This means that constraint (8.5) is too weak to encode $\mu_M > \mu_L$. The reason is that the constraint $\mu_M > \mu_L$ has more requirements than what it appears. Indeed, y should be constrained rather than free to take any value in S.

Let mpl and $m'p'l'$ two vectors. Note that $Ch_\mu(mpl) > Ch_\mu(m'p'l')$ reduces to $\mu_M > \mu_L$ when

$$Ch_\mu(mpl) = p + (l-p) \cdot \mu_{ML} + (m-l) \cdot \mu_M > Ch_\mu(m'p'l') = p' + (m'-p') \cdot \mu_{ML}$$
$$+ (l'-m') \cdot \mu_L.$$

This supposes $p \leq l < m$ and $p' \leq m' < l'$. Let $p = p' = y$, $l = m' = z$, $m = l' = x$. Thus, $\mu_M > \mu_L$ is encoded by

$$xyz \succ zyx \text{ for } x > z \geq y. \tag{8.6}$$

ii) P is more important than L: The same reasoning is made for $\mu_P > \mu_L$. It is encoded by

$$xyz \succ xzy \text{ for } y > z \geq x. \tag{8.7}$$

iii) The interaction between M and L is higher than the interaction between P and M: The inequality $\mu_{ML} > \mu_{PM}$ is equivalent to the following inequality between the two Choquet integrals:

$$Ch_\mu(mpl) = p + (l-p)\cdot\mu_{ML} + (m-l)\cdot\mu_M > Ch_\mu(m'p'l') = l' + (p'-l')\cdot\mu_{PM}$$
$$+(m'-p')\cdot\mu_M.$$

This supposes $p < l \leq m$ and $l' < p' \leq m'$. Letting $p = l' = y$, $l = p' = z$ and $m = m' = x$, $\mu_{ML} > \mu_{PM}$ is encoded by

$$xyz \succ xzy \text{ for } x \geq z > y. \tag{8.8}$$

iv) The interaction between P and L is higher than the interaction between P and M: Similarly, $\mu_{PL} > \mu_{PM}$ is encoded by

$$xyz \succ zyx \text{ for } y \geq z > x. \tag{8.9}$$

v) M and P have the same importance:

$$xyz \approx yxz \text{ for all } x,y,z. \tag{8.10}$$

vi) As previously stated, we suppose that the Pareto ordering holds. Namely,

$$xyz \succ x'y'z' \tag{8.11}$$

for $x \geq x', y \geq y', z \geq z'$ and $x > x'$ or $y > y'$ or $z > z'$.
vii) Lastly, C being preferred to A and A being preferred to B is encoded by

$$dcc \succ abf \succ fea. \tag{8.12}$$

In sum, we have the following set of generic constraints and examples [7, 12]:

$$\mathscr{C} \cup \mathscr{E}\mathscr{Q} = \begin{cases} xyz \succ zyx & \text{for } x > z \geq y \\ xyz \succ xzy & \text{for } y > z \geq x \\ xyz \succ xzy & \text{for } x \geq z > y \\ xyz \succ zyx & \text{for } y \geq z > x \\ xyz \approx yxz & \text{for all } x,y,z \\ xyz \succ x'y'z' & \text{for } x \geq x', y \geq y', z \geq z' \text{ and } (x > x' \text{ or } y > y' \text{ or } z > z') \\ dcc \succ abf \succ fea \end{cases}$$

The application of Algorithm 3.1 over $\mathscr{C} \cup \mathscr{E}\mathscr{Q}$ returns a complete preorder with 26 strata $\succeq = (E_1, \cdots, E_{26})$. See Table 8.3. Bold vectors correspond to the grades of the students A, B and C.

Using the Choquet integral we get 77 different levels. See Table 8.4. Clearly, although the two approaches satisfy the set of constraints $\mathscr{C} \cup \mathscr{E}\mathscr{Q}$, they do not induce

Table 8.3 The complete preorder following the minimal specificity principle

$E_i, i = 1, \cdots, 26$
$E_1 = \{aaa\}$
$E_2 = \{baa, aba\}$
$E_3 = \{caa, aca, aab\}$
$E_4 = \{daa, ada, bab, abb, aac\}$
$E_5 = \{eaa, aea, cab, acb, bba, aad\}$
$E_6 = \{faa, afa, dab, bac, abc, adb, cba, bca, bbb, aae\}$
$E_7 = \{eab, cac, bad, acc, abd, aeb, dba, bda, cbb, bcb, aaf\}$
$E_8 = \{fab, dac, bae, cca, adc, afb, abe, eba, bea, dbb, bbc, bdb\}$
$E_9 = \{cad, eac, dca, aec, acd, cda, fba, bfa, ebb, cbc, bcc, bbd, beb\}$
$E_{10} = \{dad, fac, cae, eca, afc, add, ace, cea, fbb, dbc, ccb, bdc, bbe, bfb\}$
$E_{11} = \{ead, fca, dda, aed, cfa, ebc, cbd, dcb, ccc, cdb, bcd, bec, \}$
$E_{12} = \{dae, fad, eda, ade, afd, dea, fbc, dbd, cbe, ecb, \textbf{dcc}, cdc, bdd, ceb, bfc, bce\}$
$E_{13} = \{eae, fda, aee, dfa, ebd, fcb, \textbf{abf}, ecc, ccd, baf, bed, ddb, cec, cfb\}$
$E_{14} = \{fae, eea, afe, fbd, dbe, acf, fcc, dcd, cdd, caf, bbf, bfd, bde, edb, deb, cce, cfc, \}$
$E_{15} = \{\textbf{fea}, efa, ebe, adf, ecd, ced, ddc, daf, cbf, bcf, bee, fdb, dfb\}$
$E_{16} = \{fbe, aef, dce, fcd, cde, cfd, edc, dec, ddd, eaf, dbf, ccf, bdf, bfe, eeb\}$
$E_{17} = \{aff, ece, cee, fdc, dfc, edd, ded, faf, ebf, dcf, cdf, bef, feb, efb\}$
$E_{18} = \{fce, cfe, eec, fdd, dfd, dde, ffa, fbf, bff\}$
$E_{19} = \{ecf, cef, fec, efc, ede, dee, ddf, ffb\}$
$E_{20} = \{fcf, cff, fde, dfe, eed\}$
$E_{21} = \{ffc, edf, def, fed, efd, eee\}$
$E_{22} = \{fdf, dff, fee, efe\}$
$E_{23} = \{ffd, eef\}$
$E_{24} = \{fef, eff\}$
$E_{25} = \{ffe\}$
$E_{26} = \{fff\}$

the same complete preorder over $\mathscr{U} \times \mathscr{U}$. Indeed, the qualitative approach induces a more compact preorder, which means that it does not add further constraints. One, however, would expect that the Choquet integral (and numerical aggregation approaches in general) returns a more refined preorder since the gap between the values of the scale play an important role in the global evaluation. Conditional logics prove to be an appealing approach against the Choquet integral since it is not sensitive to any numerical values. In fact, notice that the main component in Choquet integral is the fuzzy measure μ. Also, the computation of μ is based on the set $\mathscr{M}$ together with the ordering on A, B and C. This makes Choquet integral very sensitive to the constraints from which it is computed, as is illustrated in the following example.

Example 8.4. (Example 8.3 continued)
Let us consider another student D having a score of 15 in physics, 15 in mathematics and 12 in literature. Using the discrete Choquet integral w.r.t. μ given in Table 8.2 we get $Ch_\mu(D) = 13.5$. Then, we have the following ordering: $C \succ A \succ B \succ D$. Let us now use another fuzzy measure μ', given in Table 8.5. It is equal to μ except for μ_{PL} and μ_{ML}. Instead, we have $\mu'_{PL} = \mu'_{ML} = 0.8$. We can check that μ' satisfies

Table 8.4 Global evaluation computed with Choquet integral

v	$Ch_\mu(v)$	v	$Ch_\mu(v)$
aaa	18	edb, deb	14.4
aba, baa	17.8	ddc	14.3
aca, caa	17.7	ced, ecd	14.25
ada, daa	17.6	dfb, fdb	14.2
aea, eaa	17.4	edc, dec	14.1
afa, faa	17.2	cfd, fcd	14.05
aab	17	aaf, ddd, bbe	14
abb, bab	16.9	cbe, bce	13.95
acb, cab	16.8	**abf**, dfc, fdc, bde, dbe, baf	13.9
adb, dab	16.7	acf, caf	13.85
bba	16.6	eea, edd, adf, ebe, ded, bee, daf	13.8
aeb, cba, eab, aac, bca	16.5	aef, eaf	13.7
abc, bda, dba, bac	16.4	efa, aff, dfd, bfe, **fea**, fdd, fbe, faf	13.6
acc, cac	16.35	cce	13.5
afb, fab	16.3	cde, dce	13.45
adc, dac	16.25	cee, ece	13.35
eba, bea	16.2	eeb	13.2
aec, eac	16.05	cfe, fce	13.15
aad, bfa, fba, bbb	16	efb, feb, dde, bbf	13
cca, cbb, abd, bcb, bad	15.9	cbf, bcf	12.95
afc, acd, cad, fac	15.85	eec, ede, dee, bdf, dbf	12.9
cda, add, bdb, dca, dbb, dad	15.8	ebf, bef	12.8
cea, aed, eca, ebb, ead, bed	15.6	efc, dfe, bff, fec, fde, fbf	12.7
bbc	15.5	eed	12.6
cbc, bcc	15.45	ccf	12.5
cfa, afd, bfb, fca, fbb, fad	15.4	cdf, dcf	12.45
bdc, dbc	15.35	efd, ffa, fed	12.4
ccb	15.3	cef, ecf	12.35
cdb, dda, dcb	15.2	cff, fcf	12.25
ebc, bec	15.15	eee, ddf	12
ceb, eda, ecb, ccc, aae, dea, bbd	15	edf, def	11.9
cbd, bfc, bcd, fbc	14.95	efe, ffb, dff, fee, fdf	11.8
cdc, abe, bdd, **dcc**, dbd, bae	14.9	ffc	11.5
ace, cae	14.85	ffd	11.2
cfb, ade, dfa, fda, fcb, dae	14.8	eef	11
cec, aee, ecc, ebd, eae, bed	14.7	eff, fef	10.9
ddb	14.6	ffe	10.6
cfc, afe, ccd, bfd, fcc, fbd, fae	14.5	fff	10
cdd, dcd	14.45		

the set of constraints on μ. Using the discrete Choquet integral w.r.t. μ' we have $C \succ A \succ D \succ B$. So, we still have $C \succ A \succ B$ but the ordering over B and D is reversed.

Moreover, the way μ is computed requires us to compute a new fuzzy measure each time an example or a constraint between criteria is added.

This observation leads to another comparison standpoint. In fact, the Choquet integral relies on the hypothesis that the set of constraints is consistent while condi-

Table 8.5 Fuzzy measure μ'

μ'_M	μ'_P	μ'_L	μ'_{PM}	μ'_{ML}	μ'_{PL}	μ'_{MPL}
0.45	0.45	0.3	0.5	0.8	0.8	1

tional logics do not. If the set of constraints is inconsistent then the preorder returned by Algorithm 3.1 is not complete but still rank-orders some evaluation vectors unless the preference relation induced by the set of constraints is a complete cycle, i.e., it involves all vectors.

The above comparison focuses on the particular case where examples and generic constraints are consistent together since this is a strong hypothesis in the Choquet integral. However, one can also have to deal with examples that contradict generic constraints. An algorithm is proposed in [4] where examples are considered as exceptions. This algorithm computes the complete preorder associated with generic constraints, which is then modified in order to satisfy the examples, provided that the Pareto principle is not violated.

8.3 Temporal Reasoning

In contrast to the previous section, this section does not compare two approaches for rank-ordering outcomes. Instead, it shows how conditional logics for preference representation can be useful in temporal reasoning frameworks [11]. The problem we will address is described in the following example [11].

A university department proposes a certificate which can be obtained by accomplishing nine courses, denoted by $C_1, \cdots, C_9$. All these courses must be completed by the candidate. They are divided into three categories: primary courses C_1, C_2, C_3, C_4, secondary courses C_5, C_6, C_7, C_8, and a mandatory internship C_9. The schedule of the courses must satisfy the following constraints:

1. **Primary courses and secondary courses**
   There are four primary courses, C_1, C_2, C_3, C_4, and four secondary courses, C_5, C_6, C_7, C_8. All these courses must be pursued. The department is flexible on the order they are scheduled; nevertheless it requires that

   - at least one primary course must be scheduled before all secondary courses,
   - all primary courses must finish before secondary courses finish, and that,
   - at least one secondary course starts before all primary courses finish.

2. **Basic knowledge**
   Courses C_4 and C_8 both introduce basic knowledge which is needed for courses C_1 and C_5. However, C_4 and C_8 are too close, so pursuing one of them is sufficient

to pursue C_1 and C_5. Accordingly, at least one of the two former courses must be achieved before the latter two start. It is worth observing that this condition does not mean that a candidate is allowed to pursue C_4 or C_8 and not necessarily both. Recall that all the courses must be pursued. Thus, the condition only expresses a requirement on the scheduling of C_4, C_8, C_1 and C_5.

Similarly, C_1 or C_2 must be achieved before C_3 and C_4.

3. **Mandatory internship**
   The mandatory internship can only be achieved after all other courses, $C_1 \ldots C_8$, are completed.

The problem now is how to schedule (or rank-order over a qualitative time scale) the nine courses according to the above constraints. For this purpose, a constraint can be seen as a constraint between two intervals: each refers to a set of courses. Let us consider the first constraint. Let $I(C_1, C_2, C_3, C_4)$ (or $I(C_5, C_6, C_7, C_8)$) be the time interval in which the courses C_1, C_2, C_3 and C_4 (or C_5, C_6, C_7 and C_8) are scheduled. Observe that the courses are not strictly ordered over the time scale, i.e., two or more courses may be scheduled at the same time. Different rank-orderings over $C_1, \cdots, C_9$ are possible for fulfilling this constraint. Figure 8.2 shows two possible solutions. It is worth observing that we do not represent the duration of a course in a time scale. Consequently, when we say that a course C_i starts or finishes before C_j, this simply means that C_i is scheduled before C_j. Note, however, that these rank-orderings have a common point; the time interval $I(C_5, C_6, C_7, C_8)$ *overlaps* the time interval $I(C_1, C_2, C_3, C_4)$. Regarding the second constraint, the time interval $I(C_4, C_8)$ (or $I(C_1, C_2)$) must start before the time interval $I(C_1, C_5)$ (or $I(C_3, C_4)$). Lastly, the third constraint states that $I(C_9)$ must start after $I(C_1, \cdots, C_8)$ finishes.

Before we investigate the way the courses can be rank-ordered over a qualitative time scale given these constraints, we need to represent these constraints in a formal framework. Handling constraints over time intervals naturally call for the qualitative interval algebra developed by Allen [1]. In the next section, we recall this algebra and show how the above example can be represented within it.

8.3.1 Qualitative Interval Algebra

Qualitative reasoning deals with constraint-based formalisms for representing and reasoning with temporal or spatial information over infinite domains. The qualitative aspect is based on relational schemas that abstract from concrete metrical data of entities (e.g., coordinate positions, time points, distances) by substituting similar topological configurations of entities into one qualitative representation.

For this purpose, various qualitative approaches have been proposed to represent and reason about temporal entities and their relations (see, e.g., [1, 15]). Mainly,

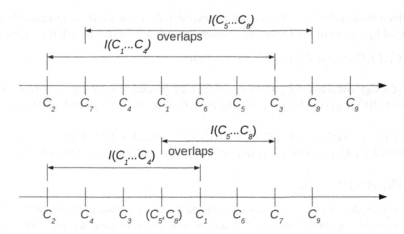

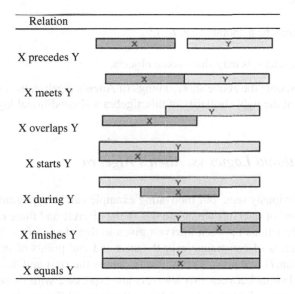

Fig. 8.2 Two possible solutions

Table 8.6 Qualitative interval algebra

Relation	
X precedes Y	
X meets Y	
X overlaps Y	
X starts Y	
X during Y	
X finishes Y	
X equals Y	

a time interval can have thirteen possible positions with respect to another interval. These positions can be combined in a disjunctive way, expressing imprecise knowledge about the way two time intervals are located. Seven of those positions are presented in the first column of Table 8.6. Reversing the positions of X and Y defines inverse relations, except for "equals", which remains identical. Note that the thirteen possible positions are jointly exhaustive and pairwise disjoint.

Given these relations, the constraints expressed in our motivating example are encoded by means of the following relations between intervals in Allen's algebra:

- $I(C_1, C_2, C_3, C_4)$ overlaps $I(C_5, C_6, C_7, C_8)$,

- $(I(C_4, C_8)$ overlaps $I(C_1, C_5))$ or $(I(C_4, C_8)$ precedes $I(C_1, C_5))$ or $(I(C_4, C_8)$ meets $I(C_1, C_5))$ or $(I(C_1, C_5)$ during $I(C_4, C_8))$ or $(I(C_1, C_5)$ finishes $I(C_4, C_8))$,

- $(I(C_1, C_2)$ overlaps $I(C_3, C_4))$ or $(I(C_1, C_2)$ precedes $I(C_3, C_4))$ or $(I(C_1, C_2)$ meets $I(C_3, C_4))$ or $(I(C_3, C_4)$ during $I(C_1, C_2))$ or $(I(C_3, C_4)$ finishes $I(C_1, C_2))$,

- $I(C_9)$ after $I(C_1 \ldots C_8)$.

However, Allen's algebra cannot go beyond a representation of our example. This is because this algebra is built on abstract and non-decomposable intervals which are only identified by their start and end points. Our example is more complicated than a simple representation by relations between intervals. In fact,

- an interval in our example is a set of discrete and finite objects which need to be rank-ordered,

- an interval may be a "point" (e.g. I_{C_9}),

- the different intervals may share some objects.

In order to overcome the above shortcomings of Allen's algebra, the authors of [11] have highlighted the tight similarity of this algebra and conditional logics.

8.3.2 Conditional Logics vs. Allen's Algebra

As we have previously seen, our motivating example can be represented in Allen's algebra by means of intervals which are sets of the discrete and finite elements to be rank-ordered. Relations between intervals given in this algebra (see Table 8.6) can be written in terms of constraints over the start and end points of intervals. More precisely, let $\min(I)$ and $\max(I)$ respectively denote the start and the end of an interval I. All relations between two intervals are expressed with those notations in the second column of Table 8.7. For instance, "an interval X *precedes* an interval Y" can be expressed in the form $\max(X) < \min(Y)$. All relations but one are encoded under several conditions. For example, "X *during* Y" needs both $\max(Y) > \max(X)$ *and* $\min(X) > \min(Y)$ to hold. It is worth observing that intervals in our framework are sets of objects which are not ordered. So, $\min(.)$ and $\max(.)$ are not known.

By considering intervals as sets of objects, the mathematical encoding of the relations between intervals enables us to build an equivalent encoding in the preference representation [11]. The latter is presented in the third column of Table 8.7. Let X^*

Table 8.7 Relations between intervals and their encoding in preference representation

Relation	Mathematical encoding	Corresponding comparative preference statements
X precedes Y	$\max(X) < \min(Y)$	$Y^* >_{st} X^*$
X meets Y	$\max(X) = \min(Y)$	$X^* \geq_{opp} Y^*$ $Y^* \geq_{st} X^*$
X overlaps Y	$\max(X) > \min(Y)$ $\min(X) < \min(Y)$ $\max(X) < \max(Y)$	$X^* >_{opp} Y^*$ $Y^* >_{pes} X^*$ $Y^* >_{opt} X^*$
X starts Y	$\min(X) = \min(Y)$ $\max(X) < \max(Y)$	$X^* \geq_{pes} Y^*$ $Y^* \geq_{pes} X^*$ $Y^* >_{opt} X^*$
X during Y	$\min(X) > \min(Y)$ $\max(X) < \max(Y)$	$X^* >_{pes} Y^*$ $Y^* >_{opt} X^*$
X finishes Y	$\max(X) = \max(Y)$ $\min(X) > \min(Y)$	$X^* \geq_{opt} Y^*$ $Y^* \geq_{opt} X^*$ $X^* >_{pes} Y^*$
X equals Y	$\min(X) = \min(Y)$ $\max(X) = \max(Y)$	$X^* \geq_{pes} Y^*$ $Y^* \geq_{pes} X^*$ $X^* \geq_{opt} Y^*$ $Y^* \geq_{opt} X^*$

be the set of objects composing the interval X. Each relation between intervals is translated into different (sets of) preference semantics. For instance, "*X during Y*" is encoded using two preference semantics. Indeed, Y^* must be preferred to X^* in an optimistic way to ensure that at least one object in Y^* is preferred to all objects in X^*. Moreover, X^* must be pessimisticly preferred to Y^* to express that there exists at least one object in Y^* that is less preferred to all objects in X^*. Therefore, the preference relation over objects of X and Y is interpreted here as a scheduling of these objects over a qualitative time scale. The less preferred an object is, the earlier it is.

The example is then translated into the following sets of preference statements:

1.
$$\begin{cases} \{C_5, C_6, C_7, C_8\} >_{opt} \{C_1, C_2, C_3, C_4\} \\ \{C_5, C_6, C_7, C_8\} >_{pes} \{C_1, C_2, C_3, C_4\} \\ \{C_1, C_2, C_3, C_4\} >_{opp} \{C_5, C_6, C_7, C_8\} \end{cases}$$

The first statement ensures that the primary courses finish before the secondary courses finish. The second statement ensures that at least one primary course is scheduled before all secondary courses. The third statement ensures that the two time intervals overlap.

2.
$$\begin{cases} \{C_1, C_5\} >_{pes} \{C_4, C_8\} \\ \{C_3, C_4\} >_{pes} \{C_1, C_2\} \end{cases}$$

These two statements ensure that at least one course of a given set must be scheduled before other courses start. For example, C_4, C_8 or both must be scheduled before both C_1 and C_5. As shown in Section 8.3.1, this constraint can be fulfilled with several interval positions, which are considered in a disjunctive way. In the preference framework, this corresponds to the pessimistic semantics. In fact, we have $(I(C_4, C_8)$ overlaps $I(C_1, C_5))$ or $(I(C_4, C_8)$ precedes $I(C_1, C_5))$ or $(I(C_4, C_8)$ meets $I(C_1, C_5))$ or $(I(C_1, C_5)$ during $I(C_4, C_8))$ or $(I(C_1, C_5)$ finishes $I(C_4, C_8))$ encoded in preference representation by

$(\{C_4, C_8\} >_{opp} \{C_1, C_5\}$ and $\{C_1, C_5\} >_{pes} \{C_4, C_8\}$ and $\{C_1, C_5\} >_{opt} \{C_4, C_8\})$
or $(\{C_4, C_8\} \geq_{opp} \{C_1, C_5\}$ and $\{C_1, C_5\} \geq_{st} \{C_4, C_8\})$ or
$(\{C_1, C_5\} >_{st} \{C_4, C_8\})$ or
$(\{C_1, C_5\} >_{pes} \{C_4, C_8\}$ and $\{C_4, C_8\} >_{opt} \{C_1, C_5\})$ or
$(\{C_1, C_5\} \geq_{opt} \{C_4, C_8\}$ and $\{C_4, C_8\} \geq_{opt} \{C_1, C_5\}$ and $\{C_1, C_5\} >_{pes} \{C_4, C_8\})$,

which is equivalent to $\{C_1, C_5\} >_{pes} \{C_4, C_8\}$.

3. $\{C_9\} >_{st} \{C_1, C_2, C_3, C_4, C_5, C_6, C_7, C_8\}$
The internship represented as $\{C_9\}$ must be the last pursued course, which is exactly captured by strong semantics.

It is worth noticing that the above encoding only holds under the hypothesis that intervals are "compact" in the sense that they are delimited (their start and end points) by the objects they are composed of. Moreover, relations between intervals first need to be described in Allen's algebra before they are encoded in terms of preference statements. For example, the direct assessment of the *overlap* relation in preference representation framework is not intuitive.

Different semantics can be used in the above encoding. Algorithms 3.5 and 3.6 deal with heterogeneous semantics. Nevertheless, they cannot be used in this case since the former only deals with strong, optimistic and ceteris paribus semantics while the latter only deals with strong, pessimistic and ceteris paribus semantics. However, the above encoding involves semantics from both sets. In [11], an algorithm has been developed which deals with all semantics at the same time. The technical details of this algorithm go beyond the purpose of the present chapter. We refer the reader to [11] for a detailed description of the algorithm.

The basic idea of the algorithm is that outcomes are not ordered following the semantics of comparative preference statements at hand. Instead, we look for (1) outcomes which dominate other outcomes w.r.t. at least one statement, but are not dominated w.r.t. any statement, and (2) outcomes which do not dominate any other outcome. The first set of outcomes is the set of the best (i.e., preferred) outcomes and the second is the set of the least preferred outcomes. Once these two sets are computed, the semantics of a given preference statement is used to check whether the statement is satisfied or not yet. Thus, the algorithm is conceptually different from those presented in Chapter 3. Unlike the latter, it does not obey minimal and maximal specificity principles. Therefore, it does not return a unique preorder following the minimal or maximal specificity principles since it combines both principles. However, the preorder is unique following the basic idea of the algorithm construction, which consists in computing the sets of outcomes which dominate other outcomes and those which do not dominate any other outcome. Therefore, at each step of the algorithm we ensure that we select all outcomes that dominate (or do not dominate) other outcomes. The two sets are respectively denoted by E_l and E'_l at an iteration l. It is worth observing that our algorithm also handles opportunistic preferences for which a unique model does not exist following minimal and maximal specificity principles when considered separately.

Let us consider again our motivating example. We have

$$\mathscr{P} = \mathscr{P}_{>opt} \cup \mathscr{P}_{>pes} \cup \mathscr{P}_{>st} \cup \mathscr{P}_{>opp}$$

with

$$\mathscr{P}_{>opt} = \{s_1 : \{C_5, C_6, C_7, C_8\} >_{opt} \{C_1, C_2, C_3, C_4\}\},$$

$$\mathscr{P}_{>pes} = \{s_2 : \{C_5, C_6, C_7, C_8\} >_{pes} \{C_1, C_2, C_3, C_4\}, s_3 : \{C_1, C_5\} >_{pes} \{C_4, C_8\}$$
$$s_4 : \{C_3, C_4\} >_{pes} \{C_1, C_2\}\},$$

$$\mathscr{P}_{>st} = \{s_5 : \{C_9\} >_{st} \{C_1, C_2, C_3, C_4, C_5, C_6, C_7, C_8\}\},$$

$$\mathscr{P}_{>opp} = \{s_6 : \{C_1, C_2, C_3, C_4\} >_{opp} \{C_5, C_6, C_7, C_8\}\}.$$

Then, $E'_1 = \{C_2\}$ and $E_1 = \{C_9\}$. We remove $(L(s_2), R(s_2))$, $(L(s_3), R(s_3))$ and $(L(s_5), R(s_5))$ since associated preferences are satisfied. We repeat this process and get $\succeq = (\{C_9\}, \{C_5, C_6, C_7\}, \{C_1\}, \{C_8\}, \{C_3, C_4\}, \{C_2\})$. The schedule of the nine courses is shown in Figure 8.3. So, C_2 is the first course to be scheduled, followed by C_3 and C_4, which can take place simultaneously. We can check that all relations between intervals are satisfied.

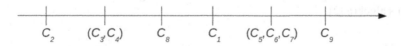

Fig. 8.3 The final schedule

8.4 Conclusion

The aim of this chapter is to stress that the preference representation framework is not an independent framework. In particular, we provide a comparative study of conditional logics and a multiple criteria aggregation approach, namely, the Choquet integral. This comparison suggests reasons to argue for each approach. In particular, conditional logics are fairly general, and agree with the way humans state their preferences in a granular manner, either in terms of generic rules or by means of examples.

A comparative discussion on an example suggests that they may be more robust and more flexible, and are more transparent to the user (who can control precisely what is expressed by means of the constraints) than the Choquet integral, which moreover requires the use of a numerical scale in order to have a sufficiently discriminative scale. On the other hand, the Choquet integral returns a more refined ordering over evaluation vectors. Therefore, it gives an indication on how large are the differences between the global evaluations.

Of interest for further research would be a general comparison of conditional logics with multiple criteria aggregation techniques such as Sugeno integrals, and a study of the extent to which it is possible to extract constraints underlying the way these aggregations handle the assessment of the relative importance of criteria.

In the second part of the chapter, we highlight the closeness of conditional logics and an apparently different framework, namely, Allen's algebra for temporal reasoning. Both frameworks deal with intervals but in different ways. While Allen's algebra handles intervals only identified by their start and end points, preference representation enables us to consider intervals composed of unordered objects which need to be rank-ordered. On the other hand, Allen's algebra is a suitable framework for representing all possible relations between intervals. Based on these observations, we provide an encoding which permits us to consider general intervals whose relations (i.e., relative positions) are expressed in Allen's algebra. This encoding translates Allen's relations into comparative preference statements obeying different semantics. Using algorithms developed in the preference representation framework, objects at hand are rank-ordered in a way that relations between intervals are satisfied. We believe that this comparison offers an interesting and promising clue for deeper investigation of the closeness of the two frameworks. In particular, if the opposite encoding is established (namely, from conditional logics to Allen's algebra) then conditional logics may benefit from efficient algorithmic tools developed for Allen's algebra [2].

References

1. Allen, J.F.: An interval-based representation of temporal knowledge. In: Hayes, P.J. (eds.), 7th International Joint Conference on Artificial Intelligence, pp. 221-226. William Kaufmann,

(1981)
2. Condotta, J.F., Ligozat, G., Saade, M.: QAT: A qualitative algebra toolkit. In: Martineau, G., Razouk, R. (eds.), Information and Communication Technologies, pp. 3433-3438. IEEE, (2006)
3. Cormen, T.H., Leiserson, C.E., R.I. Rivest, R.I., Stein, C.: Introduction to Algorithms. pp. 485-488. MIT Press and McGraw-Hill (1990)
4. Dubois, D., Kaci, S., Prade, H.: Expressing preferences from generic rules and examples- A possibilistic approach without aggregation function. In: Godo, L. (eds.), 8th European Conference on Symbolic and Quantitative Approaches to Reasoning with Uncertainty, pp. 293-304. Springer, (2005)
5. Dubois, D., Prade, H., Roubens, M., Sabbadin, R., Marichal, J.L.: The use of the discrete Sugeno integral in decision-making: a survey. International Journal of Uncertainty, Fuzziness and Knowledge-Based Systems $9(5)$, 539–561 (2001)
6. Fodor, J.: Smooth associative operations on finite ordinal scales. IEEE Transactions on Fuzzy Systems 8, 791–795 (2000)
7. Gérard, R., Kaci, S., Prade, H.: Ranking alternatives on the basis of generic constraints and examples- A possibilistic approach. In: M. Veloso (eds.), 20th Joint Conference on Artificial Intelligence, pp. 393-398. (2007)
8. Grabisch, M.: Fuzzy integral in multicriteria decision making. Fuzzy Sets and Systems 69, 279–298 (1995)
9. Grabisch, M.: The application of fuzzy integrals in multicriteria decision making. European Journal of Operational Research 89, 445–456 (1996)
10. Hansson, S.O.: What is ceteris paribus preference? Journal of Philosophical Logic 25, 307–332 (1996)
11. Kaci, S., Piette, C.: Ordering intervals: From qualitative temporal constraint problems to preference representation. In: de Givry, S., Many, F., Marques-Silva, J. (eds.), 10th Workshop on Preferences and Soft Constraints (co-located with CP 2010), pp. 1-10. Electronic proceedings, (2010)
12. Kaci, S., Prade, H.: Constraints associated with Choquet integrals and other aggregation-free ranking devices. In: Magdalena, L., Verdegay, J.L. (eds.), 12th Conference on Information Processing and Management of Uncertainty in Knowledge-Based Systems Conference, pp. 1344-1351. (2008)
13. Marichal, J.L.: Aggregation operators for multicriteria decision aid. Ph.D. dissertation (1998)
14. Mas, M., G. Mayor, G., Torrens, J.: t-operators and uninorms on a finite totally ordered set. International Journal of Intelligent Systems 14, 909–922 (1999)
15. Randell, D.A, Zhan Cui, Z., Cohn, A.G.: A spatial logic based on regions and connection. In: Nebel, B., Rich, C., Swartout, W.R. (eds.), 3rd International Conference of Principles of Knowledge Representation and Reasoning, pp. 165-176. Morgan Kaufmann, (1992)

Chapter 9
Conclusion

Preferences play an important role in our daily decisions. However, managing preferences is a hard task. We always hesitate when we are faced with multiple choices. Fortunately, work over the past decade in artificial intelligence concerning preferences has been extremely successful. In particular, there is a large number of compact preference representation languages in the literature, ranging from quantitative to qualitative languages. They are particularly appealing when the number of choices is large. Compact languages support different formats of preferences. Therefore, we distinguish between weighted logics, conditional logics and graphical languages.

Confronted with this large panel of compact languages, researchers tend to demonstrate the superiority of each language over the others. Therefore, they compare the languages with respect to complexity criteria, namely, spatial efficiency and time cost of preference queries. Moreover, according to defenders of quantitative languages, the latter outperform qualitative languages due to their higher descriptive power. On the other hand, defenders of qualitative languages raise the question "where do numbers come from?" to criticize quantitative languages. We also encounter claims that users always specify their preferences in terms of comparative preference statements. Some other researchers argue for a particular language by making a strong hypothesis on users' behavior. For example, when working with conditional preference statements, researchers claim that users systematically refer to ceteris paribus semantics and nothing else. When working with some conditional logics, researchers claim that users reject incomparabilities.

However, on reflection one should recognize that in our daily lives we may encounter different forms of preferences, such as "I like London more than Paris", "I prefer fish to meat", "If fish is served then I prefer white wine to red wine", "I really like Amsterdam", and "I like Berlin with weight .7", as repeatedly pointed out in the book. Moreover, when expressing comparative preference statements one may only refer to outcomes which are identical, apart from specified preferences (ceteris paribus semantics), but sometimes we may also wish to accommodate general preferences and specific ones, e.g., "I have a default preference for fish but if red wine is served then I would prefer meat". Moreover, one may wish to compare all outcomes or accept incomparabilities.

In light of the above observations, we believe that the different compact preference representation languages should not be in competition. While each of these languages has its merits, it appears that they do not adequately and/or intuitively cope with all forms and interpretations of preferences. Readers who agree that users' preferences show up in different formats and have various interpretations understand why different compact preference representation languages are needed.

As we already stated, compact preference representation languages can be analyzed with respect to different criteria. In the quest to compare these languages, researchers have mainly focused on spatial efficiency and time cost of preference queries. The following represent excellent references on this topic:

- *Goldsmith, J., Lang, J., Truszczynski, M., Wilson, N. The computational complexity of dominance and consistency in CP-nets. Journal of Artificial Intelligence Research **33**, pp. 403–432 (2008)*

- *Coste-Marquis, S., Lang, J., Liberatore, P., Marquis, P.: Expressive power and succinctness of propositional languages for preference representation. In: Dubois, D., Welty, C.A., Williams, M.A. (eds.), 9th International Conference on Principles of Knowledge Representation and Reasoning, pp. 203-212. AAAI Press, (2004)*

We intentionally disregarded this issue in this book because we aimed at shedding light on a less studied (but complementary) problem, namely, to establish bridges between the languages. This is not a compilation problem since we do not move from a language to another in order to improve its spatial or time complexity. Instead, we aim to understand the underpinning semantics of some key languages by making explicit their implicit priorities. It appears that conditional preference networks give priority to parent nodes while conditional logics are based on the defeasibility principle.

In the second part of the book, we addressed the problem of reasoning with preferences. We first concentrated on argumentation theory and database framework. We showed how preferences have been progressively and nicely incorporated into these frameworks. We put a particular emphasis on the use of compact preference representation languages. These works complement many other successful proposals to integrate compact languages in other frameworks. Just to cite a few, we refer to the following works where the authors respectively incorporate conditional importance networks and conditional preference networks in fair division and planning.

- *Bouveret, S., Endriss, U., Lang, J.: Conditional importance networks: A graphical language for representing ordinal, monotonic preferences over sets of goods. In: Boutilier, C. (eds.), 21st International Joint Conference on Artificial Intelligence, pp. 67-72. (2009)*

- *Brafman, R.I., Chernyavsky, X.: Planning with goal preferences and constraints. In: Biundo, S., Myers, K.L., Rajan, K. (eds.), 15th International Conference on Automated Planning and Scheduling, pp. 182-191. AAAI Press, (2005)*

We believe that we should continue to broaden the use of compact preference representation languages for an efficient and natural representation of users' preferences.

In this part we also offered a non-standard study of compact preference representation languages. In particular we first compared conditional logics and the multiple criteria aggregation approach. This work shows once again the broad range of compact languages. Then, we highlighted the closeness of conditional logics and a temporal reasoning formalism, namely, Allen's algebra. In fact, while Allen's algebra (which represents relative positions between intervals) does not explicitly use preferences, it has much in common with them. This clever comparison opens the door to a new research issue, namely, relating conditional logics and interval representation. This issue is particularly challenging since the two frameworks exhibit different behavior with respect to transitivity.

In this book we aimed at offering a coherent exposition of some problems related to the study of preferences. Therefore, we concentrated on compact preference representation languages and their use in other frameworks. We did not address problems related to reasoning about preferences, which mainly include preferences revision and aggregation of preferences provided by multiple users.

- *Li, M., Bao Vo, Q., Kowalczyk, R.: An efficient majority-rule-based approach for collective decision making with CP-nets. In: Lin, F., Sattler, U., Truszczynski, M. (eds.), 12th International Conference on Principles of Knowledge Representation and Reasoning. AAAI Press, (2010)*

- *Liu, F.: Changing for the better. Ph.D. dissertation, Amsterdam (2008)*

- *Pini, M.S., Rossi, F., Brent, K.: Aggregating partially ordered preferences. Journal of Logic and Computation 19(3), pp. 475–502 (2009)*

- *Conitzer, V.: Computational aspects of preference aggregation. Ph.D. dissertation, Pittsburgh (2006)*

Preference acquisition is the backbone of the study of preferences. We intentionally disregard the exposition of this topic as it deserves a dedicated book. In fact there are many works concerned with preferences acquisition, including preference elicitation and preference learning. We refer interested readers to the following references, among many others:

- *Boutilier, C., Regan, K., Viappiani, P.: Preference elicitation with subjective features. In: Bergman, L.D., Tuzhilin, A., Burke, R.D., Felfernig, A., Schmidt-Thieme, L. (eds.), ACM Conference on Recommender Systems, pp. 341-344. ACM, (2009)*

- *Hu, R., Pu, P.: A comparative user study on rating vs. personality quiz based preference elicitation methods. In: Conati, C., Bauer, M., Oliver, N., Weld, D.S. (eds.), International Conference on Intelligent User Interfaces, pp. 367-372. (2009)*

- *Gonzales, C., Perny, P.: GAI networks for utility elicitation. In: Dubois, D., Welty, C.A., Williams, M.A. (eds.), 9th International Conference on Principles of Knowledge Representation and Reasoning, pp. 224-234. AAAI Press, (2004)*

- *Koriche, F., Zanuttini, B.: Learning conditional preference networks. Artificial Intelligence 174(11), pp. 685–703 (2010)*

- *Cohen, W.W., Schapire, R.E., Singer, Y.: Learning to Order Things. Journal of Artificial Intelligence Research 10(1), pp. 243–270 (1999)*

- *Fürnkranz, J., Hüllermeier, E.: Preference Learning. Springer-Verlag, Heidelberg (2010)*

As we repeatedly stated, the study of preferences in artificial intelligence and related fields has been extensively investigated. This has led to successful proposals ranging from preferences acquisition to preferences modeling and representation, to reasoning with and about preferences. However suggestive these works, we are still largely ignorant of how users prefer, i.e., how they interpret their partial descriptions of preferences, and whether this preference is stable or not. Indeed, while much is understood about the formal description of compact preference representation languages and their underlying semantics, relatively much less is understood about the plausibility of such semantics. Clearly, this does not need any further theoretical investigation but calls for experimental sciences. In particular, psychology is an experimental science which does not refute theoretical methods. Instead, it only gives a prescriptive analysis showing how people are likely to behave, which method is more plausible w.r.t. human behavior, etc. The need for such analysis has been recently stressed in the artificial intelligence community. For example, it has been shown that human inference is consistent with System P and that System P constitutes a psychologically sound base of rationality postulates for the evaluation of non-monotonic reasoning systems.

Preferences are not a new topic in psychology. Different problems related to the study of preferences have been addressed in this field. Unfortunately, the relevance of the results in this field for artificial intelligence is largely unexplored. We believe that a psychological study of compact preference representation languages and their underlying semantics is an avenue of a particularly challenging and valuable research topic.

Lastly, it goes without saying that preferences should have a wide range of applications. They are at work in recommender systems and e-commerce platforms, yet we believe that work on preferences in artificial intelligence is mature enough for us to consider broadening their range of applications. We also believe that the applications themselves may be the source of new theoretical issues.

Index